CONSTITUTIONAL LAW

CONSTITUTIONAL LAW

MODEL PROBLEMS AND OUTSTANDING ANSWERS

Kevin W. Saunders

Michael A. Lawrence

Stephen M. Sheppard
SERIES EDITOR, MODEL PROBLEMS AND OUTSTANDING ANSWERS

OXFORD
UNIVERSITY PRESS

Oxford University Press is a department of the University of Oxford. It furthers the University's objective of excellence in research, scholarship, and education by publishing worldwide.

Oxford New York
Auckland Cape Town Dar es Salaam Hong Kong Karachi Kuala Lumpur Madrid
Melbourne Mexico City Nairobi New Delhi Shanghai Taipei Toronto

With offices in
Argentina Austria Brazil Chile Czech Republic France Greece Guatemala Hungary
Italy Japan Poland Portugal Singapore South Korea Switzerland Thailand
Turkey Ukraine Vietnam

Published in the United States of America by
Oxford University Press
198 Madison Avenue, New York, NY 10016

Library of Congress Cataloging-in-Publication Data

Saunders, Kevin W.
Constitutional law : model problems and outstanding answers/Kevin W. Saunders and Michael A. Lawrence.
p. cm.—(Model problems and outstanding answers)
Includes bibliographical references.
ISBN 978-0-19-991626-9 ((pbk.): alk. paper)
1. Constitutional law—United States—Problems, exercises, etc.
I. Lawrence, Michael A., Prof. II. Title.
KF4550.Z9S28 2013
342.73—dc23

2012041930

Note to Readers

CONTENTS

INTRODUCTION

This book is intended to help you learn to identify and analyze issues in constitutional law. In terms of application to coursework and law school exams, it should be useful for the usual introductory Constitutional Law course focusing on the structure of the federal government and the distribution of powers between the federal government and the states. It should also be useful in a course on individual constitutional rights, as well as a course specifically devoted to the First Amendment.

Constitutional law often proves difficult for law students, because the content and analytical approach differ significantly from those in first-year courses. In many courses, because there are often many issues to identify, simply being able to identify issues may lead to a reasonably good grade. On the other hand, in a constitutional law essay question, there are likely to be fewer issues, sometimes perhaps even only one main issue. Thus, there is a greater premium on being able to provide more depth in your analysis.

This greater expected depth of analysis may make what is known as the IRAC (Issue, Relevant law, Application to facts, and Conclusion) approach to writing exam answers, repeatedly applied in an individual essay, less appropriate for Constitutional Law. For example, in an individual rights question the major issue will often simply be to identify the proper test to apply to the given facts. The "rule" to apply in a Constitutional Law essay may not be easily stated. Rather, there may be a method followed to determine the test, and there may be precedent from which guidance may be drawn. It may well be unclear, even after applying what you know, what the test should be. You may well have two, or more, tests to apply. The most sophisticated analysis will go into determining the test or tests, whereas application may be more straightforward.

Even if IRAC is not as relevant as in some other courses, the questions the method calls for are worth remembering. Whatever issues you see should be stated. Any applicable rule or rules should be explained, and where a hypothetical falls between two rules, an explanation of why the fact pattern fits between them should be offered. Most of your effort should usually go into the analysis of how the facts fit with case law. When it comes to a final conclusion, most professors will not care what your conclusion is, as long as your analysis is complete. Where a conclusion is intermediate, it is best not to be too firm in your resolution of the issue. Offer a conclusion, and then analyze the issues that conclusion raises. But, be sure then to go back and state and analyze the issues that would arise under the alternative conclusion.

A word should be said about discussing cases. The cases in a Constitutional Law course are, in a sense, more important than most of those in other courses. A case used to illustrate a point or state a rule in a Property course often could have been replaced by any of a large number of other cases, from the same or other jurisdictions, making the same point or presenting the same rule. The cases in a Constitutional Law course are more likely to be unique; they will be *the* cases presenting the relevant law.

Given the centrality of the Supreme Court's decisions, they should be discussed whenever relevant. Some professors may put a premium on being able to include case names in your discussion. Others may be happy with a brief description or a simple statement of the facts that were present in the case and the Court's analysis and decision in that case. You need to ascertain from your professor whether he or she expects your essay to include the names of the cases that you use. Whether or not case names are required, demonstrate your familiarity with the case law. A citation to a relevant case may be the best evidence of that knowledge. But, if you do not remember a case name, you may still show that you know the law by referring to the relevant facts of the unnamed case and the case's conclusion.

HOW TO USE THIS BOOK

The best approach to using this book is, first, to identify the chapters that are relevant to your course. For each such chapter, read the introduction and check the list of readings to be sure you have read all the cases. If one of the cases listed was not included among the cases covered in your course, it is unlikely that it will be relevant to a question that actually appears on your exam. It will, however, be relevant to the problems in the chapter, so you may want to take a look at it to see how closely you can come to the model answer. Before turning to the problems, review the cases that you have studied in your class and the cases on the reading list so that your level of preparation will be similar to that which you will take into the examination. Once you are ready to turn to the problems, actually take the time to sit down and answer the questions. Do not just read the hypothetical and then read the model essay. If you do that, it is too easy to convince yourself that you would have written something similar. If you actually sit down and write out an answer, you will recognize any shortcomings in that answer and will have the opportunity to think about how you should have approached the question.

If you do not have time to actually write an essay, at least write down a detailed outline of an answer. Note that the outline should be significantly detailed. For example, in individual rights cases, the major issue is often the test that should be applied. You should set out the factors that must be considered in determining what that test is. The same is true, for example, of a case involving the impact on interstate commerce of a state regulation. Which test applies goes a long way toward determining the outcome.

In writing your answers, it is important to recognize that there seems to be a correlation between longer answers and better grades. That observation should not be taken as an invitation to free associate and go into topics not at all related to the question presented. It is, however, an indication that you should keep on writing, unless you have a word limit, as long as you have anything relevant to say. It does take some judgment to recognize what is and what is not relevant, but if a thought has relevance, and you have time, include it. If the relevance is not obvious, explain it. As long as it is explained and actually does have relevance, it will not count against you, and it may be given credit.

Once you have written an answer, read the model essay, and see where that essay differs from yours. The self-analysis section will provide some insight into how the issues were identified for the model essay and what might have led you to miss an issue or to go off in the wrong direction. Do not worry if your answer is not as good as the model essay. The model essay is not intended to be an average essay but an example of a near-perfect essay. Although the model answer would likely earn the top grade on the question, essays falling short of it may still do well.

The introductions to each chapter are not intended as an adequate review of the material in any one of the courses at which the book is aimed. Reading the introductions is not a sufficient replacement for having read the cases that you were assigned and any other suggested supplementary materials. Nor are the introductions intended as replacements for any of the other substantive study aids in the area.

It is also important to recognize that the topics covered are not exhaustive of the possibilities you may face in an exam. If your course covered a topic not included, you should not take the lack of inclusion here as an indication that the topic is not likely to be covered on your exam.

Even with a topic not included here, working through the problems in this book will be of benefit. The goal of this book is not to provide substantive coverage or even to ask questions about every topic you may face. The questions that are contained here will help you to improve your ability to identify and analyze issues that arise in Constitutional Law, and that ability will carry over to any essay you may be asked to write. It should also be noted that it will be easier to identify the main focus of the hypotheticals presented in this book than on an exam, because they are presented in chapters addressing various topics. A hypothetical in the chapter on free expression clearly presents a First Amendment problem. To provide help in identifying the main subject area in an exam question, where there will not be chapter headings, chapters with mixed problems are included. There, you will not be told the subject area, and there may be more than one subject area included in a single hypothetical.

It is *extremely important* to recognize, and it is worth repeating, that the model answers provided are exactly that: model answers. They are not average answers. Answers such as those presented would be the best in any set of exams. Indeed, in most classes the best answer would still fall short of the model answer. The model answers may represent goals, but they are not goals you must attain in order to do well on your exam. They may best be seen as representing ideals against which you can measure your answers, while recognizing that even a significant difference between your answer and the model answer does not mean that you have not done at least reasonably well. Do not let the model answers discourage you—learn from them. The more problems you work through, the better you will become at answering Constitutional Law essay questions and the closer you will come to the model answers.

The authors would like to thank Professors Matthew Fletcher; Brian Kalt; Mark Kende; Mae Kuykendall; Barry McDonald; Michael Meyerson; Noga Morag-Levine; Frank Ravitch and David Thronson; the Co-Directors of the Michigan State University College of Law Academic Support Program, Meghan Short and Goldie Pritchard; and law students Jasmine Baker, Jacqueline Clarke, Ellen Durkee, Allison Kittelberger, Rachel Meerkov, Patrick O'Brien, and James Vicchairelli, for their comments and contributions to earlier drafts of this work.

FEDERAL JUDICIAL POWER

1

A. INTRODUCTION

The federal judicial power is found in the U.S. Constitution's Article III, which provides for a nuanced relationship between Congress and the judiciary in defining the contours of the judicial power. First, Article III § 1 provides that "The judicial Power of the United States shall be vested in one supreme Court, and in such inferior Courts as the Congress may from time to time ordain and establish." So, although the Constitution mandates that there shall be a supreme Court, the lower federal courts essentially exist (textually speaking) only at the pleasure of Congress. (Indeed, one of the first tasks of the First Congress was to "ordain and establish," in the Judiciary Act of 1789, a series of lower federal courts.)

Having established the federal Judiciary in § 1, Article III § 2 then defines the scope of the federal judicial power as extending only to "Cases" and "Controversies." The U.S. Supreme Court's various "justiciability" doctrines—bar on advisory opinions, standing, ripeness, mootness, political question—essentially hinge upon whether a particular dispute that a plaintiff brings to federal court meets the "case or controversy" requirement.

Article III § 2 then provides that the Supreme Court's original jurisdiction is limited only to a specific narrow range of cases, whereas its *appellate* jurisdiction extends to all cases, with one important caveat: Congress has the power to *limit* the Supreme Court's appellate jurisdiction. ("In all the other Cases before mentioned, the supreme Court shall have appellate Jurisdiction ... with such Exceptions, and under such Regulations as the Congress shall make.") So here again we see checks and balances operating, where Congress may decide *not* to allow the Supreme Court to hear a certain category of case—a principle duly recognized by the Supreme Court in Ex Parte *McCardle* (1868).

It is very possible that the first case you read in your Constitutional Law class was *Marbury v. Madison* (1803). Aside from its fascinating factual background (Chief Justice John Marshall decides a case involving the alleged impropriety of a successor president's secretary of state (Madison) refusing to deliver an individual's (Marbury's) commission as justice of the peace, which had been ordered by the prior president (Adams) but whose own secretary of state (none other than John Marshall) had failed to deliver in time before the new president (Jefferson) took office—facts that would certainly lead to a justice's recusal if encountered today), the case introduces two fundamental enduring principles: (1) the Constitution is paramount, and (2) the Court decides. The first principle is a fairly unremarkable interpretation of the Article VI Supremacy Clause: as between conflicting provisions in the Constitution and ordinary legislation, the Constitution will prevail. The second principle, however, was (and is) truly groundbreaking: that the unelected judiciary has power to declare federal laws and some executive actions as invalid under the Constitution. In a democracy, which is founded on the idea that the will of the majority is the best way to govern society, the concept of "judicial review" is fundamentally problematic, and yet, it is vitally *necessary* in order to protect minority rights from an oppressive majority. Interestingly, nowhere in the text does the Constitution expressly provide for the power of judicial review, but Chief Justice Marshall claims it nonetheless in *Marbury* through a mixture of structural and (weaker) textual arguments. The doctrine of judicial review—perhaps U.S. constitutionalism's greatest contribution to political and jurisprudential theory—has endured for over two centuries to the present day.

Problem 1 in this chapter provides a straightforward review of the principles of the Supreme Court's original and appellate jurisdiction described above. Problem 2 addresses the issue of justiciability, touching upon the various doctrines of standing, ripeness, mootness, and political question. In order for the federal judiciary to have jurisdiction to decide a matter, the plaintiff must truly have a "Case or Controversy," which is defined under the Supreme Court's "standing" doctrine to mean that there must be (1) actual injury, (2) causation, and (3) court redressability. Problem 3 then focuses on the "political question" doctrine in the context of political redistricting. A "political question" is one that the court determines is better answered by one of the "political" branches—that is, those that are elected in the political process—rather than by the judiciary. In *Baker v. Carr* (1962), the Court provided a six-question (in descending order of importance) framework for determining when a political question may exist:

> [1] a textually demonstrable constitutional commitment of the issue to a coordinate political department; or [2] a lack of judicially discoverable and manageable standards for resolving it; or [3] the impossibility of deciding without an initial policy determination of a kind clearly for nonjudicial discretion; or [4] the impossibility of a court's undertaking independent resolution without expressing lack of the respect due coordinate branches of the government; or [5] an unusual need for unquestioning adherence to a political decision already made; or [6] the potentiality of embarrassment from multifarious pronouncements by various departments on one question.

Because the last four *Baker* factors are substantially similar and are much less "weighty" than numbers (1) and (2), they may be conflated into a consolidated third factor, which may read: "(3) Prudential considerations of comity and separation of powers suggest that a court should not decide the matter."

B. READINGS

Before attempting the problems in this section, you should have read the following material. You may have already read most, if not all, of the cases. Edited versions of the cases contained within casebooks will be adequate for your purposes here.

Marbury v. Madison, 5 U.S. (1 Cranch) 137 (1803).
Ex parte *McCardle*, 74 U.S. (7 Wall.) 506 (1869).
Poe v. Ullman, 367 U.S. 497 (1961).
Flast v. Cohen, 392 U.S. 83 (1968).
Allen v. Wright, 468 U.S. 737 (1984).
Abbott Labs. v. Gardner, 387 U.S. 136 (1967).
U.S. Parole Commission. v. Geraghty, 445 U.S. 388 (1980).

Baker v. Carr, 369 U.S. 186 (1962).
Vieth v. Jubelirer, 541 U.S. 267 (2004).
Davis v. Bandemer, 478 U.S. 109 (1986).

C. PROBLEMS

Problem 1
(30 minutes)

HYPOTHETICAL

Marcus is the ambassador to the United States from the sovereign nation of Centralia. In addition to being an able diplomat, Marcus is also a fiery orator and radio personality. Over four hundred radio stations across the United States and internationally air his show, *Moderate Mondays*, which originates from a Washington, DC studio each Monday morning. Marcus's political and social views—which are representative of the views of most citizens in his own nation of Centralia—are very controversial to many U.S. citizens because the views come from the center of the political spectrum. In fact, many critics label Marcus as the moderates' equivalent to the conservative Rush Limbaugh or the liberal Bill Maher.

Senator Smith, inflamed by Marcus's centrist rhetoric, introduces a bill in Congress that is quickly passed with strong support by both the House and Senate and signed by the president. The bill reads:

(1) Any speech that espouses the offensive ideas of radical "moderatism" is hereby banned from the radio waves.
(2) Any radio personality found to be in violation of this act shall be fined $1,000 and jailed for not less than a year.
(3) The Supreme Court is not authorized appellate review of any cases involving the aforementioned act.
(4) The Supreme Court shall not have original jurisdiction to hear cases from ambassadors, other public ministers and consuls, and states involving the aforementioned act.

Outraged at what he believes is a violation of his First Amendment rights, Marcus brings a federal lawsuit claiming that Senator Smith's law is unconstitutional. The federal district court agrees with Senator Smith that the law does not violate the First Amendment. The Federal Court of Appeals then affirms the lower court's decision.

Marcus appeals to the U.S. Supreme Court. Senator Smith contends that under section (3) of the bill that the Supreme Court may not hear Marcus's appeal. Marcus argues that section (3) of Senator Smith's law cannot preclude the Supreme Court from hearing an appeal in a claim involving the alleged unconstitutionality of a federal statute. Who is correct? Explain.

Totally separately from the question of whether he is able to appeal the lower court decision in the Supreme Court, Marcus also claims that he may bring his suit directly in the Supreme Court. Senator Smith responds that section (4) of the bill prevents Marcus from bringing the case directly to the Supreme Court. Who is correct? Explain.

SAMPLE ESSAY

You have asked me to discuss whether Senator Smith's bill, prohibiting Marcus's ability to speak his radical "moderatism" views via public airways, validly precludes the Supreme Court from hearing Marcus's case by restricting the Court's appellate and original jurisdiction.

Article III, § 2 specifies that the Supreme Court's original jurisdiction extends only to (1) cases involving ambassadors or other public ministers and consuls, and (2) those in which a state is a party, and that its appellate jurisdiction extends to all other cases "with such exceptions and under such regulations as Congress shall make." These provisions involving the Supreme Court's original and appellate jurisdiction are at the center of two important cases, *Marbury v. Madison* and Ex parte *McCardle*, respectively, which themselves guide the analysis of Senator Smith's bill.

In *Marbury v. Madison*, William Marbury sued to require Secretary of State James Madison to deliver a commission that was granted to him by the outgoing President John Adams, but which outgoing Secretary of State John Marshall (ironically, the chief justice who would later decide *Marbury*) failed to deliver to Marbury in time. When Madison refused to deliver the commission, Marbury sued directly in the U.S. Supreme Court under the Judiciary Act of 1791, which gave the Supreme Court original jurisdiction to issue a writ of mandamus (an order from the Court). But Chief Justice John Marshall observed that Article III of the Constitution conferred original jurisdiction only in a narrow set of cases—that is, those affecting ambassadors, other public ministers and consuls, and those where a state is a party—none of which factors were involved in Marbury's case. Chief Justice Marshall thus explained that where, as here, a statute and the Constitution are in conflict, under basic Supremacy Clause principles the Constitution must prevail ("the Constitution is paramount"). Therefore, the Judiciary Act of 1791, which expanded the jurisdiction of the Supreme Court to allow original jurisdiction over a case such as Marbury's, could not be given the effect of law—and a writ of mandamus could *not* be issued by the Supreme Court. (Incidentally, *Marbury v. Madison* is *most* famous for recognizing the federal judiciary's power of "judicial review": that is, the power of federal courts to review the constitutionality of many laws and executive actions).

Answering the second question first—whether Senator Smith or Marcus is correct that section (4) of the bill is (or is not) constitutionally proper in preventing Marcus from bringing his case directly to the Supreme Court—in applying the text of Article III, § 2 to the hypothetical facts, it would seem that as an ambassador, Marcus would be able to bring his case directly to the Supreme Court. Yet, section (4) of Senator Smith's Act ("The Supreme Court shall not have original jurisdiction to hear cases from ambassadors, other public ministers and consuls, and states involving the aforementioned act") purports to limit the Court's original jurisdiction so that the ambassadors and others would *not* be able to bring a specific case involving banning moderate radio speech directly to the Court. Senator Smith and other supporters of the bill would no doubt argue that section (4) is constitutional, reasoning perhaps that whereas the facts in *Marbury* involved an attempt by Congress to *expand* the Supreme Court's original jurisdiction, here Congress is *limiting* original jurisdiction, which should be recognized in our system of constitutional checks and balances as being within Congress's authority. Marcus would respond that *Marbury v. Madison* firmly established the principle that any statute that seeks to adjust *in any way* the Court's original jurisdiction must fail, under the reasoning that "the Constitution is paramount." On this point, because the principle established in *Marbury* regarding the sanctity of the Supreme Court's original jurisdiction is among the most axiomatic in constitutional law, Marcus is likely correct that section (4) of Senator Smith's bill is unconstitutional—in which case he *may* bring his case directly to the Supreme Court.

Regarding the first question—whether Senator Smith or Marcus is correct that section (3) of the bill is (or is not) constitutionally proper in preventing Marcus from bringing the case on *appeal* to the Supreme Court—in applying Article III, § 2 to the hypothetical facts it would seem that Congress *may* make such "exceptions" and "regulations" to the Court's appellate jurisdiction. Marcus might argue, however, that the Supreme Court should be able to review the constitutionality of *all* laws, based on the reasoning that the Constitution's text itself states that "the judicial power shall be vested in one supreme court [Article III, § 1] ... [and] shall extend to all Cases ... and Controversies. [Article III, § 2]"; and that in all the cases other than those where it has original jurisdiction, the Supreme Court shall have appellate jurisdiction. It would be *structurally* anomalous, he might add, to *remove* from that "one" Supreme Court the power to decide an entire category of case and controversy. On the other hand, Senator Smith would point back to the Article III, § 2 "exceptions and regulations" clause, which expressly gives Congress the power to limit the Court's appellate jurisdiction. Senator Smith could cite to the important Ex parte *McCardle* case, in which the Court refused to address a habeas corpus claim because an act of Congress effectively precluded the Supreme Court's appellate jurisdiction over the matter. *McCardle* thus stands for the proposition that Congress may constitutionally limit the Supreme Court's appellate jurisdiction under Article III. The Court wrote in *McCardle* that although the Constitution confers appellate jurisdiction upon the Supreme Court, it is conferred "with such exceptions and under such regulations as Congress shall make." Accordingly, Senator Smith is likely correct that section (3) of the bill is constitutional—meaning that the Supreme Court may not hear Marcus's case on appeal.

SELF-ASSESSMENT

First, for purposes of answering this hypothetical you must suspend your own knowledge that Senator Smith's bill is entirely absurd from a First Amendment perspective, and almost certainly would not become law in the first place. Then you are asked to believe that a federal district court and federal court of appeals would uphold the law. (Welcome to the world of law school hypotheticals—where absurdity is the norm!) Nonetheless, taking the facts as they come, you should fairly quickly recognize that the issue the hypothetical is driving at is the extent to which the Supreme Court's original and appellate jurisdiction may be altered by Congress.

The heart of your answer to this question must be Article III, § 2[2], which governs the Supreme Court's original and appellate jurisdiction:

> In all cases affecting ambassadors, other public ministers and consuls, and those in which a state shall be party, the Supreme Court shall have original jurisdiction. In all the other cases before mentioned, the Supreme Court shall

have appellate jurisdiction, both as to law and fact, with such exceptions, and under such regulations as the Congress shall make.

Unless you are given a copy of the U.S. Constitution for reference on your exam (Constitutional Law classes will vary on this), it is unlikely that you would be required to quote the constitutional provisions verbatim; however, you should have good familiarity with the *substance* of the provisions that have been covered in your class. For purposes of Article III, § 2[2], then, you should know that:

- the Supreme Court's original jurisdiction extends to cases involving ambassadors, public ministers, and consuls, and those in which a state is a party;
- the Supreme Court's appellate jurisdiction extends to all other cases and controversies (enumerated earlier in Article III, § 2[1]); and
- the Supreme Court's appellate jurisdiction may be limited by Congress.

Your answer should also note, as does the sample essay, that two landmark cases interpreting Article III, § 2[2] are key in the analysis: *Marbury v. Madison* (1803), for the proposition that the Court's *original* jurisdiction is fixed in the Constitution, and may not be altered by Congress, and Ex Parte *McCardle* (1868), for the proposition that the Court's *appellate* jurisdiction *may* be limited by Congress.

In sum, knowledge of the Supreme Court's original and appellate jurisdiction is foundational to a proper understanding of the U.S. Constitution's system of separation of powers. Specifically, when viewed together, Article III, § 2[2]'s provisions detailing the Court's original and appellate jurisdiction demonstrate the Constitution's "finely wrought" system of checking and balancing the three branches of the federal government against one another. On the one hand, the Supreme Court's authority to hear certain types of cases is unalterable and "sacrosanct," whereas on the other hand, its authority to hear other types of cases is subject to alteration by its coequal branch of government, Congress.

VARIATIONS ON THE THEME

Consider the following variations on the facts.

1. Imagine that Congress passes a law withdrawing the Supreme Court's appellate jurisdiction in *all* cases and controversies. Would this Act of Congress be constitutional?
2. Article III, § 1 provides, "The judicial Power of the United States shall be vested in one Supreme Court, and in such inferior Courts as the Congress may from time to time ordain and establish." Imagine Congress passes a law completely eliminating the lower federal (ie, "inferior") Courts. Would this Act of Congress be constitutional?

Problem 2
(75 minutes)

HYPOTHETICAL

Billy and Bethany are having a difficult time. The unmarried couple lives together with their two young children in a cramped apartment in the State of Oblivion.

Bethany has just recently learned that she's pregnant again—this time with twins, due in seven months. Neither Billy nor Bethany is traditionally employed outside of the home. Bethany cares for the couple's two children, and they rely mainly on government welfare and revenue from Billy's marijuana farm for survival. Billy grows the marijuana in a warehouse that he has rented a couple of miles from Billy and Bethany's home. Medical marijuana is legal in the State of Oblivion, and Billy complies with all requirements of the local law.

Following a change in administration, the U.S. attorney general, at the urging of the new president, begins to systematically enforce the Controlled Substances Act (CSA), a federal statute that criminalizes the growing of marijuana in states that have legalized medical marijuana.

Billy, who is a prominent activist in the marijuana legalization movement, files in federal court a lawsuit on behalf of himself, as the named party, and an unnamed class of members. The suit asks the court to grant an injunction against prosecution of compliant medical marijuana growers under the CSA. Out of fear of prosecution while the lawsuit is pending, Billy temporarily halts his operations.

With no income from Billy's marijuana business, the family is forced to rely primarily on $200 in food stamps that Bethany receives monthly to make ends meet. The food stamps are supplied under the Food Stamp Assistance Program (FSAP), a federal statute that allows families below a certain income to receive the benefits. FSAP enables families with up to two children to receive $100 in food stamps for each child, and then $50 per child for each additional child. Congress has just amended the FSAP, and although the amendments do not change the benefits for the first two children, they *reduce* the benefits available to families with more than two children by $25 per additional child. In other words, when Bethany's twins are born, she will now receive just $150 total per month ($100 for each of her older children, and -$25 for each of the newborn twins).

Worried that once the twins are born they will no longer be able to make ends meet, Bethany decides to hire an attorney and sues the United States in federal court. Her lawsuit asks the court to strike down the amendments to the FSAP on the ground that the statute violates her fundamental right to family autonomy as guaranteed by the Fifth Amendment's Due Process Clause.

Please discuss whether Billy's and Bethany's lawsuits are justiciable. (Do *not* discuss the merits of the underlying constitutional claims.)

SAMPLE ESSAY

You have asked me to discuss whether Billy's and Bethany's lawsuits are justiciable. Based on the Article III, § 1 "Case or Controversy" requirement, "justiciability" refers to whether the federal judiciary has "jurisdiction" to decide a particular dispute. The Supreme Court has developed five justiciability doctrines:

- no advisory opinions—case or controversy does not exist;
- standing—for a "case" to exist, a plaintiff must have "injury," the defendant must have "caused" the injury, and the court must be able to "redress" the plaintiff;
- ripeness—case or controversy does not yet exist (i.e., injury is speculative or premature);
- mootness—case or controversy no longer exists;
- political question—matter is inappropriate for judicial branch to consider; rather, it is for the political branches (legislative and/or executive) to decide.

Billy's lawsuit.

Regarding Billy's lawsuit, we would ask first if he has standing. The Court has stated that standing contains three mandatory constitutional elements (injury, causation, and redressability) and two prudential elements (no third-party standing, no generalized taxpayer or citizen standing). Billy can argue that he has been injured in the sense that he was forced to abandon his operation of a legal business that provides for his livelihood for fear of prosecution under the attorney general's heightened enforcement of the CSA; there is causation because it is the AG whose threat of prosecution has led to Billy's ceasing his operation, and there is redressability because the court can issue declaratory or injunctive relief that would allow Billy to resume his lawful business. The government could argue in response that the requisite injury is lacking—Billy has not himself been arrested, so his claim is premature or merely speculative (i.e., it is not "ripe"), and that there is neither causation nor redressability because the attorney general did not create the underlying law (the Controlled Substances Act) but is merely enforcing it, which will still be on the books *regardless* of whether the court grants Billy's request for relief. Regarding the prudential elements, the claim is made on Billy's own behalf, and he is not asserting his claim on the basis of his taxpayer/citizen standing. On balance, Billy likely has standing, because he arguably has a cognizable injury that is caused by the AG's enforcement, and the court can give him relief.

It is worth saying a few more words about ripeness, which is mentioned in the paragraph above. In determining whether a case is ripe, a court will look to whether a finding of non-ripeness will cause substantial hardship to the plaintiff and to the fitness of the issue/record for judicial review (the more the case involves a "legal" issue not dependent on the facts, the more likely the court will find ripeness). Here, Billy will argue he is being caused substantial hardship by being forced to give up his business for fear of prosecution, which seemed inevitable given the AG's heightened enforcement; but again the government can reply that his prosecution was not imminent or even likely. Moreover, the government might suggest that the issue—whether the AG should or should not enforce an existing statute—is not fit for judicial review, based on the reasoning that the AG is charged with enforcing *all* laws, and it is not appropriate for the judiciary to instruct the AG on such discretionary matters as enforcement. On balance, Billy's substantial hardship likely makes the case ripe.

This last point above, regarding fitness of judicial review, is also relevant in the discussion on whether this case presents a "political question," which is where the judicial branch may determine that a particular matter is more appropriately resolved among the "political" branches of government—the executive and/or legislature. *Baker v. Carr* (1962) provides a list of six factors (conflated here to three, as the Court has done) that a federal court should consider, in descending order of importance, in deciding if a case is a political question: (1) whether the text of the Constitution expressly commits a particular issue to one of the political branches of government, (2) whether there is a lack of judicially discoverable and manageable standards for resolving the issue, or (3) whether deciding the case would otherwise disturb principles of comity and respect as required under constitutional separation of powers principles. Here, the government could suggest that it would be inappropriate, from the standpoint of comity and respect for the judiciary's coequal legislative and executive branches, for a court to tell the executive (AG) how to do its job of executing the laws. Billy could respond that ever since *Marbury v. Madison* (1803) it has been clear that this is what courts do—they decide cases and controversies, even those involving the other branches of the federal government—so this does not constitute a political question (especially because it does not trigger one of the first two "weightier" *Baker* factors). This would likely not be found to be a political question.

Finally, mootness occurs when there is no longer a case or controversy. The government could perhaps suggest that when Billy stopped his cultivation of marijuana, his injury (i.e., the imminent threat of prosecution, assuming *arguendo* that the case was ripe) was no longer present and the case is mooted. Billy would respond that his injury is in fact still present (i.e., his having to give up a lawful business), but even assuming *arguendo* that that case is mooted, the *class action* mootness exception exists because he has properly filed a class action. (Neither of the other mootness exceptions—voluntary cessation by defendant, capable of repetition yet evading review—would apply here.) Therefore, this case is probably not moot.

In sum, Billy's case is arguably justiciable, because it is not an advisory opinion, he likely has standing, the case is probably ripe and not moot, and it is likely not a political question.

Bethany's lawsuit. Please see the above response for Billy's lawsuit for a description and brief discussion of the five justiciability doctrines: no advisory opinions, standing, ripeness, mootness, and political questions.

We would first ask if Bethany has standing. She would argue she has injury (half the amount of aid for twice the number of children), which is caused by the defendant United States (Congress), and the Court can redress the problem by striking down the FSAP amendments. Moreover, she is bringing the claim on behalf of herself (not a third party), and not on the basis of her taxpayer or citizen status. The government could argue that she does not *yet* have an injury (she is not due for a cut in her benefits for another seven months, when her twins are born). On balance, however, arguably she does have standing because her injury is not speculative, but rather is imminent (albeit in seven months).

This last point regarding Bethany's injury in fact applies to a discussion of ripeness, as well. The government could argue that because her injury will not occur until sometime in the future (seven months) (and, indeed, may not happen at all if she does not eventually give birth), her suit is premature. *Poe v. Ullman* (1961) (where the Court held that a claim challenging an anti-contraception law long on the books was premature because the state had only very rarely enforced the law) is the classic case the government may cite for the proposition that a case is not ripe. On the second matter for ripeness—whether the issue/record is fit for judicial review—Bethany will argue that her case involving a fundamental due process right to procreate is the sort of "legal" issue (not heavily dependent on the factual context) for which a court should find ripeness. Bethany's case probably is ripe.

Finally, Bethany's case is not moot, and does not raise any political question issues. In sum, it is likely that a court would find that Bethany has standing and that her case is ripe; therefore, her case is justiciable.

SELF-ASSESSMENT

Be careful in answering this hypothetical to pay attention to the call of the question: "Please discuss whether Billy's and Bethany's lawsuits are justiciable. (Do not discuss the merits of the underlying constitutional claims.)" Accordingly, you should limit your discussion to justiciability, and not go to the merits.

As noted in the sample essay, the Supreme Court's jurisprudence on the topic of justiciability (i.e., whether and when the federal judiciary has jurisdiction to decide a particular matter) is based in the Article III, § 2[1] "Case or Controversy" requirement:

> The judicial Power shall extend to all *Cases*, in Law and Equity, arising under this Constitution, the Laws of the United States, and Treaties made, or which shall be made, under their Authority;—to all *Cases* affecting Ambassadors, other public Ministers and Consuls;—to all *Cases* of admiralty and maritime Jurisdiction;—to *Controversies* to which the United States shall be a Party;—to *Controversies* between two or more States;[—between a State and Citizens of another State,]—between Citizens of different States,—between Citizens of the same State claiming Lands under Grants of different States, and between a State, or the Citizens thereof, and foreign States, Citizens or Subjects.

In your answer you should then enumerate and briefly describe the five justiciability doctrines: no advisory opinions, standing, ripeness, mootness, and political questions. An exam question involving justiciability, more than some other issues raised in exam questions, requires you to rather formulaically work your way through the elements: first, the five doctrines, then the rules within each of the five doctrines. And in this particular hypothetical, you have *two* claimants addressing two separate allegedly unconstitutional government actions, so you need to work through both of them. That said, you generally do *not* need to write all of the same rules twice for each of the claims that appear in a single hypothetical. It should be sufficient, in discussing the second claim, for you to reference your listing and discussion of the elements in your response to the first claim (see the sample essay, for example, which stated in the discussion of Bethany's claim: "Please see the above response for Billy's lawsuit for a description and brief discussion of the five justiciability doctrines: no advisory opinions, standing, ripeness, mootness and political questions."). That said, you should not expect that a grader will look to an entirely separate essay to find a discussion.

Note that the discussion on ripeness (especially the fitness of the issues for judicial review) may be more detailed than you might have received in your Constitutional Law class, so this sample essay—as elsewhere throughout this book—provides an *ideal* answer that even an exam earning the highest grade in a class might not address.

Finally, regarding the political question doctrine, you will note that the sample essay conflates (as have some courts) the six *Baker v. Carr* factors into three factors, which makes sense because the last four *Baker* factors are so amorphous (and ultimately similar). See the chapter introduction for the full list of the six *Baker* factors. You should always be especially familiar with the first two *Baker* factors, however—"textually demonstrable to another political branch of government" and "lack of judicially cognizable and manageable standards"—because they are the factors most often cited by courts in cases involving political questions.

VARIATIONS ON THE THEME

Consider the following additional facts. Bethany, in addition to suing to strike down the FSAP, also sues to enjoin the attorney general's heightened enforcement of the Controlled Substances Act (here she is making essentially the same claim as Billy in his lawsuit). Discuss whether she has standing to bring this added suit.

Problem 3
(45 minutes)

HYPOTHETICAL

The Republicrat Party controls the West Dakota State House and Senate, as well as the governorship. After the last census, the state's delegation to the U.S. House of Representatives was split eighteen Republicrats to twelve Whogs, which was roughly proportionate to the party representation in the State House. This distribution also closely approximates the number of voters in West Dakota who have identified as Republicrats and Whogs (i.e., there are about 60 percent Republicrats and 40 percent Whogs in the state).

When a Whog member of the West Dakota's House delegation voted against a federal law that would provide universal healthcare for all Americans, the speaker of the West Dakota State House announced, "This is a Republicrat state, and we ought to have a Republicrat delegation. We need to make sure West Dakota is more well-represented with Republicrats in Congress."

The West Dakota legislature then redistricted the state to give Republicrats a majority of registered voters in all but one of the thirty districts. The resulting map was composed of bizarrely shaped districts, some of which traveled for miles along interstates or state highways without capturing a single residence. When asked about the strange map, the speaker of the State House said:

> Our only goal was to rid our federal delegation of Whogs. We didn't care about anything else—not geography, size, or whatever. And if there were enough Republicrats in this state to go around, we might have gotten there. As it is, we will have to settle for twenty-nine out of thirty. For now.

When asked whether she agreed with the speaker's view of the redistricting, the West Dakota governor replied, "Yes—that's what we did." The legislative history of the new map does not reveal any other factors that determined the size or location of any of the congressional districts.

Several West Dakota voters brought suit in federal court to challenge the redistricting as an unconstitutional political gerrymander. The voters argued that a political gerrymander is unconstitutional when the state's *sole* motive is to *completely disenfranchise* the voters of a political party. The state moved to dismiss the case as a nonjusticiable political question.

You are a research assistant to a law professor who is writing an article analyzing the constitutionality of political gerrymandering. She asks you to write a concise memo analyzing how the U.S. Supreme Court might decide the suit by West Dakota voters if it were to reach the Court. She asks you to focus on: (1) whether the case is a nonjusticiable political question, and (2) the merits of the voters' argument (assuming the case is justiciable). In constructing your answers, be sure to discuss *Vieth v. Jubelirer* (2004).

SAMPLE ESSAY

You have asked me to discuss the issue of the political redistricting in West Dakota. Voters in the State of West Dakota have bought the suit alleging that the redistricting constitutes political gerrymander, which is unconstitutional when the state's only motive is to "completely disenfranchise" the voters of a political party. The state has moved to dismiss the case on the grounds that the case is a nonjusticiable political question. I will first examine whether the case is a political question; then, assuming the case is justiciable, I will analyze the merits of the argument that the political gerrymander is unconstitutional when the only motive is to "completely disenfranchise" the voters of a political party.

1. Justiciability (political question)

The State of West Dakota claims the case is nonjusticiable, specifically on the grounds that the case is a political question. The judicially created political question doctrine states that courts will refuse to hear a case addressing a "political question" because such issues should be left to the political branches of government to interpret and enforce. The Supreme Court has defined a political question as a matter where: (1) the text of the Constitution expressly commits a particular issue to one of the political branches of government; (2) there is a lack of judicially discoverable and manageable standards for resolving the issue; or (3) deciding the case would otherwise disturb principles of comity as required under constitutional separation-of-powers principles. (This conflates, as has the Court, the last four (of six) political question factors provided by the Court in *Baker v. Carr* (1962).)

The Supreme Court fairly recently discussed the political question doctrine in the context of political gerrymandering in *Vieth v. Jubelirer.* In that case, a plurality dismissed the gerrymandering claim, stating that it was a political question and nonjusticiable. Writing for the plurality, Justice Scalia stated that the issue of political gerrymandering, after having been found by the Court to be justiciable some twenty years earlier in *Davis v. Bandemer,* had shown itself in the intervening years to be essentially unworkable, without judicially discoverable or manageable standards. Four dissenting justices disagreed, setting forth a number of what they suggested were eminently manageable judicial standards (discussed below). Justice Kennedy's concurring opinion agreed with the plurality that there was no workable standard *at present,* but held out the possibility that a workable standard might be found at some time in the future. As such, Justice Kennedy's opinion was claimed by both the plurality and dissent as the fifth vote in support of their respective positions on the question of justiciability.

Unlike racial gerrymandering, which is justiciable due to the fact that race is a suspect classification, in this case the Supreme Court could rule either way on the question of whether political gerrymandering is (or is not) a nonjusticiable political question. In sum, the question would hinge in the particular case on whether the Court believes there exist judicially manageable standards for determining whether political gerrymandering exceeds constitutional bounds. Given that there were four separate dissents in *Vieth,* each with its own "judicially manageable standard," plus Justice Kennedy's concurring opinion declining to find such a standard, it seems highly unlikely that a majority of the Court in reviewing the West Dakota voters' case would now suddenly agree upon one—so, on balance I believe the Court would likely find the case to be a nonjusticiable political question for lack of a judicially discoverable and manageable standard.

2. Merits of voters' argument

Assuming for the sake of argument, however, that this question of political gerrymandering is not a nonjusticiable political question, I will analyze the merits of the case at hand. In *Vieth,* the dissenting opinions provide what their authors suggest are "judicially discoverable and manageable standards" for determining when political gerrymandering is unconstitutional. These proposed standards follow more or less from the Court's earlier suggestion in *Davis v. Bandemer* (1986) that political gerrymandering fails to withstand constitutional scrutiny where it dilutes the vote of any group in violation of the equal protection clause's "one-person, one-vote" mandate.

If the four *Vieth* dissenting opinions are consolidated, they essentially apply rational basis review, suggesting that political gerrymandering would be found invalid if it were done "in a way unrelated to any legitimate legislative objective." They suggest that bizarrely shaped districts, by themselves, can demonstrate an illicit purpose; and, similarly, that acts of redistricting done solely for political purposes, or to intentionally dilute the votes of some, are likewise not legitimate. Finally, they suggest that to the extent purely political gerrymandering fails to advance any plausible democratic objective while simultaneously threatening serious democratic harm, courts are justified in finding that the action violates the equal protection clause.

If we apply this analysis, the voters in West Dakota may argue that any law whose "only goal was to rid our federal delegation of Whogs," as quoted by the Republicrat speaker of the House (and confirmed by the Republicrat governor) cannot be a "legitimate" objective under any metric. (The speaker continued, "We didn't care about anything else—not geography, size, or whatever.") This is a case, the voters would suggest, where the state, through the dominant political party, admits to intentionally diluting the voters' vote. They would argue that such sentiments and outcomes—where a party constituting 40 percent of the voters in the state is only able to capture one out of thirty seats (roughly 3 percent) in the House of Representatives, effectively completely disenfranchising the voters of a prominent political party—must surely violate equal protection principles of "one-person, one-vote," as first established in *Reynolds v. Sims* (1964). Additionally, the redistricting in West Dakota resulted in very bizarre district shapes, some of which do not capture a single residence for miles. Moreover, such disenfranchisement might violate First Amendment associational rights by "punishing" voters who associate with the Whogs (Justice Kennedy, in his *Vieth* concurrence, actually suggested the First Amendment might be a sounder basis for such analysis than the Equal Protection Clause).

On the other hand, the dominant Republicrats would argue that precedent is on their side—never has the Court struck down the redistricting in a partisan gerrymandering case. The Court has properly been very hesitant to invalidate gerrymandered districts, they would argue, because the politics (an area typically outside of the judiciary's authority) are largely inseparable from redistricting and apportionment. They would suggest that in this case there is neither discrimination against any racial group nor violation of "one-person, one-vote." Every person may still vote in an election, and each person's vote counts as much as another's, regardless of the voter's political affiliation.

In sum, if ever there is an instance where the Court would find that political gerrymandering is unconstitutional, this would seem to be the case. The admitted purpose of the controlling party is to totally *get rid of* representation of approximately 40 percent of the voters in the state—which would seem under most any definition to constitute "vote dilution."

SELF-ASSESSMENT

In order to put this hypothetical and sample essay into context, it is worth briefly discussing the issue of "gerrymandering" (which has commanded a lot of attention from the Supreme Court) a bit more broadly. A threshold inquiry in determining the constitutionality of a specific act of gerrymandering involves determining what is the primary motivation of those who are doing the gerrymandering (typically, the political party that holds the majority in the state legislature when redistricting occurs every ten years after the census): that is, whether it is *politically* motivated, or whether it is motivated by other factors, such as race.

If the gerrymandering is politically motivated, then we have the case such as that provided in the hypothetical and sample essay. The big question in *Vieth v. Jubelirer* (and afterward, as well, because the case left the question so unsettled) is whether political gerrymandering is even justiciable—that is, whether "a lack of judicially discoverable and manageable standards" (factor number two in the *Baker v. Carr* list) renders the matter to be a nonjusticiable "political question." As described in the sample essay above, the plurality in *Vieth* believed the answer to be "yes" whereas four dissenters believed the answer to be "no," and the one concurring justice (Kennedy) believed the answer to be "yes" in this case, but potentially "no" in other cases. Doing the math, we see that although five justices thought the issue of political gerrymandering was a political question on the facts of the *Vieth* case, five justices also thought that the issue of political gerrymandering might *not* be a political question under other circumstances. IF a political gerrymandering case is found not to be a political question (as the Court had earlier held in *Davis v. Bandemer* (1986)), then the redistricting will be upheld unless it fails to satisfy rational basis review or otherwise violates a constitutional right (e.g., equal protection right of "one-person, one-vote"; First Amendment rights of expression and association).

On the other hand, if gerrymandering is found to be motivated by race (which appears not to be the case in this hypothetical), the case will not be found to be a political question, and, according to *Bush v. Vera* (1996), will be decided using a strict scrutiny standard where the redistricting will be presumed to be unconstitutional, and upheld only if the government proves that the redistricting was necessary to accomplish a compelling government interest.

But back to the hypothetical: the call of the question throws you a bone by asking you to be sure to discuss *Vieth v. Jubelirer.* This hint is included because it is *possible* that you did not study this case in law school (a survey of the leading Constitutional Law casebooks shows that although some include an edited version of the case, others do not)—if this is so, then you will know to read *Vieth* before attempting the sample essay.

As noted in the previous problem as well, you will note that the sample essay conflates the six *Baker v. Carr* political question factors (see chapter introduction) into three—which the high Court has done, and which makes sense because the last four *Baker* factors are so amorphous (and ultimately similar). You should always be especially familiar with the first two *Baker* factors, however—"textually demonstrable to another political branch of government" and "lack of judicially cognizable and manageable standards"—because they are the factors most often cited by courts in cases involving political questions.

As for part two of the question, as instructed, you should provide an analysis even if you have concluded in part one that the case is a nonjusticiable political question under *Vieth*. The *Vieth* case involved four separate dissenting opinions and one concurring opinion that all had different takes on what particular "judicially discoverable and manageable standards" should be applied to determine the constitutionality of the political redistricting. Unless you have been instructed otherwise, generally you would not be expected to discuss each of the opinions in detail separately on an exam; rather, it will usually be enough for you to summarize the major *consolidated* arguments of the majority and/or of the dissents. The sample essay was written accordingly.

As noted in the answer, the Supreme Court's discussions of the constitutionality of political gerrymandering will involve whether the redistricting fails to meet rational basis review or otherwise violates constitutional rights protected by, for example, the Equal Protection Clause (*Davis v. Bandemer* (1986), suggesting that partisan gerrymandering violates the equal protection principles of "one-person, one-vote" established in *Reynolds v. Sims* (1964)) or the First Amendment (Justice Kennedy, suggesting in his *Vieth* concurrence that a better basis for analyzing partisan gerrymandering cases might be the First Amendment, with its protections of various rights such as expression and association). If you have not yet studied the Equal Protection Clause or First Amendment, these nuances likely will not be obvious to you. As suggested in the sample answer, it would seem that if ever there is an example of a political gerrymandering case that violates the Equal Protection Clause and/or the First Amendment, this hypothetical would seem to be it, in light of the blatant comments and actions of the dominant party. The problem is that never has the Court found there to be a gerrymandering case that fit that bill—indeed, in recent years the Court has failed even to consider the merits of such claims (eg, *Vieth; League of United Latin American Citizens v. Perry* (2006)).

VARIATIONS ON THE THEME

Consider the following facts.

Paula Bergen is a federal district court judge who is married to a prominent real-estate developer, James Weeden. Congress passes a controversial statute that gives substantial tax breaks to real-estate developers who meet certain requirements. Weeden will benefit greatly by this new law.

The statute's constitutionality is challenged in federal district court, and Judge Bergen is the judge who would hear the case. She refuses to recuse herself from hearing the case, despite calls from many (including many members of Congress) to do so because of her relationship to Weeden. Judge Bergen then hears the case, and upholds the law.

Many members of Congress are outraged by the decision. Thereafter, a majority in the U.S. House of Representatives votes to bring articles of impeachment against Judge Bergen. Judge Bergen brings suit in federal district court, claiming that she cannot be impeached because she has not committed any impeachable act of "Treason, Bribery, or other high Crimes and Misdemeanors," as required by Article II, § 4.

What will the federal district court decide?

D. OPTIONAL READINGS

The following sources present the topics covered in this chapter in more depth than the chapter introduction. The sources are in increasing levels of detail. The first provides an overview, the second provides more detail, and the third and fourth provide the greatest coverage of the material.

MICHAEL C. DORF & TREVOR W. MORRISON, CONSTITUTIONAL LAW (2010), chapter 1, pp. 119–124.

JOHN E. NOWAK & RONALD D. ROTUNDA, PRINCIPLES OF CONSTITUTIONAL LAW (4th ed. 2010), chapters 1, 2.

ERWIN CHEMERINSKY, CONSTITUTIONAL LAW: PRINCIPLES AND POLICIES (4th ed. 2011), chapter 2.

JOHN E. NOWAK & RONALD D. ROTUNDA, CONSTITUTIONAL LAW (7th ed. 2000), chapters 1, 2.

FEDERAL LEGISLATIVE POWER 2

A. INTRODUCTION

Under the U.S. Constitution, Congress is a body of limited governmental authority, while states retain all residual governmental power. Article I provides, "All legislative Powers herein granted shall be vested in a Congress of the United States, which shall consist of a Senate and House of Representatives." The Tenth Amendment observes that Congress must have a specific provision in the Constitution in order to act; absent that express authority, governmental power resides in the states (and, ultimately, the people): "The powers not delegated to the United States by the Constitution ... are reserved to the States respectively, or to the people."

So anytime we are asked to assess the constitutionality of federal legislation, we must ask two questions: (1) what provision of the Constitution gives Congress the power to enact the legislation, and (2) are there any independent constitutional *limits* on Congress's action?

The first three problems in this chapter address question (1), examining three of the most important of Congress's express powers: the commerce power; the taxing and spending power; and the Fourteenth Amendment section 5 power. The fourth problem explores the second part of the inquiry for the constitutionality of federal legislation: whether—even assuming Congress is operating within one of its constitutional powers—there are any independent constitutional limits that would foreclose Congress's specific exercise of the power.

The commerce power is derived from the Commerce Clause of Article I, § 8[3], which states: "The Congress shall have the power ... To regulate commerce with foreign nations, and among the several states, and with the Indian Tribes." We focus on the second of these, the *interstate* commerce power—although, incidentally, the third of these (the Indian commerce power) is a matter of great controversy because over the centuries, Congress and the Supreme Court have read the clause as granting Congress the power to regulate the commerce not only *with* the tribes, but also the commerce *of* the tribes—thus assigning Congress a paternalistic role over the tribes likely not intended in the original Constitution. The Supreme Court's evaluation of the interstate commerce power has fluctuated wildly over the past 150 years. During the second half of the nineteenth century, the Court mostly deferred to Congress's commerce clause legislation; then from the late 1890s until 1937 the Court actively reviewed Congress's legislation, striking down numerous pieces of legislation as being beyond the commerce power. From 1937 until 1995 the Court was extremely deferential to Congress's determinations of when it could exercise the commerce power. Finally, from 1995 to present, the Court has once again inquired more closely into Congress's commerce clause legislation.

Problem 1 addresses the Court's current doctrine for reviewing whether Congress is properly exercising the interstate commerce power. Problem 2 addresses the taxing and spending power of Article I, § 8[1], which provides: "The Congress shall have Power To lay and collect Taxes, Duties, Imposts and Excises, to pay the

Debts and provide for the common Defence and general Welfare of the United States; but all Duties, Imposts and Excises shall be uniform throughout the United States." Of all of Congress's expressly enumerated powers, the taxing and spending power probably receives the greatest deference from the Supreme Court, chiefly because the power is authorized for the "general welfare of the United States"—a phrase that seems to give Congress an almost police-power–like authority within this realm. (It is axiomatic that generally the *states*—*not* the federal government—possess the police power to regulate for the peoples' health, safety, and welfare.) Even during the height of the *Lochner* era in the mid-1930s, when the Supreme Court was frequently striking down federal legislation as exceeding Congress's enumerated powers, the Court recognized in *United States v. Butler* (1936) that Congress's taxing and spending power is broad. Problem 2 also addresses the issue of the *conditions* that Congress often attaches to its spending—generally, according to the Court in *South Dakota v. Dole* (1987), Congress *may* attach conditions upon states in order for them to receive federal funds, so long as "the financial inducement offered by Congress [is not] ... so coercive as to pass the point at which pressure turns into compulsion."

Next among the important powers of Congress is the power to enforce the provisions of the so-called "Reconstruction Amendments" (the Thirteenth, Fourteenth and Fifteenth Amendments), proposed and ratified in the several years toward the end of and following the Civil War. Although the Reconstruction Amendments did *not* signal a fundamental change in the federalist system of dual state and federal sovereignty, they did dramatically alter the balance of power between Congress and the states by removing power from the states in favor of Congress. The reason for this dramatic shift was that many states, by perpetuating slavery, had failed to adequately protect liberty and equal justice during the four-score years following the Constitution's ratification. So, the people amended the Constitution to authorize Congress to force the states to abide by these principles of liberty and equality. Problem 3 deals with the power often asserted by Congress (in civil rights legislation, for example) to enforce the guarantees of due process and equal protection through section 5 of the Fourteenth Amendment, which reads: "The Congress shall have power to enforce, by appropriate legislation, the provisions of this article." Among the provisions of "this article" are those in section 1 guaranteeing citizenship to all persons born or naturalized in the United States, prohibiting states from depriving any persons of due process and equal protection, and banning the states from abridging the privileges or immunities of citizens.

Almost 150 years later, there is still great disagreement about the scope of Congress's Fourteenth Amendment, section 5 power. At one point, notably during the Warren Court era of the 1960s, the Court took a broad view of Congress's section 5 enforcement power (see, e.g., *Katzenbach v. Morgan* (1965)). In recent decades, the Court has substantially narrowed its view (see, e.g., *City of Boerne v. Flores* (1997)). Problem 3 also addresses that aspect of the section 5 power that allows Congress to abrogate states' Eleventh Amendment sovereign immunity.

Finally, Problem 4 deals with the second question we ask when inquiring into the constitutionality of any Act of Congress: whether there are any independent constitutional limits that would foreclose Congress's specific exercise of the power. Congress may technically have power under the Commerce Clause to blatantly favor the sales of a particular item to one racial group over another, for example, but the Equal Protection Clause would independently forbid it from doing so. It is especially important to ask this second question anytime Congress passes a law that may affect some aspect of state governance, for the Court may consider the Tenth Amendment as an independent limit on Congress's power. In assessing this last, the Court has held that where the effect of Congress's law is to essentially "commandeer" the states' legislative process or officials, the Tenth Amendment forbids Congress from so acting. (See, for example, *Printz v. United States* (1997) and *New York v. United States* (1992)).

B. READINGS

Before attempting the problems in this section, you should have read the following material. You may have already read most, if not all, of the cases. Edited versions of the cases contained within casebooks will be adequate for your purposes here.

Lochner v. New York, 198 U.S. 45 (2005).
United States v. Lopez, 514 U.S. 549 (1995).
United States v. Morrison, 529 U.S. 598 (2000).
Gonzales v. Raich, 545 U.S. 1 (2005).
National Federation of Independent Business v. Sebelius, 132 S.Ct. 2566 (2012).
United States v. Butler, 297 U.S. 1 (1936).
Sabri v. United States, 541 U.S. 600 (2004).
South Dakota v. Dole, 483 U.S. 203 (1987).
New York v. United States, 505 U.S. 144 (1992).
Printz v. United States, 521 U.S. 898 (1997).
The Civil Rights Cases, 109 U.S. 3 (1883).
Katzenbach v. Morgan and Morgan, 384 U.S. 641 (1966).
City of Boerne v. Flores, 521 U.S. 507 (1997).
Fitzpatrick v. Bitzer, 427 U.S. 445 (1976).
Seminole Tribe v. Florida, 517 U.S. 44 (1996).
Kimel v. Florida Board of Regents, 528 U.S. 62 (2000).
Tennessee v. Lane, 541 U.S. 509 1978 (2004).
Reno v. Condon, 528 U.S. 141 (2000).
Alden v. Maine, 527 U.S. 706 (1999).

C. PROBLEMS

Problem 1
(60 minutes)

HYPOTHETICAL

Coffee is big business in the United States, with annual sales of over 18 billion dollars. Nearly 54 percent of the population—over 150 million Americans—drink some form of coffee beverage every day (with an average daily consumption of 3.1 cups), much of which is sold at the nation's more than forty thousand coffee shops.

Recently it has come to light that all coffee beans—but only those roasted under certain complicated conditions—can contain substantial amounts of a compound chemically similar to that found in coca, the plant used to manufacture cocaine. Cocaine, a powerful stimulant, is regulated as a Schedule II drug under the federal Controlled Substances Act (CSA). According to the CSA, Schedule II drugs have a high potential for abuse, which may lead to severe psychological or physical dependence.

Congress, concerned about possible increases in violence against individuals that may arise because of this newfound potential source for cocaine in a product as popular as coffee, passes the Federal Coca-Coffee-Bean Control & Violence Act (FCCVA), which has the following major provisions that:

(1) prohibit the possession of "coca-coffee-beans" and the roasting of coffee beans in a manner that would produce coca-coffee-beans.
(2) provide federal civil remedies for a person injured by another who is in possession of coca-coffee-beans.

For its part, the State of Mellow has passed a law that allows individuals to acquire a license to roast and possess coca-coffee-beans solely for the individuals' own use within the state (applicants are required to sign an affidavit stating that they will not sell or give away the coca-coffee-beans). (Assume that this state law is not preempted by the FCCVA.)

Bob Bannery, who lives in the town of Manana, State of Mellow, is a coffee connoisseur who has long roasted his own coffee beans. He particularly enjoys the flavor of coffee brewed using the new coca-coffee-bean process, so he has acquired a state license to roast coca-coffee-beans for his own use. He does not sell or traffic in the beans.

Federal Drug Enforcement Agency (DEA) agents receive a tip that Bannery is roasting coca-coffee-beans, so they contact the local sheriff's department in Manana to coordinate a raid. Despite the Manana sheriff's explanations to the DEA agents that the laws in the State of Mellow do not prohibit Bannery's activities, the DEA agents visit Bannery's property to seize his coca-coffee-beans. The agents seize all of Bannery's coffee beans and roasting equipment.

As the DEA agents are seizing Bannery's coffee beans and roasting equipment, Bannery objects, and as he is arguing with the agents, he uncharacteristically pushes one of them, Shirley Jones, who trips over a carpet and falls, breaking an arm.

Bannery sues, claiming that Congress has exceeded its constitutional power in enacting FCCVA provision (1). In a separate claim, DEA agent Jones sues Bannery under FCCVA provision (2) for damages for the injuries she suffered while seizing Bannery's coca-coffee-beans. Bannery counterclaims that Congress has also exceeded its commerce power in enacting provision (2).

You are a law clerk for the federal judge who will hear both of these cases. She asks you to provide an objective memo considering Bannery's claims that Congress lacks the power under the Commerce Clause to enact the FCCVA provisions (1) and (2). Please provide me with your memorandum.

SAMPLE ESSAY

You have asked me to discuss whether Congress has the power under the Commerce Clause to enact provisions (1) and (2) of the FCCVA, which are challenged in the lawsuits by Bob Bannery.

It is worth noting that a proper full analysis of the constitutionality of a federal statute requires answering two questions: (1) what provision of the Constitution gives Congress the power to enact the legislation; and (2) are there any independent constitutional *limits* on Congress's action? Because you only asked me about (1) (i.e., to "consider[] Bannery's claims that Congress lacks the power under the *commerce clause* to enact the FCCVA provisions (1)"), I will not address question (2) about constitutional limits.

The U.S. Supreme Court's Commerce Clause analysis has undergone many changes over the years, from the pre-1937 "*Lochner*-era" when the Court read the commerce power quite narrowly; to the post-1937 era when the Court adopted an extremely deferential view regarding Congress's exercise of the commerce power; to the present day (since the mid-1990s) when the Court has scaled back on its deference to Congress and undertaken a more exacting review of the commerce power. Under the Court's current doctrine ("*Lopez* test"—first enunciated in *United States v. Lopez* (1995)), Congress has the power to regulate (1) channels of interstate commerce, (2) instrumentalities of interstate commerce, and (3) matters that substantially affect interstate commerce. An important limiting aspect of part (3) is that the matters affecting interstate commerce must be "economic" in nature. Here, the FCCVA regulates neither the channels nor instrumentalities of interstate commerce; so if anything, in order to be upheld, the FCCVA's provisions must regulate matters that substantially affect interstate commerce.

Regarding the FCCVA's provision (1), which "prohibit[s] the possession of 'coca-coffee-beans' and the process of roasting of coffee-beans in a manner that would produce coca-coffee-beans," Bob Bannery will argue that his possession and roasting of coca-coffee-beans does not at all involve interstate commerce—rather, the activity is solely *intra*state (for his own use within the state), as authorized by state law. Also, his roasting of a few coffee beans for his own use surely cannot rise to the level of "substantially" affecting interstate commerce. Finally, he might argue that the possession and roasting of coffee beans is not inherently an *economic* activity—just as Congress could not use the Commerce Clause to regulate guns in school zones (*United States v. Lopez*) or violence against women (*United States v. Morrison*), it cannot use the clause to regulate the possession/roasting of coffee beans.

Congress, on the other hand, will argue that the possession and production of coca-coffee-beans substantially affect interstate commerce. Well-established precedent since 1937 suggests that intrastate activities (such as manufacturing) that occur with products that will travel or have traveled across state lines are sufficiently within the stream of commerce to constitute "interstate commerce" for purposes of Congress's regulatory power. Bannery's coffee beans were certainly not grown in his home state of Mellow, so by definition they had to have crossed state lines; as such they may be reached by the commerce power. Even a small producer such as Banning whose production does not alone "substantially" affect interstate commerce may be regulated under the commerce power because the cumulative effects of many such producers *do* substantially affect supply and demand of a regulated commodity power. Moreover, Congress can argue that the provision is a smaller part of a comprehensive national scheme to regulate dangerous drugs under the Controlled Substances Act (CSA), an argument by Justice Scalia that was crucial in the Court's upholding the federal government's seizure of marijuana grown and used solely for home use (in compliance with state medical marijuana law) in *Gonzales v. Raich* (2005). Finally, Congress will argue that the FCCVA does indeed regulate an "economic activity": coffee as a commodity is the source of an 18 billion-dollar fully integrated national (and international) industry. As the Court explained in *Raich,* economics are inherently about supply and demand—and just as the Court found relevant the possibility that some of the marijuana grown for home use in *Raich* could reach the interstate market and increase supply, so too here some of the coca-coffee-beans, despite the state law mandating home use only, may reach the interstate market and increase the supply of this dangerous drug.

In conclusion, Congress will likely prevail in its arguments that FCCVA provision (1) is within its commerce power. The key fact here is that Congress is regulating the possession and production of a controlled substance, because it places the facts within the realm of *Raich,* which strongly affirmed Congress's power to regulate controlled substances even in intrastate settings.

You have also asked me to discuss whether Congress exceeded its commerce power in passing FCCVA provision (2), which "provid[es] federal civil remedies for a person injured by another who is in possession of coca-coffee-beans." In short, Bob Bannery may have greater success in arguing the unconstitutionality of the FCCVA's second provision. Bannery's strongest argument will be that the activity Congress is attempting to regulate in provision (2), violence by people possessing coca-coffee-beans, is not inherently an *economic* activity, and thus it may not be said to be a matter that substantially affects interstate commerce. This provision somewhat resembles the statute that the Supreme Court struck down in *United States v. Morrison,* where Congress had provided civil remedies for victims of violence against women. There the Court found that violence against women simply is not an economic activity. Similarly, Banning will argue here that violence by those in possession of coca-coffee-beans simply is not an economic activity, and that Congress therefore may not regulate it.

DEA Agent Shirley Jones's strongest argument may be the same as Congress's strongest argument regarding provision (1) above—that is, that FCCVA provision (2) is constitutional because it is but a small part of a larger regulatory scheme to control drugs. (*Gonzalez v. Raich*). She might suggest that this is how the FCCVA provision may be distinguished from the statute in *Morrison,* which stood alone.

In conclusion, both of these arguments have merit. On balance, especially because the modern Supreme Court has been more skeptical of Congress's commerce power (and *Gonzales v. Raich* may be seen as something as an anomaly), perhaps the most likely outcome is that the Court will find that Congress has exceeded its commerce power in passing FCCVA provision (2).

SELF-ASSESSMENT

It is important to pay attention to the prompt in this hypothetical. Specifically, as explained in the sample essay, the question asks only whether Congress is authorized under its commerce power to enact the statute, so you should answer only that precise question. Had the question asked instead whether the statute is "constitutional," then it would be appropriate to answer the second part of the general constitutionality-of-Acts-of-Congress inquiry of as well: whether there any independent constitutional *limits* to Congress's action (e.g., Bill of Rights and Fourteenth Amendment protections, Tenth Amendment federalism limits). The final hypothetical in this chapter addresses this second part of the inquiry. This hypothetical question could also give rise to preemption issues, but because it specifically asks you to "assume that the state law is not preempted by the FCCVA," you should not address preemption.

Because questions regarding Congress's commerce power have been such a major part of the Court's jurisprudence over the years (and of your Constitutional Law class, in all likelihood), it is worth spending a sentence or two summarizing the history. Unless the question asks for more specific information, it is enough simply to comment that the Court has gone through various stages where it was much less deferential to Congress (pre-1937), much more deferential (1937–1995), and then again marginally less deferential (1995–present).

The Court's current Commerce Clause doctrine focuses heavily on whether the activity being regulated is fundamentally an *economic* matter. This inquiry is part of the analysis of whether Congress's regulation falls within the third prong of the *Lopez* test, which provides that Congress may regulate "matters that substantially affect interstate commerce." Your answer should spend substantial time on the "economic/noneconomic" distinction—indeed, FCCVA provision (2) is especially vulnerable on this point, because it attempts to allow civil remedies for acts of violence associated with possession of coca-coffee-beans, which resembles the statute allowing civil remedies for violence against women that was struck down by the Court in *United States v. Morrison* (2000). In discussing FCCVA provision (1), a key point is whether the regulated activity is sufficiently "interstate" in nature to justify Congress's use of its commerce power. Here your analysis should pick up on *Gonzales v. Raich* (2005), which held that Congress *may* regulate what appears to be purely local activity if the regulation is part of a larger comprehensive regulatory scheme (and if the "cumulative effects" of the activity might leak across state borders). Indeed, *Raich,* like the facts in the hypothetical, also involved Congress's larger regulatory efforts through the "Controlled Substances Act" to control illegal drugs.

VARIATIONS ON THE THEME

Consider the following additional facts. Congress, as part of the process in passing the Federal Coca-Coffee-bean Control & Violence Act (FCCVA) described above, conducts lengthy legislative hearings and studies on the issue of coca-coffee-beans and violence. These hearings and studies provide strong evidence that violence against individuals will likely increase substantially with the introduction of "coca-coffee-beans" into the market.

Discuss how (if at all) this additional information affects your analysis above.

Problem 2
(60 minutes)

HYPOTHETICAL

The medical field has seen numerous developments in recent years. For example, many states have authorized the use of medical marijuana for the treatment of medical conditions. The State of Utopia has recently passed legislation that authorizes marijuana to be prescribed within the state and used by persons with terminal illnesses. As part of the state legislation, cultivators of medical marijuana and doctors who prescribe marijuana for medicinal purposes are exempt from state criminal prosecution.

Congress still believes marijuana use is harmful, as demonstrated by its continued listing of marijuana as a Schedule I drug under the Controlled Substances Act. Accordingly, Congress is considering passing the "Medical Marijuana Management Act." This Act would impose a special federal tax on doctors who prescribe medical marijuana to persons with terminal illnesses, as well as on cultivators and treatment centers that supply medicinal marijuana. Specifically, the Act requires doctors who choose to prescribe medical marijuana to pay a federal tax of $1,000 annually; doctors who do not prescribe medical marijuana will not incur this tax.

In addition to the tax requirements on doctors, cultivators, and treatment centers, the Medical Marijuana Management Act also requires doctors to report the names of those patients to whom they have prescribed marijuana as well as what illness the drug is treating.

The Act will also impose limitations on cultivators and treatment centers. Persons who cultivate marijuana for non–personal medicinal purposes are limited to a maximum of forty mature marijuana plants at one time. Any cultivator who is growing in excess of this limit will incur an annual tax of $10,000. Treatment centers that sell marijuana to persons with terminal illnesses are limited to keeping a maximum of two pounds of marijuana.

Additionally, the Act contains the following Medicaid-funding provisions:

1. A State will receive one hundred percent (100%) of its federal Medicaid funding for any particular year if the State enacts and enforces a statute requiring all cultivators and treatment centers to: (a) register with the State; and (b) submit monthly reports to the State listing the names of customers and patients (including their prescribing physicians) they have served during the month.
2. A State will receive seventy-five percent (75%) of its federal Medicaid funding for any particular year if the State fails to enact and enforce either item 1(a) or 1(b) above.

Dr. Roberts is an ophthalmologist in the State of Utopia. Dr. Roberts treats several glaucoma patients, to whom he has prescribed medical marijuana in order to help improve their vision. If the Act is passed, Dr. Roberts will be subject to the $1,000 annual federal tax. Dr. Roberts is quite affluent, and the $1,000 does not place a large burden on his annual salary; however, he is concerned about the constitutionality of such a tax. By contrast, Dr. Roberts's close friend, Mary Jane Smith, who owns a treatment center and cultivates marijuana for non–personal medical use, is not as affluent. She currently has around sixty mature plants; so the Act would cause her to incur a tax of $10,000. Mary Jane is concerned that the Act could put her out of business.

In addition, for its part, the State of Utopia believes the Act's Medicaid-funding provisions are an unconstitutional exercise of Congress's spending power.

Dr. Roberts and Mary Jane have filed a lawsuit in federal district court challenging the constitutionality of the Medical Marijuana Management Act, and the State of Utopia has filed a separate suit in the same court. You are a law clerk for the judge who will hear these two cases. She asks you to draft an unbiased memo discussing the merits of these two challenges to the constitutionality of the Medical Marijuana Management Act under the Taxing and Spending Clause.

SAMPLE ESSAY

You have asked me to discuss the merits of the lawsuits of (1) Mary Jane and Dr. Roberts, and (2) the State of Utopia, both challenging the constitutionality of Medical Marijuana Marijuana Act ("Act") under the taxing and spending power.

Suit 1: Mary Jane and Dr. Roberts—Taxing Power

Congress's taxing and spending power comes from Article I, § 8[1] of the U.S. Constitution, which states:

> The Congress shall have power to lay and collect taxes, duties, imposts, and excises, to pay the debts and provide for common defence and general welfare of the United States; but all duties, imposts, and excises shall be uniform throughout the United States.

The U.S. Supreme Court has adopted a broad interpretation of the Taxing and Spending Clause (*United States v. Butler* (1936)). In *Butler*, the Court explained that a broad interpretation was originally urged by Alexander Hamilton, who suggested the clause confers a distinct power separate from (and not limited by) those later enumerated; and that the taxing and spending power is limited only by the requirement that it be for the general welfare of the United States. By contrast, James Madison advocated a narrower view, whereby Congress's authority to tax and spend would be limited to the other direct grants of legislative power to Congress. By adopting the broad Hamiltonian view in *Butler*, the Court held that Congress's taxing and spending power is not limited to direct grants of legislative power, but may be exercised to provide for the general welfare. Moreover, it does not matter what Congress's underlying purpose may be in imposing the tax—so long as the purpose is for the general welfare and the law raises revenue, it is said to be within Congress's power.

Here, the constitutionality of the "Medical Marijuana Management Act" will likely be upheld as long as the tax is found to provide for the general welfare. Because Congress believes that marijuana use is potentially harmful, a regulatory tax that would perhaps make it more difficult to acquire the drug and thus reduce its use among Americans would likely be found to provide for the general welfare. Dr. Roberts and Mary Jane could argue that the tax is merely a punishment for legal users, but given the Court's broad deference to Congress on what constitutes a constitutional "tax" under the taxing clause, they would likely be unsuccessful.

Whether the *reporting* requirements fall within Congress's taxing and spending power is a closer question. On one hand, Dr. Roberts may argue that the requirement to provide information on patient names and conditions is unrelated (and thus beyond) Congress's taxing and spending authority; on the other, Congress may respond that the reporting of names and medical conditions of medical marijuana patients is *necessary* and *proper* (under the Article I § 8 Necessary and Proper Clause) in order to monitor the proper collection of taxes. The Supreme Court has fairly recently held, in *Sabri v. United States* (2004), that the Necessary and Proper Clause works in conjunction with the taxing and spending power to allow Congress to create rules to assure that taxpayer dollars are not "frittered away." (Although it is beyond the scope of this question, Dr. Roberts's argument on this point may be bolstered by healthcare privacy laws.)

In sum, based on the Court's previous interpretations of the taxing and spending clause, the taxes imposed by the Medical Marijuana Management Act are likely within Congress's taxing and spending power. The reporting requirements, however, are a closer question.

Suit 2: State of Utopia—Spending Power

In *South Dakota v. Dole* (1987), the Court set out a four-step test to determine the constitutionality of conditional grants by Congress under Congress's spending power. For a limitation on a grant of federal funds to be valid, the limitation must be (1) pursuant to the providing for the general welfare of the United States, (2) clear and unambiguous, and (3) related to a particular national project or program, and (4) there must not be any independent constitutional bar.

Here, the State of Utopia is challenging the Medicaid-funding provisions of the Medical Marijuana Management Act, specifically claiming they are not within Congress's spending power. When analyzing the Act's Medicaid-funding provision, we must first determine if it is in pursuit of the general welfare. Similar to the taxing provisions of the Medical Marijuana Management Act, the Medicaid-funding provision is arguably in pursuit of the general welfare. The exercise of Congress's spending power under this Act provides for stricter regulations on the use of medical marijuana to promote the general welfare of the United States and protect against abuse of the drug. Given the U.S. Supreme Court's historically broad reading of the Taxing and Spending Clause on what constitutes the "general welfare," objections by Utopia on this point would likely be unavailing.

Second, any limitation on federal funds needs to be clear and unambiguous. Here, the terms of the Medicaid-funding provisions likely satisfy this requirement. The terms provide specifically what is required of the state to receive 100 percent of funding: to "enact and enforce a statute requiring all cultivators and treatment centers to: (a) register with the State; and (b) submit monthly reports to the State listing the names of customers and patients (including their prescribing physicians) they have served during the month."

Third, we consider whether the Medicaid-funding limitation is related to a particular national project or program. Utopia would argue that limiting the funding for Medicaid (with a general goal of improving health) is in fact *un*related to Congress's desire to decrease the use of marijuana. In this sense Utopia would agree with the dissenters in *Dole,* who argued that there must be a closer nexus between the funding limit and the federal program Congress is promoting than exists here. Congress, on the other hand, would argue that the relationship here is just as high (if not higher) than was upheld in *Dole*; and that the requirement here that the state require all treatment centers and cultivators to register and submit monthly patient/customer reports to the state is reasonably related to the federal goal of reducing marijuana use.

Last, there must not be any constitutional provisions that provide an independent bar to the grant of federal funds. Utopia would argue that *Dole* stands for the proposition that the Tenth Amendment places certain limitations on congressional spending; namely, that Congress cannot place restrictions so burdensome—such as depriving the state of federal funds upon which it has come to rely—as to compel the state to participate in the "optional" legislation. Whereas the amount of funds South Dakota stood to lose in *Dole* was just 5 percent of the total federal highway funds, Utopia would explain that here the state would lose 25 percent of the federal contribution to Medicaid. Thus, Utopia could conclude that the legislation is unconstitutionally coercive in that it crosses the point where federal "pressure turns into compulsion." Congress would counter that the state *does* maintain a real choice in the matter—if it does not like Congress's terms, for example, the state could create and fund programs of its own. Moreover, Congress would add that *Dole* did not draw any fixed percentages beyond which federal conditions could not go. Although 25 percent here is more than the 5 percent in *Dole*, it comes nowhere near to being even a majority of the federal funds provided to the state. On balance, in light of the fact that the Supreme Court has never to date struck down federal conditional spending on these grounds, this fourth prong of the test would probably be found to be met, and the condition would likely be upheld.

In conclusion, because all four prongs of the *Dole* test are likely met, the Medicaid-funding provision of the Medical Marijuana Management Act will probably be upheld as constitutional.

SELF-ASSESSMENT

In your answer, you should note that perhaps more than any other of Congress's powers, the Supreme Court has recognized a broad authority in the Taxing and Spending Clause ("Congress shall have Power to lay and collect Taxes, ... to pay the Debts for the common Defence *and general Welfare of the United States*"). As long as a tax raises revenue, it is legitimate, and the Supreme Court will not question Congress's motives for raising the tax. All taxes, the Supreme Court has explained, are in a sense "regulatory," so the Court will not become involved in trying to distinguish when a given tax is or is not too "regulatory" to qualify as a legitimate tax.

Even during the height of the *Lochner* era, when the Court did not hesitate to strike down federal laws (and state laws too) as falling beyond Congress's scope, the Court acknowledged that the taxing and spending power was different. As discussed in the sample essay, for example, in *United States v. Butler*, decided in 1936 (reviewing the constitutionality of the Agricultural Adjustment Act which authorized payments of grants to farmers in order to regulate production and prices), the Court held that the taxing and spending power, contrary to what James Madison had argued, is *not* "confined, to the enumerated legislative fields committed to Congress. [If this were so,] the phrase is mere tautology.... Hamilton, on the other hand, maintained the clause confers a power separate and distinct from those later enumerated and is not restricted in meaning by the grant of them." Under this latter interpretation, which the Court adopts in *Butler*, the only limitation on the exercise of the power is that it be done "for the general Welfare of the United States." So, although the *Butler* Court in the end struck down the Agricultural Adjustment Act on Tenth Amendment grounds, the case stands for the proposition of an expansive taxing and spending power.

This broad reading is confirmed more recently in *Sabri v. United States* (2004), where the Court upheld a federal criminal statute punishing individuals who bribed officials of public entities receiving more than $10,000 in federal funds:

> Congress has authority under the Spending Clause to appropriate monies for the general welfare, and it has a corresponding authority under the Necessary and Proper Clause to see to it that taxpayer dollars appropriated under that power are in fact spent for the general welfare, and not frittered away in graft or on projects undermined when funds are siphoned off or corrupt public officers are derelict about demanding value for dollars. Congress does not have to sit by and accept the risk of operations thwarted by local and state improbity.

Sabri is also instructive regarding the hypothetical's reporting requirements. Although the Taxing and Spending Clause per se likely does not authorize the reporting requirement, the Necessary and Proper Clause likely *does*. Rephrasing the *Sabri* quote above to fit the hypothetical, we might say: "Congress ... has a corresponding authority under the Necessary and Proper Clause to see to it that taxpayer dollars ... [are] not frittered away in *a system that fails to adequately account for who is responsible for paying the tax*. Congress does not have to sit by and accept the risk of operations thwarted by *inadequate or inaccurate recordkeeping*." Incidentally, if you have knowledge outside of the class that is relevant to the question but is beyond the scope of the question, it does not hurt to insert a parenthetical such as in the sample essay: "(Although it is beyond the scope of this question, Dr. Roberts's argument on this point may be bolstered by healthcare privacy laws.)" A cautionary note, however: do *not* get carried away with adding such outside information—anything beyond a very brief statement is excessive.

Regarding the State of Utopia's challenge to the Medicaid-funding provisions, the sample essay properly works through the four factors enunciated in *South Dakota v. Dole* (which you should use whenever talking about conditional grants—i.e., Congress authorizing spending *if* the state does something in return). As noted in the essay, in order to be valid the limitation must be (1) pursuant to providing for the general welfare of the United States, (2) clear and unambiguous, and (3) related to a particular national project or program; and (4) there must not be any independent constitutional bar. The first two factors are usually met fairly easily, and the third will be the source of some dispute (as in *Dole* itself, for example, between the majority and dissent). But it is the fourth factor that likely will create the most questions in this era of a seemingly revitalized Tenth amendment. (You may note, incidentally, that the fourth *Dole* factor is essentially the same (second) question that is asked *anytime* we review the constitutionality of an Act of Congress. *See* the Self-Assessment discussion of *New York v. United States* in the final problem of this chapter.) In short, this sort of quid pro quo is constitutional, *unless* the federal government's condition amounts to coercion—that is, where the state is left with no real choice in the matter. In other words, is "the financial inducement offered by Congress ... so coercive as to pass the point at which pressure turns into compulsion"? There is no clear answer to where this point occurs—so the best you can do in answering the question is to present arguments for both sides, and draw your best conclusion.

The very issue of alleged Medicaid-fund coercion as posed in the hypothetical was raised by the plaintiffs in the recent landmark case of *National Federation of Independent Business v. Sebelius* (2012), which involved the constitutionality of the Affordable Care Act (ACA). In that case, states claimed that the ACA (which sought the states' participation in an expansion of Medicaid, whereby the federal government would bear nearly all of the costs, but states would pay incidental administrative costs associated with the expansion until 2016, after which time they would bear an increasing percentage of the cost capping at 10% in 2020) was unduly coercive. In a fractured opinion, a majority of justices agreed that the Medicaid expansion could survive, but that the states could not be compelled to participate.

(The *Sebelius* case also discussed whether the ACA's "individual mandate" exceeded Congress's commerce power.)

VARIATIONS ON THE THEME

Consider the following. As part of the Medical Marijuana Management Act (which, as stated in the hypothetical above, imposes a special federal "tax" on doctors who prescribe medical marijuana to persons with terminal illnesses, as well as on cultivators and treatment centers that supply medicinal marijuana), Congress also imposes a $500 "penalty" on any patient who fails to report to the government that he or she has received a prescription for medical marijuana. (Assume there are no healthcare privacy issues.) This penalty is to be collected on the individual's income tax return. The Act repeatedly refers to this required payment as a "penalty," not as a "tax"—even though the Act elsewhere refers to the annual payments and fees described in the hypothetical above as "taxes." The language within the Act itself pegs the power to require this "penalty" to the Commerce Clause, as part of Congress's larger regulatory scheme under the Controlled Substances Act to control illegal drugs: "The individual responsibility requirement provided for in this section ... is commercial and economic in nature, and substantially affects interstate commerce.... "

Shane Bayley is an Oblivion resident who has a prescription for medical marijuana. He does not believe he should have to inform the federal government of his prescription, and he objects to being penalized. Shane argues that the $500 "penalty" provision of the Act does not fall within Congress's taxing and spending power. Based on the Supreme Court's decision in *National Federation of Independent Business v. Sebelius* (2012), discuss whether the penalty provision falls within the taxing and spending power. (Do not discuss the Commerce Clause.)

Problem 3
(45 minutes)

HYPOTHETICAL

Discrimination against women is an unfortunate fact of U.S. history. In light of this history, under its current equal protection doctrine the Supreme Court subjects governmental gender classifications to heightened (intermediate) scrutiny, requiring that classifications be substantially related to an important governmental objective. Even with great improvements in opportunities for women, vestiges of the past discrimination remain. Recognizing this fact, Congress initiates an investigation into discriminatory state hiring practices. After a comprehensive set of hearings, two separate congressional committees strongly conclude that many states around the country have indeed failed to protect women from bias in state hiring.

Based on additional information revealed in the hearings, the committees also conclusively determine that hiring biases exist in many states against persons who happen to be poor. Under its current doctrine the Supreme Court has not subjected wealth classifications to heightened scrutiny.

Acting upon the committee reports, Congress passes the Fairness in Hiring Act, a civil rights act that states:

(i) Every State shall take necessary steps to assure that all hiring for state employment is conducted in a fair and unbiased manner without regard to a person's gender or wealth;
(ii) This Act intends to abrogate State sovereign immunity. Any person who believes a State has violated Section (i) of this Act may bring a suit against

that State or state officials in federal court for such relief as the court may deem appropriate.

Janis Johnson lives in Oblivion, a state with a historically patriarchal and economically hierarchical social structure. Janis, a part-time waitress who receives federal food-stamp assistance, is active in social causes in the state, and she is incensed with the biases she believes exist in the State of Oblivion's hiring policies. For example, she is particularly angered by a billboard along the interstate highway she takes to work every day, which says, "The State of Oblivion is looking for a 'few good men.' Discover the economic satisfaction that a good job brings. Call for employment opportunities."

When Janis applies for a job in state government and is denied in favor of a middle-class man whom she believes to be less qualified, she brings suit against the state for declaratory relief and money damages in federal district court under the Fairness in Hiring Act, claiming that Oblivion has used her poverty and gender as factors in its decision not to hire her. Oblivion argues in response that both provisions (i) and (ii) of the Fairness in Hiring Act are unconstitutional exercises of Congress's power.

You are the law clerk for the judge hearing the suit. In preparation for the case, the judge asks you to provide an objective discussion of the merits of the State of Oblivion's arguments. Please provide your discussion. (For purposes of this discussion, do not discuss Oblivion's Tenth Amendment arguments.)

SAMPLE ESSAY

You have asked me to discuss the State of Oblivion's arguments concerning whether provisions (i) and (ii) of the Fairness in Hiring Act are unconstitutional. This set of facts raises constitutional issues involving equal protection, Congress's powers under section 5 of the Fourteenth Amendment, and Eleventh Amendment state sovereign immunity. Specifically, your request deals with Congress's section 5 powers and Eleventh Amendment state sovereign immunity, so I will focus on those.

As a preliminary matter, the U.S. Supreme Court has long held that Congress may not regulate private conduct under its section 5 power, a position it reaffirmed in 2000. This issue is not implicated under these facts, because the civil rights law at issue, the Fairness in Hiring Act, reaches only government action.

Regarding provision (i) of the Fairness in Hiring Act ("Every State shall take legislative steps to assure that all hiring for state employment is conducted in a fair and unbiased manner without regard to a person's gender or wealth"), Congress would claim constitutional authority in the Fourteenth Amendment, section 5, which provides that "The Congress shall have power to enforce, by appropriate legislation, the provisions of this article."

The issue can be thus stated: does the Fairness in Hiring Act properly "enforce" a provision of the Fourteenth Amendment? As for the rule, whereas at one time the Supreme Court took a highly deferential approach to Congress's exercise of its section 5 power, the current rule, as established through Court precedent, is that Congress's power is "remedial," not "substantive": "Congress cannot 'decree the substance of the Fourteenth Amendment's restrictions on the States.... It has been given the power 'to enforce,' not the power to determine what constitutes a constitutional violation.'" The Court further explained that "the ultimate interpretation and determination of the Fourteenth Amendment's substantive meaning remains the province of the judicial branch." And the Court has determined that in order for Congress to properly exercise its section 5 power, "[t]here must be a congruence and proportionality between the injury to be prevented or remedied and the means adopted to that end."

Given these guidelines, Congress will likely explain that its intent with the Act is to remedy past episodes of state hiring biases against women and the poor—episodes that thus violate the Fourteenth Amendment section 1 equal protection clause forbidding any state from "deny[ing] to any person within its jurisdiction the equal protection of the laws." As demonstrated in the legislative record, there has been a history of state discrimination against hiring women and the poor, so, the argument goes, Congress is justified in taking this "enforcement" action of requiring states to legislate to guarantee fairness and equal consideration in hiring decisions. Congress will argue that there is the necessary congruence and proportionality between the injury to be remedied (i.e., hiring discrimination) and the means adopted to that end (i.e., the requirement that states take necessary steps to prevent hiring discrimination). For its part, the State of Oblivion may counterargue that there is no congruence and proportionality in the absence of specific evidence of discrimination by the State of Oblivion, as opposed to a general finding of discrimination in "many" states. This argument likely fails, however, because for section 5 purposes there is no requirement to show discrimination by the specific state.

Regarding provision (ii) of the Fairness in Hiring Act, the issue is whether Congress may abrogate a state's Eleventh Amendment sovereign immunity. Supreme Court precedent holds that to successfully abrogate the states' sovereign immunity, Congress must (1) "unequivocally express its intent to abrogate the immunity," and (2) show that the act is "pursuant to a valid exercise of powers." See *Seminole Tribe v. Florida* (1996).

Here, Congress clearly expressed its intent to abrogate the states' sovereign immunity in section (ii) of the Fairness in Hiring Act. As for the second element, *Seminole Tribe* held that Congress may abrogate a state's sovereign immunity pursuant only to its Fourteenth Amendment section 5 power, but *not* pursuant to its Article I powers (for example, the commerce power). The Fairness in Hiring Act is enacted pursuant to Congress's section 5 power, so this element would seem to be met as well.

This is not the end of the analysis, however, because the Supreme Court has determined that only certain types of actions fall with the scope of Congress's section 5 authority to abrogate state sovereign immunity. Specifically, the Supreme Court has held that Congress has more authority to act under section 5 when dealing with classifications and rights that trigger heightened scrutiny under its equal protection, due process, or other rights analyses. Here, the facts note that gender classifications are subjected to heightened scrutiny, whereas wealth classifications are *not* subjected to heightened scrutiny. Accordingly, it would seem that pursuant to its section 5 power, Congress *may* abrogate state sovereign immunity in order to enforce the gender classification, but it may *not* do so in order to enforce the wealth classification.

In policy terms, supporters of the Court's current narrow reading of the section 5 power, where Congress is limited to enacting laws that remedy or prevent violations of rights of the sort the Supreme Court has already recognized, argue that this approach properly recognizes Congress's limited role in a federal system where states possess sovereign immunity as well and retain residual power to regulate for inhabitants' health, safety, and welfare. Critics of the current approach suggest, on the other hand, that in so limiting Congress, the Court improperly intrudes upon terrain constitutionally delegated to Congress; they add, moreover, that the Court's Eleventh Amendment doctrine vastly overstates the scope of state sovereign immunity embraced by the text of the amendment and its framers' intentions.

SELF-ASSESSMENT

As we have stated previously, be sure to pay close attention to the call of the question in deciding how to approach constructing a response to any essay problem. If the question asks for a letter, for example, provide a letter; if it asks for a memo, provide a memo. Moreover, when asked for an *objective* discussion, as here, do not try to persuade the reader of the superiority of one position; rather, dispassionately discuss the merits of alternative approaches. Also, please note that you are generally not required to cite case names in your answer.

It is worth briefly mentioning in your response the "state action" rule of the *Civil Rights Cases,* as recently reaffirmed in *United States v. Morrison,* even though the facts do not involve private action. As a general principle, unless the exam instructions state otherwise, it is good strategy to briefly address closely related rules that are not directly implicated by the facts. The key here is brevity—do not waste time on a lengthy discussion. State in one or two sentences the rule and the conclusion that the rule does not apply to the facts, then get out and move on.

Beyond that, be careful not to fall into the trap of discussing more than the question requests. Although it may be tempting to discuss the merits of Janis Johnson's equal protection claim, for example, you are asked only to provide an objective discussion of the merits of Congress's responses to Johnson's suit. The question does *not* ask for the merits of her claim, so resist the temptation. Moreover, the question expressly says not to address Oblivion's possible Tenth Amendment arguments. There is more than enough to discuss with the precise questions asked.

This particular problem requires you to understand the nature of the Congress's Fourteenth Amendment, section 5 power under the current U.S. Supreme Court doctrine. The *scope* of the section 5 power as recognized by the Court is especially important, because the Court's view has undergone a fundamental change since the days of the Warren Court (where the Court during the 1950s–1960s was highly deferential to Congress's determinations of the scope of its Section 5 power), to the point where Congress's power today is limited to enacting only laws that remedy past particularized discrimination, and the Court will be much more inclined to step in to limit Congress's section 5 power.

In answering this hypothetical, be sure to identify the root of the issue: how the Supreme Court interprets the meaning of the section 5 text that gives Congress the power to "enforce" the provisions of the Fourteenth Amendment. Because the Court is so closely divided between the current majority "remedial" view and the dissent's "substantive" view (of the former Warren Court majority), an objective analysis must address both sides of this divide. The discussion must attempt to apply the *City of Boerne v. Flores* "congruent and proportional" language to the facts—even though this language in fact has been the source of much confusion and ambiguity in the years since the case was decided (1997).

The analysis should also demonstrate an understanding of the relationship of the section 5 power to the issue of Congress's power to abrogate Eleventh Amendment state sovereign immunity. Indeed, all of the half dozen or so section 5 cases the Court has heard since *Boerne* in 1997 have involved this aspect of the power. In those cases, as expressed in the sample essay, the Court has indicated that Congress may only abrogate state sovereign immunity when the particular right or form of state discrimination is of the sort to which the Court has previously applied heightened scrutiny. This may involve rights protected in the Bill of Rights or otherwise recognized by the Court through the due process clause, and in the equal protection context, it will include classifications previously identified as "suspect": race, national origin, alienage, gender, nonmarital children, and perhaps sexual orientation.

Finally, unless you are asked to do so, it is not strictly necessary to go into a policy discussion of the sort illustrated in sample essay's last paragraph; but if you have time, it is rarely a bad idea to discuss (however briefly) policy considerations.

VARIATIONS ON THE THEME

Answer the same problem, but with the following changes. You represent Janis, who, in an effort to persuade the state to reconsider its decision not to hire her, asks you to draft a letter that sets forth her most persuasive arguments to the state official in charge of hiring.

Answer the same problem, but with the following changes. Section (ii) of the Fairness in Hiring Act authorizes suit in *state* court instead of federal court, and Janis accordingly sues in state court. The State of Oblivion now has an additional argument for the Act's unconstitutionality. Discuss this additional argument.

Problem 4
(45 minutes)

HYPOTHETICAL

Recent scientific studies have demonstrated conclusively that the use of certain chemicals in the production of fruits and vegetables poses substantial dangers to human health. These reports are widely reported in the media over a period of months, and the matter becomes a major political issue of the year.

In an attempt to assure that all citizens are protected from the dangers of chemicals commonly used in growing produce, Congress passes "The Organic Produce Act" ("Act"), which mandates

> All produce offered for sale in the United States which is transported in any way across state lines shall be organically grown.

To encourage states to enact similar state statutes for produce offered for sale solely within the state, Congress also includes the following provisions in the Act:

1. Every State shall either (a) pass legislation designed to enforce, at the state and local levels, the terms of the Act; or (b) assume strict liability for the citizen health problems that are proximately caused by the use of chemicals in producing fruits and vegetables.

2. Any legislation enacted pursuant to 1(a) above shall include a provision requiring State agricultural officials to conduct, as part of their regular duties, spot checks of farming activities to ensure full compliance with the Act.

You are a clerk in the federal district court located in the Western District of Oblivion. In anticipation of an expected suit from the State of Oblivion against the United States challenging the constitutionality of the Organic Produce Act, the judge for whom you work asks you to analyze the constitutional issues that may potentially be involved in the case. Please provide me with your discussion. Do not discuss justiciability. (Note: For purposes of this question, assume that it is agreed that Congress *does* have the power under the Commerce Clause to enact the legislation.)

SAMPLE ESSAY

You have asked me to discuss and analyze the issues involved in a lawsuit by the State of Oblivion against the United States regarding the constitutionality of implementing the Organic Produce Act ("Act"). This set of facts raises an issue involving the Tenth Amendment's potentially limiting effect on the federal legislative power among the sovereign states.

As a preliminary issue, Congress is able to exercise only legislative authority granted to it in the Constitution. Therefore, Congress must point to a specific power when exercising its legislative power. Here, Congress has invoked its Article I commerce power in creating the Act. (And, I am instructed to assume that Congress *does* have the power under the Commerce Clause to enact the legislation.) However, Congress's power to enact legislation is not unlimited in scope: it is subject to the limitations contained in the Constitution. In the modern era, the Supreme Court has recognized that Congress's legislative power may be limited under the Tenth Amendment (as well as under, typically, the Bill of Rights and the Fourteenth Amendment). This power is not found in the words of the Tenth Amendment per se, but exists in the Tenth Amendment's confirmation that federal legislative power is subject to limits that reserve powers in the states.

The issue can thus be stated: does the implementation of the Act overstep the constitutional boundary between state and federal power preserved by the Tenth Amendment? The applicable rule comes from *New York v. United States* where the Supreme Court applied Tenth Amendment principles and held that although the federal government may influence state legislation, it may not compel the states to take such action, thereby commandeering the state legislative process. Further, the Court found in *Printz v. United States* that federal legislation may not compel or commandeer state or local *officials* to implement or administer a federal regulatory program.

With *New York* and *Printz* as guides, the court would very possibly find that both sections of the Act "commandeer" state legislative processes and officials. The Act's use of the word "shall" is arguably a directive commandeering the legislative process and leaving no room for independent state action or choice. Essentially, the states are offered a non-choice similar to the "take title" provision found to be unconstitutional in *New York*; similarly here, the State of Oblivion may elect to follow the federal mandate of the Act or accept strict liability punishment. Such a notion is seemingly at odds with the Court's conception of the boundaries of state and federal authority.

However, proponents of the Act will likely argue that safeguarding the health of all citizens against dangerous food supplies is a serious national problem, one that has drawn the attention and action of the duly elected federal legislature. Moreover, proponents will argue that a construction of the Constitution relying on a tautological interpretation of the Tenth Amendment is insufficient to find a legitimate exercise of the commerce power unconstitutional. Essentially, the Tenth Amendment does not proscribe a restriction on federal legislative power that runs counter to Congress's ability to enact laws using its commerce power or such laws necessary and proper to meet those ends.

Congress's aforementioned argument is unlikely to find success because the Supreme Court has held and reaffirmed that no matter how powerful the federal interest involved may be, the Constitution does not empower Congress to *require* state regulation. The Court has reasoned that the constitutional balance between the federal and state sovereignty is protected by the Tenth Amendment. The gravity of the dangerous health concerns that the Act seeks to alleviate is akin to the gravity of the concern over the proliferation of nuclear waste and handguns, which was the driving force behind the legislation in *New York* and *Printz*. The issue of contaminated food supply is serious, but enabling Congress to commandeer the state legislative function would distort the boundary between state and federal power and render those legislatures powerless. Therefore, the first part of the Act will likely be held unconstitutional.

Next, a court will likely also find the second part of the Act (requiring the states to include a provision forcing state agricultural officials to regularly conduct spot checks of farming activities) an unconstitutional infringement of state sovereignty. This provision of the Act is reminiscent of the provision of the Brady Hand Gun Act at issue in *Printz*. That provision required county law enforcement officials, pursuant to federal statute, to conduct background checks on prospective handgun buyers. The Supreme Court found this provision unconstitutional because empowering the federal legislature to impress state officials into its service would compromise the structure of dual sovereignty. In effect, this Act would transfer the responsibility of the executive branch to execute the federal laws enacted by Congress to the state officials. Such a proposition runs counter to the limits of federal legislative power described by the Tenth Amendment.

However, proponents of the Act will likely argue that the Act's required involvement of state officials is substantially similar to the involvement of state officials in *Reno v. Condon*. In *Reno*, the Supreme Court distinguished the federal legislation at issue, which required state officials to learn and apply the substance of that specific act, with the legislation at issue in *Printz*. The Court reasoned that the act at issue did not require the states in their sovereign capacity to regulate their own citizens or assist in the enforcement of federal statutes regulating private individuals. Here, the proponents will argue that Oblivion agriculture officials will conduct the spot checks as part of their regular duty and that this provision does not require a significant deviation from those duties. In sum, the provisions required by the Act will not compel administration of a federal regulatory scheme, but like any other federal regulation, the Act demands compliance and support from state and local officials.

Ultimately, this final argument will likely fail, because the Act is specifically creating a new state duty and subsequent responsibility to enforce those requirements. Unlike *Reno*, this provision will require states to regulate their own citizens who violate the Act. Further, this Act explicitly commands state officials to conduct spot checks to assure compliance with the Act. The Act is substantially similar to the provisions struck down in *Printz*, because Congress is directly conscripting the state officials of Oblivion. Therefore, the second part of the Act will likely be held unconstitutional.

SELF-ASSESSMENT

This hypothetical tests a topic that has become more prevalent in recent decades with the Supreme Court's conservative turn: whether Congress, independent of its constitutional *power* to pass a law (under its commerce power, for example, as in these hypothetical facts), is nonetheless limited by another constitutional provision from so legislating. You likely learned this principle in law school according to some variation of the following: "A proper full analysis of the constitutionality of a federal statute requires two questions: (1) specifically, what provision of the Constitution gives Congress the power to enact the legislation, and (2) are there any independent constitutional *limits* on Congress's action?"

To give an example, imagine a federal statute providing that only women may purchase a particular national brand of cookies. Technically this law (although ridiculous) is within Congress's commerce power—Congress may regulate "(economic) matters that substantially affect interstate commerce." Moving to question (2) of the inquiry, however, we see that the law would fail under the Fourteenth Amendment's equal protection clause, where classifications based on gender are presumed unconstitutional under an intermediate scrutiny standard of review, and will be struck down unless the government is able to show that the law substantially advances an important government interest. It is highly unlikely the government would be able to meet this burden for the given statute.

This hypothetical asks you to assume Congress has the power under the Commerce Clause to enact the Organic Produce Act, so the question that arises here is whether Congress goes too far in coopting state legislative processes and state officials in its legislative scheme. The independent constitutional provision that might limit such activity is the Tenth Amendment, which has received renewed attention in recent decades as imposing independent *substantive* limitations on Congress (as opposed to merely stating the objective "truism" that the federal government is limited whereas states have the residual governmental power). You should be sure to discuss the two cases that speak directly to the hypothetical facts in your answer: *New York v. United States* (1992), which closely resembles part 1 of the Organic Produce Act, and *Printz v. United States* (1997), which resembles part 2 of the Act. In *New York* the Court struck down a federal law's provision that gave states a "choice" of either complying with the federal law or taking title to hazardous waste and assuming strict liability for all damages incurred, commenting that the law did not give states a true choice, but rather commandeered state government—which is forbidden by the Tenth Amendment. Then, in *Printz* the Court struck down a provision of a federal law requiring state and local law enforcement officers to carry out background checks on applicants for handgun licenses, explaining that the law commandeered—in violation of the Tenth Amendment—state officials to implement a federal project. Also of note is

Reno v. Condon (2000) (mentioned in the Problem 4 sample essay in this chapter), upholding the constitutionality of federal laws that neither compel a state to enact any laws or regulations nor require state officials to assist in the enforcement of federal statutes regulating private individuals.

VARIATIONS ON THE THEME

The Organic Produce Act contains a third provision that states:

3. In order to protect the identity of farmers involved in organic farming from potential industrial sabotage, States shall be prohibited from disclosing any information about the identity of farmers involved in the interstate sale of organic produce.

Discuss whether part 3 of the Organic Produce Act violates the Tenth Amendment.

D. OPTIONAL READINGS

The following sources present the topics covered in this chapter in more depth than the chapter introduction. The sources are in increasing levels of detail. The first provides an overview, the second provides more detail, and the third and fourth provide the greatest coverage of the material.

MICHAEL C. DORF & TREVOR W. MORRISON, CONSTITUTIONAL LAW (2010), pp. 78–90, 117–119.

JOHN E. NOWAK & RONALD D. ROTUNDA, PRINCIPLES OF CONSTITUTIONAL LAW (4th ed. 2010), chapters 3–5; 15.

ERWIN CHEMERINSKY, CONSTITUTIONAL LAW: PRINCIPLES AND POLICIES (4th ed. 2011), chapter 3.

JOHN E. NOWAK & RONALD D. ROTUNDA, CONSTITUTIONAL LAW (7th ed. 2000), chapters 3–5; 15.

3 FEDERAL EXECUTIVE POWER

A. INTRODUCTION

The federal executive power may arise in three situations: (1) where expressly stated in the Constitution, (2) where expressly given by Congress, and (3) where inherent or implied in the Constitution.

Regarding the first, in marked contrast to the federal legislative power defined in Article I, Article II does not provide a long list of executive powers. The specific powers in Article II, § 2 given the president include the power to pardon; the power to enter into treaties (with the advice and consent of two-thirds of the Senate); and the power to nominate and appoint ambassadors, Supreme Court justices, and other federal officers (with the advice and consent of the Senate; and, during Senate recess, without the Senate's advice and consent). The president's other Article II powers, although potentially broad, are quite ambiguous. For example, Article II, § 1 confers the "vesting power" ("The executive Power shall be vested in a President of the United States of America"); Article II, § 2 confers the "Commander in Chief" power ("The President shall be Commander in Chief of the Army and Navy of the United States"); and Article II, § 3 confers the power to "take Care" ("he shall take Care that the Laws be faithfully executed").

So, Article II's powers given to the president are provided in mostly general terms. Indeed, there has been a long-standing debate, beginning with Alexander Hamilton and James Madison, whether the more general language of Article II ("The executive Power shall be vested in a President of the United States of America"), when contrasted with that of Article I ("All legislative Powers *herein granted* shall be vested in a Congress of the United States.... "), should be interpreted as giving the executive broad powers, essentially unbounded by the Constitution. According to Hamilton, by omitting the words "herein granted" as used in Article I, the framers intended to provide a comparatively much broader executive power in Article II. The "unbounded executive power" interpretation has *not* prevailed in the subsequent centuries, however; rather, Madison's view that separation-of-powers principles require that the executive power *is* bounded by the Constitution has instead carried the day.

Regarding the second situation where federal executive power may arise, "where expressly given by Congress," congressional legislation will commonly authorize and direct the executive to enforce particular provisions, thus providing another source of executive power.

Where neither the first nor second situation clearly apply, the third situation—the president's so-called *inherent* or *implied* power—becomes relevant. As discussed further in the problems below, inherent/implied authority is itself a nebulous concept, as it depends on subjective, structural notions of what is the proper role of an "executive" in a constitutional democracy (or, for that matter, in any governmental organization). Over time, the Supreme Court has not settled on any one approach for ascertaining the scope of the president's inherent/implied authority, instead offering a range of approaches from the narrow, where, essentially, there is *no* inherent authority (as expressed by Justice Black's majority opinion in *Youngstown*); to the legislatively dependent, where the president's inherent authority depends on the degree to which Congress has expressly or impliedly indicated its approval/disapproval of the particular executive action (as developed by Justice Robert Jackson's *Youngstown* concurrence); to the broad, where the president may act in any way that does not violate the Constitution, regardless of what Congress says (as detailed by Justice Vinson in his *Youngstown* dissent; and, in the context of foreign affairs, by Justice Sutherland in *United States. v. Curtiss-Wright Export Corp.* (1936): "The broad statement that the federal government can exercise no powers except those specifically enumerated in the Constitution, and such implied powers as are necessary and proper to carry into effect the enumerated powers, is categorically true only in respect of our internal affairs.").

The Court usually seems to fall somewhere in the middle—that is, the inherent authority may be seen as something of an "extrapolation" of the previously mentioned broad-yet-vague clauses of Article II (e.g., "take care," "vesting," "commander in chief"), with a final determination somewhat surprisingly that is somewhat dependent on Congress's implied or express opinion on the matter.

The first problem in this chapter focuses upon the president's inherent/implied power, and the role (if any) that Congress plays in the president's exercise of that power. We will see in the Supreme Court opinion most often cited for determining the scope of the president's inherent power, Justice Robert Jackson's concurrence in *Youngstown Sheet & Tube v. Sawyer* (1952), that Congress plays a substantial role indeed. Problem 2 addresses the boundaries of Congress's allocation of authority to the president. Having stated above that one of the three situations where the federal executive power is where the power has been expressly given by Congress, we see that there indeed are limits—rooted in the text of the Constitution itself—to Congress's grant of power to the executive. Problem 3 then discusses the extent to which executive agreements are treated as "treaties" (for Supremacy Clause and other purposes), and finally, Problem 4 explores the president's authority in conducting the "war on terror," specifically as related to prisoner habeas corpus rights, as discussed in several important Supreme Court cases.

B. READINGS

Before attempting the problems in this section, you should have read the following material. You may have already read most, if not all, of the cases. Edited versions of the cases contained within casebooks will be adequate for your purposes here.

Youngstown Sheet & Tube Co. v. Sawyer, 343 U.S. 579 (1952).
United States v. Curtiss-Wright Export Corp., 299 U.S. 304 (1936).
Clinton v. City of New York, 524 U.S. 417 (1998).
Powell v. McCormack, 395 U.S. 486 (1969).
Missouri v. Holland, 252 U.S. 416 (1920).
United States v. Pink, 315 U.S. 203 (1942).
United States v. Belmont, 301 U.S. 324 (1937).
Dames & Moore v. Regan, 453 U.S. 654 (1981).

Hamdi v. Rumsfeld, 542 U.S. 507 (2004).
Boumediene v. Bush, 553 U.S. 723 (2008).
Johnson v. Eisentrager, 339 U.S. 763 (1950).
Ex parte *Quirin*, 317 U.S. 1 (1942).
Hamdan v. Rumsfeld, 548 U.S. 557 (2006).

C. PROBLEMS

Problem 1
(60 minutes)

HYPOTHETICAL

The states of Middleton, Westbury, and Easton (the Tri-State Region) have the most extensive network of interstate highways in the United States. The major shipping and trucking companies often travel through the Tri-State Region, as this route is the fastest way to get from coast to coast. Recently, the number of trailer hijackings has dramatically increased along the region's highways, despite the efforts by state and local officials to prevent the thefts. Because all major shipping companies travel through the Tri-State Region, the trucking industry has been drastically affected. One option is to send the trucks around the Tri-State Region; however, this option is prohibitive in terms of time and cost.

The president of the United States, Bryan Willink, is very concerned with the high number of hijackings occurring in the Tri-State Region. Frustrated with the ineffectiveness of the states' response, and believing the situation has created a national emergency, President Willink issues an executive order to increase the regulation of the interstate highways in the Tri-State Region.

The executive order states:

> Tractor-trailers, with a length of 40 feet or more, shall be equipped with a dual locking system, which shall include a primary and secondary locking system. The secondary locking system must serve as a backup which automatically triggers upon the wrongful unlocking of the primary system. Armed Federal Agents shall be authorized to conduct spot checks of all trucks traveling in the Tri-State Region (Middleton, Westbury, Easton). Failure to incorporate a locking system as required in this Order will result in both:
>
> (a) a $10,000 fine to the truck's owner; and
> (b) seizure of the truck by the Federal Agents, who will drive it to the closest boundary of the Tri-State Region, at which time the truck's owner may retrieve the truck. Expenses for the Federal Agents' time will be charged to the truck's owner.

For its part, Congress has not spoken on this particular crisis. However, during a period several decades earlier when acts of piracy of merchant vessels were occurring with some regularity in U.S. territorial and international waters, Congress passed legislation giving the president authority to fine the owners of merchant vessels who failed to install certain anti-piracy protective devices on the vessels. The legislation was silent on whether federal agents could seize the vessels and pilot them to safer waters.

United States Freight and Travel (USFT) is the largest trucking company in the United States. Based out of Delaware, USFT ships primarily to cities in the southwestern United States. With a fleet of over five thousand vehicles, USFT will incur a large expense in the installment of the newly required locking system. However, for USFT trucks to avoid the Tri-State Region would incur even higher expenses for the company. USFT also believes that the hijacking problem is not as large as President Willink believes and could be better managed through regulations on the perpetrators of the crimes.

USFT files suit in federal district court seeking an injunction and invalidation of the executive order. USFT specifically alleges that the president does not have the constitutional authority to enact the provisions within this executive order.

You are a law clerk for the judge who will hear these cases. He has asked you to draft an objective memo discussing whether the president has acted within his constitutional authority in issuing the executive order. Please provide me with your memo.

SAMPLE ESSAY

You have asked me to discuss the constitutionality of the president's executive order addressing the rising number of trailer hijackings in the Tri-State Region of Middleton, Westbury, and Easton.

This set of facts raises constitutional issues involving the inherent presidential power. As a preliminary matter, executive power arises in three situations; (1) when the power is authorized or given by Congress to the president, (2) when the power is expressly stated as a power of the president in the Constitution, and (3) when a power is implied or inherent to the president. Here, there is neither express authorization by Congress nor express power in the Constitution for the president to deal with the specific piracy situation in the Tri-State Region, so if he is to have any power in this situation, it must be pursuant to his inherent power.

In *Youngstown Sheet & Tube v. Sawyer* (1952), the Supreme Court struck down the president's executive order to seize steel mills and keep them operating (in the face of a strike) during the Korean War, reasoning that the president's action was essentially "legislative" in nature. Only *Congress* may legislate, and the executive branch may execute—but not make—laws. It may be argued that President Willink's executive order creates a similar scenario: by ordering fines and seizure of trucks that do not comply with certain anti-piracy requirements, the president is essentially legislating—and that he may not do. Indeed, legislating on matters of commerce is a power expressly given to Congress in Article I.

On the other hand, the president may point out that the greatest impact of the *Youngstown* case has been Justice Jackson's concurring opinion, which spoke of the importance of *Congress* in determining inherent executive power, and identified three categories for classifying inherent presidential power. First, presidential power is at its maximum when the president acts pursuant to an express or implied authorization of Congress. In such situations there is a presumption in favor of authorizing presidential power, which consists of all of the power he has of his own plus all that Congress can delegate. Second, when Congress has neither granted nor denied the president's authority in a particular area, power is limited to his own independent powers, but there is a kind-of "twilight" zone where he and Congress may have concurrent authority or where the distribution is uncertain. Last, Justice Jackson stated that presidential power is at its lowest ebb when the president takes measures incompatible with the express or implied will of Congress, in which case the president may act only pursuant to his own constitutionally granted power, minus any power of Congress over the matter.

Applying this three-step approach here, with respect to the executive order's imposition of *fines*, Congress *has* previously passed (several decades earlier) legislation authorizing the president to fine owners of merchant vessels who fail to install proper anti-piracy protective devices on their vessels. Therefore, because both situations similarly authorize the president to fine the owners of vessels/ vehicles who fail to install certain anti-piracy equipment, President Willink will argue that he acted pursuant to an express or implied authorization of Congress and his power is therefore at its highest ebb. Under this reasoning, the president could argue that the executive order on fines should be upheld.

On the other hand, there has not been any express congressional authorization for this exact situation—Congress's earlier authorization to fine was focused on merchant vessels, not on tractor-trailer trucks. Likewise, Congress has not spoken as to whether *seizure* of the vehicles is a proper step to take. (The president could argue expansively, however, that Congress's authorization of fines could be inferred to extend its permission to other sorts of penalties as well—such as seizure. But opponents could argue that specifically authorizing one scenario is the equivalent of denying all nonspecifically authorized scenarios.) In such cases where Congress is silent, Jackson's *Youngstown* concurrence suggests that the president and Congress share authority in this area, and that the president's executive order will be constitutional if he has independent inherent power to take the action. Here the president may argue that his inherent power may be extrapolated through the "Vested" Clause, the "Take Care" Clause, and the "Commander-in-Chief" clause. The Vested Clause states that the executive power shall be vested in a president of the United States. Thus, the president has the inherent power to do whatever an "executive" in a system of separated powers would ordinarily do—including, he would argue, protect the nation's economic base, especially during times of emergency. (Whether the instant facts constitute an "emergency" is debatable.) The Take Care Clause states that the president shall take care that the laws be faithfully executed. Applying the Take Care clause, the president may argue that because the number of hijackings has seen a substantial increase, the federal laws of the United States involving interstate criminal activity are not being faithfully executed, and he thus has the inherent power to issue the executive order in order to "take care" that the laws are complied with more faithfully. His "commander-in-chief" argument will be his weakest, because the interstate highways are not a "theater of war"; thus, the president's commander-in-chief power does not extend to the national highways.

Opponents of President Willink's executive order might argue that because Congress has the express power in Article I to regulate commerce, the president is interfering with Congress's authority when he is essentially regulating the interstate trucking industry by imposing equipment requirements and penalties for noncompliance. (The president may respond, though, that Congress's power to regulate interstate does not foreclose the president's exercise of his own powers in ways that might involve matters of interstate commerce.) Moreover, to the extent the Supreme Court has reasoned in *Curtiss-Wright* that the president has greater authority to operate in matters involving *foreign affairs* (thus perhaps justifying his action in the earlier case involving piracy of merchant vessels in territorial waters, because the pirates may have entered the territorial waters from the high seas), in the instant case there is no such international component.

Summing up, if we must rely solely upon the president's express constitutional authority, the executive order likely fails. If we consider also the effect of Congress's actions, however, the executive order will likely be found to be constitutional if the previous congressional authorization to fine owners of merchant vessels is found under the instant facts to extend to fining owners of trucks. It will be a closer call for the seizure penalty, however, because Congress has not previously spoken of seizure, per se, as a possible punishment for failure to comply with antitheft requirements (likewise for the fines if they are found not to have been authorized by the prior action). In such case of congressional silence, where the distribution of authority between the president and Congress is uncertain, the president's power is lower (but still not at its lowest), and the executive order will be upheld so long as his action can be justified through the operation of one or more of his independent powers (such as found in the Take Care Clause or Vesting Clause).

SELF-ASSESSMENT

This hypothetical is a bit tricky at first glance, because the facts initially resemble those that you may commonly see in a question about Congress's commerce power, yet here the hypo focuses on the *executive* power. It is worth saying again that each of the sample essays in this book (including the essay for this question) represent the highest "A" paper in the class, so you should not be discouraged if your answer does not completely cover everything included in the samples—your answer may well still be an "A"-quality paper.

Whenever answering a question about the executive power, a good place to start is by explaining, as does the sample essay, that executive power originates either from: (1) an express provision of the Constitution, (2) an express Act of Congress, or (3) "inherent" (or "implied") executive authority. Where, as in this hypothetical, neither (1) nor (2) clearly apply, the issue of the president's so-called (3) *inherent* power may come into play.

Regarding (3), inherent authority is itself a nebulous concept, as it depends on subjective, structural notions of what is the proper role of an "executive" in a constitutional democracy (or, for that matter, in any governmental organization). Over time, the Supreme Court has not settled on any one approach for ascertaining the scope of the president's inherent authority, instead offering a range of approaches from the narrow to the very broad, but falling usually somewhere in the middle—that is, where the inherent/implied authority may be seen as something of an "extrapolation" of Article II's previously mentioned broad yet vague clauses (the Vesting Clause, Commander-in-Chief Clause, and the Take Care Clause), with the final determination somewhat dependent on *Congress's* implied or express opinions on the matter. The sample essay does a decent job of discussing the effect of Congress's opinion—especially in the context of Justice Jackson's three-part *Youngstown* concurrence, and your answer should similarly spend time with the Jackson concurrence, because it has played such a prominent role in the constitutional analysis of recent decades. In sum, as demonstrated in the sample essay, when dealing in an area such as this that is especially "lawless," it is important to offer the competing arguments.

VARIATIONS ON THE THEME

Recall the following facts from the hypothetical:

> For its part, Congress has not spoken on this particular crisis. However, during a period several decades earlier when acts of piracy of merchant vessels were occurring with some regularity in U.S. territorial and international waters, Congress passed legislation giving the president authority to fine the owners of merchant vessels who failed to install certain anti-piracy protective devices on the vessels. The legislation was silent on whether federal agents could seize the vessels and pilot them to safer waters.

Consider also the following additional facts. For the first time in decades, recently there has been another outbreak of piracy of merchant vessels (including many U.S.-flag vessels) in international waters. Congress considers whether to take action pursuant to its power under Article I, § 8 "to define and punish piracies and felonies committed on the high seas, and offenses against the law of nations," but ultimately it does not pass any legislation. (This is consistent with this Congress's recent tendencies to pursue very isolationist, nonconfrontational approaches.) In its discussion of the potential legislation, Congress considers, but *rejects*, authorizing the president to fine the owners of U.S.-flag merchant vessels who fail to install certain anti-piracy protective devices on the vessels, and also rejects allowing U.S. agents or troops to seize the vessels and pilot them to safer waters.

Thereafter, President Willink issues an executive order which is substantively virtually identical to the executive order in the hypothetical above, requiring owners of U.S.-flag vessels to install anti-piracy protection devices on the vessels and allowing U.S. agents or troops to seize the vessels and pilot them to safer waters.

Discuss the constitutionality of President Willink's executive order.

Problem 2
(45 minutes)

HYPOTHETICAL

Congress has recently been engaged in heated political discussions over the backlash from citizens concerning the rise in petroleum prices. As often happens when it debates such contentious issues, Congress finds that it cannot efficiently resolve the debate into productive outcomes. Frustrated with the deadlock that often results when it attempts to discuss important legislation (and perhaps finally fed up with its very low single-digit public approval ratings), Congress passes the Emergency Debate Enforcement Act (EDEA).

The Emergency Debate Enforcement Act provides:

(1) As determined by the President of the United States, an Emergency Debate shall be found after Congressional debate has:
   (a) Occurred for a period of at least 60 days,
   (b) Been at a stalemate for at least 30 days, and
   (c) Such stalemate does not have a likelihood of reconciliation toward passage of a bill.
(2) When an Emergency Debate has been declared, the President of the United States shall be the deciding vote with relation to the issue within the debate, such that the President shall:

(a) hear the arguments of Congress; and
(b) take action to resolve the stalemate in whole or in part in order to move a bill toward passage. Any decision made by the President under this section shall be immediately binding.

(3) The President may discipline any member of Congress for disorderly behavior which caused or is determined to be the cause of the extended stalemate leading to the Emergency Debate situation. Punishment may include but is not limited to sanctions, probation, or expulsion of such member.

With the passage of the above Act, Congress seeks to have the president assist in resolving the stalemate that has arisen in the petroleum price debate. Gretchen Stone, a U.S. senator for the State of Seaside, knows that as a result of the Emergency Debate Enforcement Act, her position in the petroleum debate will not be adequately represented because she is from the president's rival political party.

Senator Stone, who is a strong advocate of constitutional separation of powers, has approached your boss, Clive Edwards, a well-known constitutional law attorney in whose office you are working as a law clerk. Edwards has asked you to analyze the Emergency Debate Enforcement Act and determine whether Ms. Stone has a valid claim in questioning the constitutionality of the Act. Please provide me with your memo.

Given:

> Article I, § 2: "No person shall be a Representative who shall not have attained the Age of twenty five Years, and been seven Years a Citizen of the United States, and who shall not, when elected, be an Inhabitant of that State in which he shall be chosen."
>
> Article I, § 5[2]: "Each House may determine the rules of its proceedings, punish its members for disorderly behavior, and, with the concurrence of two thirds, expel a member."
>
> Article I, § 7: "Every Bill which shall have passed the House of Representatives and the Senate, shall, before it becomes a Law, be presented to the President of the United States; If he approve he shall sign it, but if not he shall return it.... If after such Reconsideration two thirds of that House shall agree to pass the Bill, it shall be sent ... to the other House, ... and if approved by two thirds of that House, it shall become a Law."

SAMPLE ESSAY

You have asked me to analyze the Emergency Debate Enforcement Act (EDEA) and discuss its constitutionality. Ms. Stone, a U.S. senator from the State of Seaside, has brought to our attention this issue and has alleged that the EDEA is unconstitutional. Specifically, I will discuss separation of powers and the boundaries on Congress and the president to extend the president's powers. The analysis of the EDEA will involve two separate constitutional provisions; first, Article 1, § 5 (regarding Section (3) of the EDEA); and second, Article 1, § 7 (regarding Sections (1) and (2) of the EDEA).

Under Article I, § 5[2] of the Constitution, "Each House may determine the rules of its proceedings, punish its members for disorderly behavior, and, with the concurrence of two thirds, expel a member." Section (3) of the EDEA, by contrast, gives the *president* the authority to discipline any member of Congress for disorderly conduct that has led to the extended stalemate and triggered an Emergency Debate. Additionally, under the EDEA the *president* may expel that member of Congress if he so chooses. These delegations of power from Congress to the president seem to be in direct conflict with the express terms of Article I, § 5[2], which expressly grants to each House of Congress the authority to punish and expel its own members. Such cases as *Powell v. McCormack,* where the Supreme Court struck down the House of Representatives's attempt to exclude a member from being seated for failure to comply with requirements above and beyond those expressly mentioned in Article I, § 2 of the Constitution (age, citizenship, and residency), suggest that congressional efforts to alter the basic constitutional terms of membership will likely fail.

Sections (1) and (2) of the EDEA are also arguably unconstitutional because they increase the president's powers beyond those that are found in the Constitution. As noted in *Clinton v. New York,* in which the Supreme Court struck down the Line Item Veto Act as improperly expanding the president's powers, Article I, § 7 governs how laws shall be made. Specifically, Article I, § 7 specifies that every bill shall be passed by both the House and Senate ("bicameralism"), and then presented to the president for approval ("presentment"), who may approve or return (veto) the bill at his discretion (Congress may then override a presidential veto with a two-thirds vote by both the House and Senate). The Court in *Clinton v. New York* held that, by giving the president the power to excise specific provisions of already-passed bills, the Line Item Veto Act violated the framers' "finely-wrought process" of lawmaking as set out in Article I, § 7. (As an aside, Congress need not abide by the Article I, § 7 process for *every* action it ever takes—but it *must* abide by the section whenever its action is "essentially legislative in purpose and effect." A congressional action is "legislative" when it alters a person's legal rights.)

In the instant case, the EDEA arguably similarly unconstitutionally alters the Framers' finely wrought Article I, § 7 lawmaking process. The EDEA specifically allows the president to insert himself into Congress's lawmaking debates and to be the deciding vote in case of any stalemate ("the President shall: (b) make a determination resolving the stalemate in whole or in part in order to move a bill toward passage. Any decision made by the President ... shall be immediately binding."). This makes a mockery of congressional debate, and by giving the president the authority to be the deciding vote in any stalemated debate (indeed, "stalemated" as finally defined by the president himself), the EDEA vastly expands the president's powers in the lawmaking process. Moreover, by making the president's decision "immediately binding," the EDEA violates the Article I, § 7 requirement that the House and Senate be able to reconsider and overcome (by two-thirds' vote) the president's action.

Finally, and more generally, Congress for its part might argue that the duly-elected branches of the federal government, all acting together and passing legislation toward a common goal, may adjust how the Constitution shall be interpreted in certain areas. It follows, the argument goes, that the EDEA is such a case of cooperation among the elected branches to deal with a serious governance problem—and it is not as if such an arrangement is necessarily permanent, as it can later be reversed by a simple majority of Congress. Ultimately this argument is a non-starter, however. Members of Congress and the president, as powerful as they may be, do not have the authority to alter the Constitution. Although they may be in temporary possession of the keys to the national government, congresspeople and the president cannot "give away the store."

SELF-ASSESSMENT

In this hypothetical you must suspend your disbelief (once again) about a law that purports to give such massive authority to the president—one that not only allows him to unilaterally decide disputes in the lawmaking process, but also enables him to punish a member of Congress with "sanctions, probation, or expulsion of such member." It is difficult to imagine a Congress ever passing such a law, but here again we are in "law-school-hypothetical-land," where unusual facts are the norm. The hypothetical gives you a major assist by including a couple relevant constitutional provisions: Article I, § 5[2] (conditions for punishment/removal of House member), and Article I, § 7 (lawmaking process). You may or may not receive such an assist on your exam—it will depend upon your professor—but we include them here in order to point you in the proper direction. That said, the hypo also includes something of a red herring—in particular, Article I, § 2 (qualifications for election to the House) is not relevant to the facts of the hypothetical (although it *was* at issue in the important *Powell v. McCormack* case cited by the sample essay).

The sample essay covers the hypothetical's issues fairly well. Each part of this statute raises constitutional concerns. Congress's attempt in Sections (1) and (2) of the EDEA to assign to the president the authority to resolve legislative stalemates somewhat resembles the facts in *Clinton v. New York* (1998), where Congress attempted to give the president the authority in the "Line Item Veto Act" to strike specific spending items from completed laws. There the Court said that the Act interfered with the "finely-wrought" process for lawmaking established in Article I, § 7. Article I, § 7 states:

> Every Bill which shall have passed the House of Representatives and the Senate, shall, before it become a Law, be presented to the President of the United States: If he approve he shall sign it, but if not he shall return it, with his Objections to that House in which it shall have originated, who shall enter the Objections at large on their Journal, and proceed to reconsider it. If after such Reconsideration two thirds of that House shall agree to pass the Bill, it shall be sent, together with the Objections, to the other House, by which it shall likewise be reconsidered, and if approved by two thirds of that House, it shall become a Law.

There is a reason Article I, § 7 (with its provisions regarding "bicameralism," "presentment," and "veto") is the stuff of eighth-grade Civics class as well as law school Constitutional Law classes—it sets forth the sacrosanct process set forth in the Constitution for lawmaking, which cannot be altered (except by constitutional amendment) even by the agreement of the elected branches. The president and members of Congress certainly may (and must) themselves *interpret* the Constitution, but when that interpretation crosses the line to actually *altering* its terms, they have gone too far. Simply stated, just because the president and members of Congress temporarily hold the nation's most powerful seats of government does not mean they can alter the Constitution without engaging the Article V amendment process.

Section (3) of the hypothetical statute, which purports to give the president the authority to punish and even expel members of Congress, touches upon a similar principle—that is, the allocation of authority to the president directly contradicts the express constitutional provision (Article I, § 5[2]) governing the circumstances under which a House member may be expelled; therefore, the statute is likely unconstitutional.

VARIATIONS ON THE THEME

Consider the following facts. As a result of a massive reformist sentiment throughout the nation, the most recent presidential and congressional elections placed individuals in office who are determined to dramatically change the way the federal government operates. Thereafter, each House of Congress establishes new, vastly different rules and regulations for how it considers, passes, and reconciles bills to be presented to the president. For her part, the president establishes brand new procedures by which the president shall decide whether to sign a bill.

Discuss whether these changes in Congress and the executive raise constitutional concerns.

Problem 3
(45 minutes)

HYPOTHETICAL

Texas encounters a massive plague of Japanese beetles that destroy many of the state's staple items of food, including tomatoes and corn. The Texas restaurant industry, specializing in delicious Tex-Mex creations, takes a heavy hit when restaurants are unable to turn out some of their signature dishes on a nightly basis. Although Texas farmers attempt to regrow many of their crops, heavy pesticides are necessary to ensure that the crops are not destroyed by the Japanese beetles. Testing of the crops reveal that they are not safe to eat because they contain dangerous levels of pesticides.

U.S. President John Smith, a long-time lover of Tex-Mex food, concludes an executive agreement with Mexico to allow tomatoes and corn grown in Mexico to be imported into the United States. One issue that President Smith faces, however, is that the Mexican corn and tomatoes also do not meet Texas pesticide standards, although they are much safer than the products currently grown within the state.

Cornelia Conner, a produce seller in Texas, is prosecuted in Texas for selling Mexican-grown tomatoes that do not comply with Texas law. Conner approaches Jackson Browning, a partner at the law firm where you work as an associate, to discuss her legal position. Browning asks you to research the following question: does the executive agreement between President Smith and Mexico bar enforcement of the state law against Conner? Also discuss how your analysis would change (if at all) if President Smith's executive agreement was concluded in accordance with a valid *treaty* between the United States with Mexico under which each country agreed to encourage the exchange of agricultural produce. In answering the question, please discuss the preemption doctrine in general terms only (i.e., do not discuss the elements of preemption).

SAMPLE ESSAY

You have asked me to discuss whether President Smith's executive agreement with Mexico will bar enforcement of the Texas law against Conner. To the extent a valid executive agreement is treated for constitutional purposes much like a treaty, it will likely preempt conflicting state laws under the Article VI Supremacy Clause, which states that the Constitution, laws, and treaties of the United States are the supreme law of the land, to which state laws and constitutions are subsidiary. So, the issue here is whether the executive agreement concluded by President Smith is valid. If it is valid, the executive agreement would likely bar enforcement of the Texas law against Conner.

Unlike a treaty, which requires a two-thirds' vote from the Senate, an executive agreement does not need to be ratified by the Senate under Article II, § 2[2] in order to be valid. The Supreme Court has never struck down an executive agreement, so for all intents and purposes that which may be done by treaty may also be done by executive agreement (until the Supreme Court says otherwise, at least). The Court has inferred from the Constitution that the president's power to enter into executive agreements may be traced to his constitutional authority as chief executive to represent the nation in foreign affairs, his authority as "Commander-in-Chief," and his power to "take care that the laws be faithfully executed." Despite the fact that the Court has never struck down an executive agreement, there are likely constitutional limits to the president's authority to enter into such agreements. To wit, the cases upholding executive agreements, such as *Dames & Moore*, all involve issues where Congress had at least implicitly authorized the president's action; if, by contrast, a case ever arises where the president is acting in a way inconsistent with legislation enacted by Congress in the exercise of its constitutional authority, it is possible the Court will find the executive agreement unconstitutional. Here, Texas may argue that President Smith has exceeded his constitutional authority because the executive agreement with Mexico regulates interstate and foreign commerce, a task traditionally assigned to Congress under Article I, § 8[3]. The state can maintain that this executive agreement with Mexico violates separation of powers by infringing on Congress's sphere of authority.

On the other hand, President Smith can argue that his power to enter into executive agreements is broad, as demonstrated by every Supreme Court case that has addressed the constitutionality of such agreements. This is especially true to the extent that Congress has not regulated commerce with Mexico in a way inconsistent with the executive agreement (the facts here are silent). Specifically, he could suggest that the mere fact that Congress has the power to regulate foreign commerce does not forbid the president from exercising his authority to represent the nation in foreign affairs by entering into an executive agreement that happens to touch upon that area. Accordingly, President Smith would argue that the executive agreement should stand. In sum, based on the fact that the Supreme Court has never struck down an executive agreement, and has spoken in broad terms about the president's power and autonomy to enter into executive agreements with foreign nations, this executive agreement (entered into in the context of congressional *silence*) is likely constitutional.

You have also asked me to discuss how my analysis would change (if at all) if President Smith's executive agreement was concluded in accordance with a valid *treaty* between the United States with Mexico under which each country agreed to encourage the exchange of agricultural produce. Briefly stated, the outcome would be more decisive in President Smith's (and Conner's) favor if the executive agreement was entered into in order to carry out the terms of a treaty. First, although there might be some ambiguity as to whether an executive agreement would preempt state law under the Supremacy Clause, under long-standing precedent there is no question that a valid *treaty* will preempt state law. Second, the executive agreement to import corn and tomatoes from Mexico seems to be in furtherance of the treaty in that it encourages an exchange of agricultural produce. As such, the executive agreement can arguably be said to be a valid exercise of the president's Article II duty to take care that the laws (and treaties) of the United States be faithfully executed.

SELF-ASSESSMENT

Note that the hypothetical asks specifically if the executive agreement between President Smith and Mexico bars enforcement of the state law against Conner—that is, whether the executive agreement supersedes state law. (And note again the technique in answering the hypothetical for repeating the precise wording of the question as the first sentence in the answer; by using this technique, you are less likely to become sidetracked by peripheral issues.) Like the doctrine of legislative "preemption" discussed in Chapter 4, this question necessarily involves an interpretation of the Article VI Supremacy Clause. The Supremacy Clause states:

> This Constitution, and the Laws of the United States which shall be made in Pursuance thereof; and all Treaties made, or which shall be made, under the Authority of the United States, shall be the supreme Law of the Land; and the Judges in every State shall be bound thereby, any Thing in the Constitution or Laws of any State to the Contrary notwithstanding.

So your sample essay should initially ask whether the executive agreement should be treated as a "treaty." If so, the state law is barred under the Supremacy Clause. As noted, in the several cases where the Supreme Court has considered the issue, the Court has always upheld the president's power to enter into executive agreements, despite the seeming incongruity with the treaty power requirements, and treated them the same as treaties. Indeed, the Court has commented that the president's power is at its most expansive in the realm of foreign relations, suggesting that great deference should be given to the president by the Court in such cases (*Curtiss-Wright*).

Accordingly, as the sample essay suggests, it would seem that the state law is barred in this case—assuming the executive agreement is valid. Each of the cases where the Court has reviewed an executive agreement has involved a situation where the president was operating pursuant to congressional authority, whether express or implicit. This leaves open the question of the constitutionality of an executive agreement where the president entered into the agreement despite congressional *dis*approval, or even silence (as in the hypothetical). Your answer should discuss how on one hand, a broad view of executive power would suggest that the president should be given deference in the realm of foreign relations, whereas a narrow checks-and-balances view would suggest that the president's power should depend in part on whether Congress is in agreement with the president's action.

Be sure in your answer to address the additional question of "how your analysis would change (if at all) if President Smith's executive agreement was concluded in accordance with a valid *treaty* between the United States with Mexico." As noted in the sample essay, under these changed facts "the outcome would be more decisive in President Smith's (and Conner's) favor if the executive agreement was entered into in order to carry out the terms of a treaty designed 'to encourage the exchange of agricultural produce.'"

Incidentally, regarding executive agreements—international agreements that become effective simply when signed by the president and the head of another country—students are often puzzled in light of the fact that Article II, § 2[2] seems so clearly to indicate that the president's Treaty Power is qualified by the requirement that all treaties must be agreed to by two-thirds of the Senate. This begs the question of why the president would ever even feel the need to resort to the treaty process, if the much simpler process of entering into an executive agreement is equally valid. The answer is that there are potential political costs to the president by entering into executive agreements as opposed to treaties. The treaty process is likely more credible in the public's view, because it involves negotiation and discussion between the president and Senate; if the president is seen as circumventing this process, the public may not support the action to the same degree, which may ultimately harm the prospects for the president and his political party at the next election.

Finally, on a tactical note, it is a useful test-taking device to state (parenthetically or otherwise) that "the facts are silent" where you are aware that certain unstated facts would be relevant to the analysis. (This device is used in paragraph 3 of the sample essay.) By stating certain assumptions, you are able to further demonstrate the depth of your knowledge. Be careful, however—you do not want to overuse this device and unintentionally go too far afield from the stated facts and the call of the question.

VARIATIONS ON THE THEME

Consider the following facts. The United States is currently involved in a tumultuous relationship with the Persian Gulf nation of Gramon. U.S. President Joyce Jones anticipates that military hostilities are imminent. Jones believes that the key to a U.S. victory lies in a surprise naval attack on Gramon, but she realizes that conducting Navy maneuvers and exercises in U.S. waters would raise suspicion. Furthermore, the water and climate conditions on the U.S. Atlantic and Pacific coasts are not equivalent to what the conditions would be in Gramon. Jones begins negotiations with President Gonzalez of Mexico in order to allow the U.S. Navy to begin conducting exercises in the Atlantic Ocean off the coast of Mexico. Jones also realizes that it would be strategically wise to strengthen the U.S. ties with Mexico in order to ensure that the U.S. naval maneuvers can continue and that the United States may have an ally in the impending conflict with Gramon.

In fewer than 250 words, please discuss (a) whether ordering the naval exercises are within President Jones's power, and (b) what additional constitutionally acceptable action (short of entering into a treaty) she may undertake to ensure that Mexico will allow the naval exercises to continue well into the future. Briefly discuss the advantages and disadvantages of such an action.

Problem 4
(75 minutes)

HYPOTHETICAL

U.S. troops are stationed in western Afghanistan, whose border is shared with Iran to the west. There has been an uneasy escalation of skirmishes with groups appearing to have ties with the al Qaeda terrorist network near the border over the past several months, and satellite and drone surveillance show that Iran appears to be dramatically building up its forces and military capabilities in the region. Congress has recently extended the Authorization for Use of Military Force (AUMF) to include the current dispute with Iran, because Congress has reason to believe that al Qaeda members responsible for the 9/11 attacks are now operating with impunity in Iran. The AUMF authorizes the president "to use all necessary and appropriate force against those nations, organizations, or persons he determines planned, authorized, committed or aided the terrorist attacks that occurred on September 11, 2001 ... in order to prevent any future acts of international terrorism against the United States.... " Furthermore, other countries in the region have begun to take preliminary precautions of arming themselves in case major fighting breaks out.

One afternoon, a group of U.S. soldiers near the border is attacked by a group of individuals in civilian clothes. At the time of the fray, the U.S. troops are unaware whether the enemies are Iranian military members, military members of another country, members of al Qaeda, or civilians. During an exchange of gunfire, U.S. soldiers manage to capture Mohammad Mashaei and Odah Gambia. It is later revealed that they are nationals of Syria, a nation with which the United States is not at war. Each denies he is a member of al Qaeda or of the Taliban regime that provided sanctuary for al Qaeda, but rather is operating in sympathy with Iran. Both men appear before a U.S. Department of Defense Field Review Tribunal and are found to be enemy combatants with ties to al Qaeda.

Both Mashaei and Gambia are imprisoned along with uniformed Iranian soldiers in a temporary prison run by U.S. soldiers located within a U.S.-occupied region in Afghanistan. Both Mashaei and Gambia have been in the temporary prison for several years. Mashaei is given some opportunity to speak with U.S. military personnel about his acts of violence against the United States, and is presented with some evidence of his activities; Gambia has been denied the opportunity to speak with counsel and does not know of any charges pending against him, if there are any at all. Both Mashaei and Gambia petition for a writ of habeas corpus. The U.S. government claims they are not entitled to habeas corpus review. What result?

Given:

> Article I, § 9[2]: "The privilege of the Writ of Habeas Corpus shall not be suspended, unless when in Cases of Rebellion or Invasion, the public Safety may require it."

SAMPLE ESSAY

As a threshold matter, the capture of Mashaei and Gambia in a combat zone and their detention is most likely authorized under the AUMF. They are fighting in a region known to be inhabited by al Qaeda, which was involved in the 9/11 attacks, and as such their detention likely falls within the "necessary and appropriate force" Congress authorized in the AUMF. Mashaei and Gambia may argue, however, that the Review Tribunal process that designated them as "enemy combatants" was procedurally flawed, and, moreover, that they have no affiliation or connection with al Qaeda or other groups involved in the 9/11 attacks and that their detention under the AUMF is therefore improper.

The U.S. Constitution permits a prisoner to seek justification for his or her imprisonment, under Article I, § 9[2], which states that "the privilege of the Writ of Habeas Corpus shall not be suspended, unless when in Cases of Rebellion or Invasion, the public Safety may require it." In other words, this clause supplies U.S. federal courts with jurisdiction to hear claims from prisoners challenging the legality of their detention.

Regarding whether the privilege of the writ of habeas corpus will extend to a particular prisoner, the Supreme Court explained in *Boumediene v. Bush* (2008) that at least three factors are relevant: (1) the citizenship and status of the detainee and the adequacy of the process through which the status determination was made, (2) the nature of the sites where apprehension and then detention took place, and (3) the practical obstacles inherent in resolving the prisoner's entitlement to the writ.

If the Court finds that a consideration of the factors suggests that the privilege *does* exist, then Congress may deny the writ only in compliance with the Suspension Clause—that is, "when in Cases of Rebellion or Invasion, the public Safety may require it"—or, alternatively, Congress may provide adequate substitute procedures for habeas corpus (e.g., meaningful hearing and opportunity for release if detention is found unlawful).

Applying the *Boumediene* factors, the first contention that the U.S. government may raise is that neither Mashaei nor Gambia is entitled to the writ of habeas corpus because they are not U.S. citizens. Prior to 9/11 it was not clear whether aliens held by U.S. military authorities as enemy combatants were entitled to bring a federal habeas corpus proceeding. In *Hamdi v. Rumsfeld* (2004), the U.S. Supreme Court held that an *American citizen* captured outside of the country and being held as an enemy combatant outside U.S. sovereign territory (in Guantanamo Bay, Cuba) had access to habeas corpus review. The *Hamdi* holding was then extended in *Boumediene,* where the Court held that *noncitizen* detainees held outside of U.S. sovereign territory (again, in Guantanamo Bay) have the constitutional right to habeas corpus. Mashaei and Gambia will thus likely argue that *Boumediene* suggests that they—as noncitizen detainees—are entitled to the writ of habeas corpus. As discussed below, however, the government will respond that their cases are otherwise distinguishable from *Boumediene.*

As we continue with the first factor, Mashaei and Gambia will argue that their *status* as "enemy combatants" is an unsettled matter of dispute, and that they are thus entitled to further process through the writ of habeas corpus. Mashaei has been afforded some minimal process to determine his status; Gambia, on the other hand, has been given neither representation by counsel nor the ability to introduce evidence on his own behalf or to cross-examine witnesses. Accordingly, for both, there may be a question about the adequacy of the process. Mashaei and especially Gambia will argue that the procedures here have fallen far short of the minimum required for their lawful detention. They could say that their cases are thus distinguishable from *Johnson v. Eisentrager* (1950), where the Court held that prisoners convicted by a military commission with violating laws of war after the conclusion of World War II and being held in a temporary prison in Germany were *not* entitled to assert the writ, on the reasoning (in part) that the prisoners had received adequate substitute procedures in the form of numerous protections (for example, receipt of detailed factual allegations, representation by counsel, right to introduce evidence and conduct cross-examination) that helped to eliminate the need for habeas corpus review. By contrast, here, the prisoners—especially Gambia—have received virtually none of these sorts of protections. In this sense they would argue that their case more resembles the facts in *Boumediene*, where the Court held that the government's replacement procedures were *not* adequate and effective, and found that the noncitizen prisoners at Guantanamo Bay *were* entitled to habeas corpus review.

Whether inadequacy of process alone is sufficient to require that the privilege be extended to prisoners being held outside the United States is a question the Supreme Court has not precisely addressed. (*Hamdi* and *Boumediene* involved not only inadequacy of process, but also the important fact, discussed below, that they were being held in a location where the United States had long possessed de facto sovereignty.) On balance, because such a holding would entail a substantial extension of any prior Supreme Court precedent, inadequacy of process in a territory wholly outside of U.S. sovereign territory, considered by itself, probably is *not* enough to give rise to the right of habeas corpus. That said, the Court might nonetheless hold that there is a requirement, short of habeas corpus, for *some* form of due process—and that here the government, especially with Gambia, has failed to meet that basic responsibility.

Looking to the second factor (the nature of the sites where the prisoners were apprehended and detained), the U.S. government can argue that the writ of habeas corpus does not extend to prisoners held outside of the sovereign territory of the United States, and, therefore, that neither Mashaei nor Gambia are entitled to assert the writ of habeas corpus. The government would likely cite *Eisentrager*, where the Court held that noncitizen prisoners being held in a temporary prison in Germany were *not* entitled to assert the writ. For their part, the prisoners could cite *Hamdi* and *Boumediene*, in which the Court held that citizen and noncitizen enemy combatants, respectively, held outside U.S. sovereign territory in Guantanamo Bay, Cuba, *are* entitled to the writ, because the United States for many decades had complete de facto sovereignty over the base at Guantanamo Bay. But the government would respond that the instant facts—where the alien enemy combatants are being held outside of the United States in a territory over which the United States does not exercise de facto sovereignty—more resemble *Eisentrager* than *Boumediene*, so the writ should not extend to the prisoners.

The fact that the temporary prison is in a remote location outside of the United States speaks also to the third *Boumediene* factor for determining whether the privilege of the writ of habeas corpus shall apply: the practical obstacles inherent in providing the prisoner with the writ. In the instant case, where both Mashaei and Gambia have been detained in a remote area far outside the sovereign United States, the practical obstacles to arranging for the federal judiciary to hear habeas claims from prisoners are likely excessive, as compared to the facts in *Boumediene* where the United States exercised long-standing de facto sovereignty in Guantanamo Bay, and the Court therefore found that the practical obstacles to providing the writ would *not* be excessive. Accordingly, on this factor the Court would likely find that the writ does not extend to these prisoners. Also consistent with *Eisentrager*, however, the Court could possibly hold that the government must still provide these prisoners some minimal degree of due process, which has certainly *not* been satisfied here—especially with Gambia, who has received *no* process.

In sum, in evaluating this case, the Court will probably hold that the privilege of habeas corpus does *not* extend to Mashaei and Gambia, because they are being held in a distant foreign land over which the United States does not possess de facto sovereignty. This case is thus distinguishable from *Boumediene*. That said, the Court might also hold that fundamental principles of due process require that the prisoners receive at least *some* minimum degree of process.

SELF-ASSESSMENT

Again, as a preliminary note, you will most likely not need to memorize provisions of the Constitution; therefore, Article 9, § 2[2] is provided in the hypothetical.

Do not be surprised if you find this problem involving habeas corpus to be especially challenging. The cases in this area raise difficult questions that are vigorously disputed in the U.S. Supreme Court (with caustic 5–4 opinions), and where the events and holdings are still of recent enough vintage that they have not yet achieved the "seasoning" within the judiciary and academy of other major doctrinal constitutional issues. (On a more practical note, the cases' recent vintage is reason to expect that your answer for this issue might be required to include the case names *and* dates—which has been reflected in this sample essay.) A survey of major Constitutional Law casebooks, for example, reveals a distinct lack of consistency in how these "war on terror" cases and issues are approached. Accordingly, this problem attempts to extract some useful basic principles that you very possibly did not study during your law school Constitutional Law class.

More generally on the substance, the president's prosecution of the "war on terror" since September 11, 2001, has given rise to profound questions about the scope of the executive authority—questions that are not limited to those of detention and habeas corpus discussed in this hypothetical, but which also extend to knotty issues involving, for example, the constitutionality of various interrogation techniques (torture), use of military tribunals, withholding of state secrets, and warrantless eavesdropping.

It would be useful to include in your answer to any such "war on terror" hypothetical some general sense of the competing arguments concerning the scope of executive authority. On one hand, supporters of a broad executive power argue that, in times of emergency, the president should be unencumbered by restrictions from Congress and the Court. This viewpoint is epitomized by Justice Scalia's dissent in *Boumediene v. Bush* (2008):

> [T]oday's opinion ... will almost certainly cause more Americans to be killed.... What competence does the Court have to second-guess the judgment of Congress and the President on such a point? None whatever. But the Court blunders in nonetheless.... Today the Court warps our Constitution in a way that goes beyond the narrow issue of the reach of the Suspension Clause, invoking judicially brainstormed separation-of-powers principles to establish a manipulable "functional" test for the extraterritorial reach of habeas corpus (and, no doubt, for the extraterritorial reach of other constitutional protections as well).... It breaks a chain of precedent as old as the common law that prohibits judicial inquiry into detentions of aliens abroad absent statutory authorization.... The Nation will live to regret what the Court has done today.

Others suggest, on the other hand, that the very purpose of the Constitution is to impose limits on the political branches, *especially* during times of emergency, lest the government overstep its bounds and resort to oppression and tyranny, and that in our system of separation of powers, it is certainly within the province of the Court to insert itself into such decision making. This perspective is demonstrated by Justice Kennedy's majority opinion in *Boumediene:*

> The Framers viewed freedom from unlawful restraint as a fundamental precept of liberty, and they understood the writ of habeas corpus as a vital instrument to secure that freedom.... The [Suspension] Clause protects the rights of the detained by affirming the duty and authority of the Judiciary to call the jailer to account.... Even when the United States acts outside its borders, its powers are not "absolute and unlimited" but are subject "to such restrictions as are expressed in the Constitution." Abstaining from questions involving formal sovereignty and territorial governance is one thing. To hold that the political branches have the power to switch the Constitution on or off at will is quite another ... [, and] would permit a striking anomaly in our tripartite system of government, leading to a regime in which Congress and the President, not this Court, say "what the law is." *Marbury v. Madison* (1803).

Finally, this hypothetical too contains a modest red herring in its statement, "Furthermore, other countries in the region have begun to take preliminary precautions of arming themselves in case major fighting breaks out." This fact may have practical implications for the policies the president (and Congress) may decide to pursue, but it has no bearing on the constitutional question.

VARIATIONS ON THE THEME

Consider the following facts. Pursuant to an executive order, the president provides for the trial of enemy combatants by military tribunal. Congress is silent. As created by the president, the military tribunal process does not include many of the procedural protections contained within the Bill of Rights.

Discuss: (1) whether the president has the authority to create military tribunals, and (2) whether the lack of Bill of Rights protections renders the military tribunals unconstitutional.

D. OPTIONAL READINGS

The following sources present the topics covered in this chapter in more depth than the chapter introduction. The sources are in increasing levels of detail. The first provides an overview, the second provides more detail, and the third and fourth provide the greatest coverage of the material.

Michael C. Dorf & Trevor W. Morrison, Constitutional Law (2010), pp.104–117, 122–24.

John E. Nowak & Ronald D. Rotunda, Principles of Constitutional Law (4th ed. 2010), chapters 6, 7.

Erwin Chemerinsky, Constitutional Law: Principles and Policies (4th ed. 2011), Chapter 4.

John E. Nowak & Ronald D. Rotunda, Constitutional Law (7th ed. 2000), chapters 6, 7.

LIMITS ON STATE REGULATORY AUTHORITY

4

A. INTRODUCTION

Under the U.S. Constitution, the federal government, within its area of authority,[1] is supreme. The Supremacy Clause (Article VI) states:

> This Constitution, and the Laws of the United States which shall be made in Pursuance thereof; and all Treaties made, or which shall be made, under the Authority of the United States, shall be the supreme Law of the Land; and the Judges in every State shall be bound thereby, any Thing in the Constitution or Laws of any State to the Contrary notwithstanding.

In other words, valid federal authority will supersede conflicting state actions, even if state constitutions or laws say otherwise. State judges, moreover, are sworn under the Supremacy Clause to recognize this federal supremacy.

Limits on state regulatory and taxing power arise under two scenarios, yielding a total of three judicially created doctrines: (1) where Congress has acted (preemption doctrine), and (2) where Congress has *not* acted (Dormant Commerce Clause doctrine and Privileges and Immunities Clause doctrine). This section will provide discussions (including hypotheticals and sample answers) for each of these three doctrines.

The preemption doctrine, rooted in the Supremacy Clause, holds that Congress may act to preempt state law. In any preemption case the key question is: what is Congress's *intent?* If Congress intends to preempt, state authority is preempted.

The easy preemption case is when Congress *expressly* states its intent to preempt. In express preemption we look to the plain meaning and clear language of the statute to ascertain Congress's intent. The difficult questions are often about the scope and extent of state laws that are thus preempted.

The more difficult preemption case is where Congress is silent on the issue of preemption, in which case we attempt to ascertain Congress's *implicit* intent through the context, legislative history, or any other available materials. The Supreme Court has identified three areas of "implied" preemption: field preemption (where the scheme of federal regulation is so pervasive as to create a reasonable inference that Congress intended to leave no room for states to supplement it), conflict preemption (where compliance with both federal and state regulations is physically impossible), and federal objective preemption (where state/local law impedes the achievement of federal objective) (this third area is sometimes conflated into field preemption).

1. The threshold question of the constitutionality of the federal law, treaty or action must first be satisfied in order for the Supremacy Clause to operate (see discussion in Chapters 1, 2, and 3 above).

In contrast to the preemption doctrine, the Dormant Commerce Clause (DCC) doctrine arises in the absence of action by Congress. The DCC (sometimes also called the "negative Commerce Clause") doctrine is a negative inference derived from the Article I interstate Commerce Clause ("Congress shall have Power ... To regulate Commerce ... among the several States ... ") that states shall not legislate or act in ways that discriminate against out-of-staters. Under the DCC doctrine, the Court first asks whether the given state measure intentionally (or "facially") discriminates against out-of-state interests. If so, the measure is presumed to be virtually per se invalid, and will be struck down unless the government is able to rebut this heavy presumption. If the state does not intend to discriminate, the Court balances the state's interest against the burdens that the measure imposes on interstate commerce, with greater weight against the measure if it discriminates in *effect* against out-of-staters, and greater weight *for* the measure if it affects in-staters and out-of-staters equally. Some of the nuances of the Court's DCC analysis are presented below in Problem 2.

The Article IV Privileges and Immunities Clause ("The Citizens of each State shall be entitled to all Privileges and Immunities of Citizens in the several States") also places limits on state regulatory and taxing authority. As interpreted by the Supreme Court, the Article IV Privileges and Immunities Clause (to be distinguished from the entirely separate Fourteenth Amendment Privileges or Immunities Clause) requires states to treat citizens of other states as they would treat their own citizens with respect to "fundamental" rights. In determining what qualifies as a fundamental right, the Court has looked in contemporary cases such as *United Building. & Construction Trades v. Camden* (1984) and back to the early case of *Corfield v. Coryell* (1823), where Justice Bushrod Washington wrote that the Clause protects those interests:

> which are fundamental; which belong, of right, to the citizens of all free governments; and which have, at all times, been enjoyed by the citizens of the several states which compose this Union, from the time of their becoming free, independent, and sovereign. What these fundamental principles are, it would perhaps be more tedious than difficult to enumerate. They may, however, be all be comprehended under the following general heads: Protection by the government; the enjoyment of life and liberty, with the right to acquire and possess property of every kind, and to pursue and obtain happiness and safety; subject nevertheless to such restraints as the government may justly prescribe for the general good of the whole.[2]

This definition offers only limited practical assistance, however; what has emerged over decades of the Supreme Court's jurisprudence is that the Privileges and Immunities Clause applies where a state is discriminating against out-of-staters on matters concerning either (1) constitutional interests (for example, rights protected by the Bill of Rights or the Fourteenth Amendment), or (2) important economic interests. The protected interest that has been at issue in most of the Supreme Court's cases involving the Privileges and Immunities Clause is the important economic interest of the ability to earn a livelihood.

---

2. Corfield v. Coryell 6 F.Cas. 546, 551–52 (C.C.E.D. Pa. 1823).

It is also well to mention an example of the sort of matter that does *not* qualify as a protected interest under the Privileges and Immunities Clause as either a constitutional right or sufficiently important economic interest. As identified in the sample essay for Problem 3, the classic case for this proposition is *Baldwin v. Fish & Game Commission of Montana* (1978), where the Court held that a state law that charges out-of-staters substantially more for hunting licenses than it charges in-staters does *not* implicate the Privileges and Immunities Clause, because a law regulating a *recreational* interest is not a sufficiently "important economic interest."

Once it is established that the plaintiff's claim involves a privilege or immunity that is covered by the clause, the doctrine applies a heightened standard of review (essentially a cross between intermediate scrutiny and strict scrutiny). Under this review, the statute is presumed to be unconstitutional and will be struck down unless the state is able to meet its burden of showing that there is a substantial reason for the difference in treatment and that the discrimination practiced against nonresidents bears a substantial relationship to the state's objective (which is interpreted to mean that there are no less restrictive alternatives available).

As noted throughout this book, it is crucial that you understand the standards of review that the Court uses in reviewing legislative and/or executive actions, so we will briefly review them again here. Separation-of-powers principles require that courts, in exercising the power of judicial review, generally defer to acts of the legislature and executive. Accordingly, unless special circumstances exist that would lead a court to scrutinize the law/action more carefully, the law is presumed to be constitutional and will be upheld unless it is not *rationally related* to a *legitimate* government purpose. This "rational basis test" is a highly deferential standard. By contrast, where special circumstances exist that lead a court to apply "heightened scrutiny" (either "intermediate scrutiny" or "strict scrutiny") to the law/action, the presumption shifts against the government. Under intermediate scrutiny, unless the government meets the burden of demonstrating that the law/action *substantially advances* an *important* government purpose, a court will strike it down. And likewise, under strict scrutiny, a court will strike down the law/action unless the government meets the burden of demonstrating that it is *necessary* to accomplish a *compelling* government purpose. (Note that as part of the strict scrutiny analysis, if any "less discriminatory alternatives" to the law/action are available, a court will find that the government has failed to meet its burden and will strike down the law/action.)

B. READINGS

Before attempting the problems in this section, you should have read the following material. You may have already read most, if not all, of the cases. Edited versions of the cases contained within casebooks will be adequate for your purposes here.

Gade v. National Solid Waste Management Ass'n, 505 U.S. 88 (1992).
Lorillard Tobacco Co. v. Reilly, 533 U.S. 525 (2001).
Florida Lime & Avocado Growers, Inc. v. Paul, 373 U.S. 132 (1963).
Hines v. Davidowitz, 312 U.S. 52 (1941).
Pacific Gas & Electric v. State Energy Resources Commission, 461 U.S. 190 (1983).

Granholm v. Heald, 544 U.S. 460 (2005).
Hughes v. Oklahoma, 441 U.S. 322 (1979).
Maine v. Taylor, 477 U.S. 131 (1986).
Hunt v. Washington State Apple Advertising Comm'n, 432 U.S. 333 (1977).
Dean Milk Co. v. City of Madison, 340 U.S. 349 (1951).
Pike v. Bruce Church, Inc., 397 U.S. 137 (1970).
Hughes v. Alexandria Scrap Corp., 426 U.S. 794 (1976).
Reeves, Inc. v. Stake, 447 U.S. 429 (1980).
Supreme Court of New Hampshire v. Piper, 470 U.S. 274 (1985).
Toomer v. Witsell, 334 U.S. 385 (1948).
Baldwin v. Fish and Game Commission of Montana, 436 U.S. 371 (1978).
United Building Building & Construction Trades Council v. Mayor & Council of Camden, 465 U.S. 208 (1984).

C. PROBLEMS

Problem 1
(60 minutes)

HYPOTHETICAL

In 1970, President Richard Nixon and Congress passed the Clean Air Act to protect the public's health, safety, and welfare against harmful air contaminants. Under the Clean Air Act, Congress has established standards for limiting emissions from coke ovens. A coke oven produces coke by heating coal in a controlled environment and is often used for the production of iron ore. However, the emissions from coke ovens have been scientifically demonstrated to be very dangerous to humans, particularly by causing various forms of cancers and tumors.

The Clean Air Act states:

> Coke oven batteries will not exceed 8 per centum leaking doors, 1 per centum leaking lids, 5 per centum leaking offtakes, and 16 seconds visible emissions per charge, with no exclusion for emissions during the period after the closing of self-sealing oven doors.

By contrast, the law in Mountonia, the nation's top state for production of coal and iron ore, which has somewhat surprisingly undertaken an effort to lead the way in protecting the environment, imposes more stringent standards:

> Coke oven batteries will not exceed 6 per centum leaking doors, 1 per centum leaking lids, 4 per centum leaking offtakes, and 13 seconds visible emissions per charge, with no exclusion for emissions during the period after the closing of self-sealing oven doors.

Over a period of six months, the Mountonia Department of Environmental and Natural Resources (DENR), the agency responsible for enforcing the state's environmental standards, conducted a series of spot checks on the largest coke oven plant in Mountonia, which is operated by New Hill Industries, Inc. These spot checks yielded conclusive data showing that the visible emissions per charge from the New Hill Industries plant regularly reach 16 seconds, that the doors leak in amounts up to 8 per centum, and that there are 5 per centum leaking offtakes.

Thereafter the DENR sent an official notice to New Hill Industries, Inc. informing the company that it will be fined for noncompliance with the state emissions standards. New Hill responded with a letter to the DENR stating that it believes the federal Clean Air Act was intended to preempt the state emissions law, and that the state law is therefore void and unenforceable.

Please provide an objective discussion of whether the Mountonia emissions law is preempted by the federal Clean Air Act.

SAMPLE ESSAY

You have asked me to discuss whether the Mountonia emissions law is preempted by the federal Clean Air Act. The Supremacy Clause found in Article VI, § 2 of the U.S. Constitution lays the foundation for the concept of preemption. The Supremacy Clause states:

> This Constitution, and the laws of the United States which shall be made in pursuance thereof; and all treaties made, or which shall be made, under the authority of the United States, shall be the supreme law of the land; and the judges in every state shall be bound thereby, anything in the Constitution or laws of any State to the contrary notwithstanding.

Thus, if a state or local law conflicts with a federal law, the state or local law will be invalidated. Additionally, under the doctrine of preemption, a congressional action may limit or prohibit a state or local regulation on the same subject matter or in the same field of law.

When analyzing a potential preemption issue, we first look to see if Congress has acted. If Congress has not acted, an analysis under the Dormant Commerce Clause or the Privileges and Immunities Clause of the Constitution would be appropriate. The Clean Air Act was enacted by Congress and President Nixon in 1970 to protect the public's health and welfare against harmful air contaminants. Because the Clean Air Act is an Act of Congress, the first question within the preemption framework has been answered in the affirmative, and we now turn to the second inquiry.

The second inquiry in a preemption analysis is whether the congressional action was proper under the Constitution. The Clean Air Act almost certainly falls within Congress's Article 1, § 8 power to regulate interstate commerce, because pollutants emitted into the air, which are byproducts of commercial activity, certainly cross state lines. In addition, there appear to be no independent constitutional limits here on Congress's exercise of the power. Thus, the Act is likely a proper congressional action under the Constitution. Because the second inquiry has also been answered in the affirmative, we now move to the third inquiry.

The third inquiry is whether the congressional action preempted the state or local law. In answering this question, the key is to try to understand what was Congress's *intention*—that is, did Congress intend to preempt the states? Congress's intent to preempt may be either express or implied. Express preemption occurs when a federal law contains language providing that the state law is preempted. In *Lorillard Tobacco Co.*, for example, the Court found that a federal law, stating that no requirement or prohibition based on smoking or health shall be imposed under state law with respect to advertising or promotion, expressly preempted states from passing regulations on the marketing and advertisement of cigarette sales. Here, if there is additional language in the Clean Air Act (beyond what we have been given) that expressly preempts state or local laws on coke oven emissions, the Mountonia law is invalid; otherwise, we must continue the analysis to ask if preemption is implied.

There are three classifications of implied preemption: (1) conflict preemption, (2) field preemption, and (3) federal objective preemption (i.e., when a state law impedes the achievement of a federal objective). Conflict preemption occurs when a federal law and a state law are mutually exclusive and an actor cannot comply with both. Here, it is unlikely that the state law is preempted under a theory of conflict preemption as it is not physically impossible to comply with both the state and federal law. If New Hill Industries was operating in accordance with the Mountonia law, it would also be in compliance with the federal Clean Air Act, as the Clean Air Act simply imposes a less strict standard on the emissions produced by coke ovens. Thus, there is no conflict preemption here because there is "no inevitable collision between the schemes of regulation, despite the dissimilarity of the standards." See *Florida Lime & Avocado Growers, Inc. v. Paul* (1963).

Field preemption occurs when a federal law wholly occupies a given field of regulation. If the congressional intent is to have a federal law fully occupy a particular area, field preemption will be found to exist. With field preemption there is often a scheme of federal regulation that is so pervasive that a reasonable inference can be made that Congress has left no room for the states to supplement it. Here, the question is whether Congress intended to enact a complete scheme for the regulation of emissions through the Clean Air Act, or, rather, whether it intended to create only a "floor" of minimum emissions standards, leaving states free to individually enact more stringent standards. If the former is the case, states cannot supplement the federal scheme with their own laws involving emissions; here, Mountonia would be preempted from entering a field (clean air and, specifically, coke oven emissions) that the Congress has intended to occupy through the Clean Air Act. Here, New Hill Industries might argue based on some unknown facts that Congress balanced the interests of the environment against the competitive interests of industry in arriving at the emissions standards, and thus there is a reasonable inference that Congress did *not* intend that states would be allowed to impose stricter standards. On the other hand, Mountonia could argue that the latter is the case, and that Congress here, in legislating pursuant to its interest in providing for clean air, has simply provided a minimum standard to which every state must adhere. Mountonia could say, moreover, that it is simply exercising its sovereign police power authority by imposing its own more stringent set of regulations that work toward the goal of reducing harmful emissions. The state would argue that under our system of federalism it retains the authority to enact health, safety, and welfare regulations of this type, unless it is eminently clear that Congress either expressly or impliedly intended to preempt—and that such a clear message is lacking here. Mountonia would conclude that it is not reasonable to infer that Congress intended to preempt states from adopting more stringent standards. It is difficult to know without additional facts whether Congress intended with the Clean Air Act emissions standards to fully occupy the field, but on balance I would conclude that Congress likely did *not* seek to preempt states from imposing their own standards, but rather intended to provide a "floor" below which states could not go. In other words, on our facts alone, a reasonable inference can*not* be made that Congress has left no room for the states to supplement the Clean Air Act's emissions standards.

The final classification of implied preemption is found when the state or local law impedes the achievement of a federal objective. When examining this form of preemption, courts must first determine the federal objective and then if the state or local law interferes with attaining that goal. In *Pacific Gas & Electric*, for example, the Court found that a federal law regulating nuclear power plants did *not* preempt a California law prohibiting the building of a new plant until the federal government developed a proper way to dispose of the nuclear waste because the laws had different objectives (the federal law concerned safety, and the California law addressed both safety and economic issues). Here, the federal objective of the Clean Air Act is to protect and improve the nation's air quality. Mountonia's law has the same objective of improving and protecting air quality, which is manifested with its even more stringent standards. This higher standard arguably does not impede the federal objective; if anything, it would seem to further the federal objective. The standards set by the Clean Air Act were determined by the federal government in an effort to meet a particular standard of air quality, so any law that meets or exceeds those standards does not impede those objectives, and Mountonia law is likely not preempted.

On balance, based on the foregoing preemption analysis, the Mountonia law is likely not preempted on a theory of implied conflict, field, or federal objective preemption. Therefore, New Hill Industries must operate in compliance with the state law.

SELF-ASSESSMENT

It is worth repeating that in an essentially single-issue hypothetical such as those presented in most chapters of this book, an effective way to begin your answer is to state the issue: "You have asked me to discuss the preemption issue.... " It is also a good idea to include the relevant constitutional provision, which in this hypothetical is the Supremacy Clause—although you will likely not be required to quote the clause verbatim unless you have been supplied with a copy of the Constitution.

In stating the rule, the sample essay above systematically runs through the steps of the inquiry that the Supreme Court has developed to address preemption questions:

1. Has Congress acted?
2. If yes, is Congress's action constitutional?
3. If yes, does Congress's action preempt the state law (Congress's *intent* is the key)?
   (a) Express preemption
   (b) Implied preemption (field, conflict, federal objective)

Each of the elements of the inquiry is provided in the sample essay in some detail. If you were to stop here and write nothing more, you would likely receive about half of the available points (under most professors' grading rubrics) for effectively stating the issue and rule of law. Even if you are confused about a question and not sure how to proceed with the analysis, go ahead and spend some time building the foundation, so to speak, of the issue and rule. You could receive valuable points for this effort alone.

Assuming, however, that you are not satisfied with receiving just 50 percent of the points, a strong analysis will get you most of the rest of the points (regardless of your conclusion). In the sample essay, the analysis is interwoven into the paragraphs along with the statement of the rules, and often prefaced with the word, "Here, ... " This is an effective way to organize the answer (i.e., include the analysis as each aspect of the rule is introduced), but it is equally effective to organize your answer by stating all of the rules in one block, then providing the entire analysis thereafter. However you organize the analysis, for any question asking for an objective discussion it is important to argue *both* sides. This is effectively indicated (as above) with the prefatory, "On the other hand, Mountonia could argue.... "

Mini-conclusions on various aspects of the analysis are included within each of the individual paragraphs, but it is helpful in wrapping up any essay answer to include a final paragraph summing up your overall conclusion to the issue. In this sample, for example, "On balance, ... the Mountonia law is likely not preempted ...."

Finally, where you simply do not have adequate facts to draw a firm conclusion, it is perfectly fine to say so, but you should go ahead and make a conclusion based on the information you have. The sample essay handles this with "It is difficult to know without additional facts whether ..., but on balance I would conclude.... " In order to stimulate a discussion where key facts are lacking, you might say, for example, something like (as does the sample essay) "[Defendant] might argue based on some unknown facts that ... " But be careful in using this technique; do not construct your own elaborate set of alternate facts that might lead you down a rabbit hole. Most professors will not give points for so-called "negative issue-spotting."

VARIATIONS ON THE THEME

You are the legal assistant to the congresswoman who is considering amendments to the Clear Air Act. She is uncertain what position she will ultimately take, but she asks you to prepare possible language for the Clean Air Act to express:

1. Congress's intent to completely preempt states' regulation in the area of coke oven emissions.
2. Congress's intent to preempt only those state laws that do not meet the minimum federal standards.
3. Congress's intent to preempt none of the state laws, but to instead allow states to set their own minimum standards.

Please provide sample language for each of these three scenarios. Then, for each of these scenarios, discuss how your analysis in the sample essay would change.

Problem 2
(60 minutes)

HYPOTHETICAL

The State of Oblivion has recently become heavily involved in the regulation and operation of day-care facilities located within the state. During this past legislative term the state enacted a statute that requires anyone who wishes to operate a day-care facility within the borders of Oblivion to obtain an operator's license. The standards for obtaining such a license are quite rigorous. In order to qualify, the applicant must show that he or she has at least five years experience in day-care management, obtained either in another state or in Oblivion. Moreover, the applicant's record during the prior five years must be clean. The fee for obtaining an Oblivion day-care operator's license is $5,000 for in-state residents and $10,000 for out-of-staters. Oblivion contends that the additional charge for out-of-staters is necessary in order to recoup the more costly exercise of verifying out-of-state records and references.

Oblivion also owns three day-care facilities in Oblivion City, the state capital. These three facilities care exclusively for the children of state workers. The state itself does not, however, operate these facilities. Instead, Oblivion contracts out the operation of these facilities on a competitive bid basis to resident day-care operators. Nonresident operators, even if properly licensed in Oblivion, are precluded from bidding on these three contracts.

KinderKids, Inc. is an experienced day-care facility operator from the neighboring State of Delirium. KinderKids is fully licensed under the State of Oblivion's recently adopted day-care operators licensing procedures. Although the company had no trouble obtaining the Oblivion license, KinderKids is angry that it had to pay $5,000 more than its Oblivion counterparts. Further, KinderKids is frustrated with the fact that it is ineligible for the three Oblivion City contracts simply because it is not from the State of Oblivion.

You are the law clerk for the sitting federal judge in Oblivion. In anticipation of a federal lawsuit by KinderKids against the State of Oblivion, the judge has asked you to prepare a legal memorandum discussing the constitutionality of Oblivion's day-care licensing and contract bidding schemes. The judge says you should *not* discuss matters of justiciability or the Privileges and Immunities Clause in your memo. Please provide him with your memorandum.

SAMPLE ESSAY

You have asked me to discuss the constitutionality of Oblivion's day-care licensing and contract bidding schemes. The issue here involves the so-called Dormant Commerce Clause (DCC). When state or local action affects interstate commerce, under the DCC the judiciary determines whether a state or local statute or action violates an implicit limitation of the Commerce Clause, which forbids states from economically discriminating against out-of-staters. (Note that Congress has the authority under its commerce power to regulate interstate commerce. It is well settled that Congress's power in this area is not exclusive; states too may regulate interstate commerce—provided that Congress has not preempted the states in the particular area.) Some have criticized the DCC doctrine on separation-of-powers grounds, as an example of the Court's overstepping its authority by reading hidden meaning into a power delegated by the Constitution to another branch of government: Congress. The DCC doctrine is also criticized on federalism grounds—that the federal Court is inappropriately limiting state authority to regulate. On the other hand, supporters of the doctrine maintain that it is a proper exercise of the judiciary's authority to prevent states from placing undue burdens on interstate commerce.

In analyzing DCC cases, the Court first asks whether the state measure "facially" discriminates against out-of-state interests. If so, the measure is presumed to be virtually per se invalid, and will almost always be struck down unless the government is able to rebut this heavy presumption. The reason for this heavy presumption of invalidity is that discrimination on the face of a measure is almost always indication of discriminatory *purpose*. And if the Constitution means anything at all in the area of interstate relations, it means (in the famous words of Justice Brandeis) that the "states will sink or swim together" economically—which therefore forbids states from purposefully discriminating against out-of-staters. For a facially discriminatory measure to survive, the state must overcome a form of "strict scrutiny" to show that it has a legitimate (i.e., nondiscriminatory) purpose, and that the purpose cannot be accomplished by available less-discriminatory means. (Quarantine-type laws, where states exclude "infected" out-of-state items, as in *Maine v. Taylor* (1986), are the rare cases that will sometimes satisfy this test.)

If the measure is facially neutral, by contrast, the Court balances the state's interest against the burdens that the measure imposes on interstate commerce, with greater weight against the measure if it discriminates in *effect* against out-of-staters, and greater weight *for* the measure if it affects in-staters and out-of-staters equally. For the former (discriminatory-in-effect laws)—especially those that exclude all or virtually all out-of-staters—the statute is presumed unconstitutional, and will be struck down unless the state proves that there is a legitimate nondiscriminatory purpose to explain the disparate impact, and that the measure is the least-discriminatory means to accomplish the legitimate purpose. (Note that this test for a facially neutral, discriminatory-in-effect state action is very similar to that for facial discrimination, but with a somewhat lower burden for states to overcome the presumption of invalidity.) For the latter (laws that are evenhanded in their effect on in-staters and out-of-staters alike), however, the statute is presumed constitutional and, according to *Pike v. Bruce Church, Inc.* (1970), "will be upheld unless the burden imposed on such commerce is clearly excessive in relation to the putative local benefits."

There are two important exceptions when states may discriminate against interstate commerce: (1) when Congress, pursuant to its commerce power, authorizes states to discriminate; and (2) when states are acting as market participants, and are thus allowed to operate as would any other private entity in the competitive marketplace—including picking and choosing with whom they will do business.

Applying the DCC framework to this case involving Oblivion's day-care licensing and contract-bidding schemes, we first ask if the state law discriminates on its face. Here, both the licensing and bidding schemes do facially discriminate against out-of-staters (specifically, higher fees for out-of-staters—$10,000 versus $5,000 for in-staters, and prohibiting out-of-staters from bidding). As such, both will be considered virtually per se invalid, and will be struck down unless Oblivion can demonstrate that there is a legitimate (nondiscriminatory) purpose for the disparate treatment, and that the purpose cannot be served as well by available less-discriminatory means. Here, Oblivion will argue that its legitimate purpose for the differing fees (found in its police power interest of protecting the health, safety, and welfare of its citizens) is to make sure that day-care operators are competent, and that the examination process of out-of-state operators is in fact more costly. Similarly, it will argue that its purpose in limiting bids on the three day-care centers to in-staters is to rely on providers with whom the state may be more familiar so as to protect children from potential harm—in other words, it is easier to get references and be comfortable with providers who are "closer to home."

For its part, KinderKids may argue that Oblivion's claimed purposes are invalid, and that the state's true purpose in requiring higher licensing fees and banning contract bids for out-of-staters is to give in-staters an economic advantage—which is strictly prohibited under the DCC doctrine. Moreover, KinderKids may argue that even if the state has legitimate purposes, there are less-restrictive alternatives available. For example, KinderKids might suggest that even assuming it costs somewhat more to check the backgrounds of out-of-state providers, that amount should be absorbed by all applicants by assigning a flat fee (say, $7,500) for all applicants, whether in-state or out-of-state. Another less-discriminatory alternative would be to charge the out-of-stater the *actual* higher cost for the state to accomplish the check of out-of-staters over in-staters (say, $500—$1,000 at the most—it is unlikely that it costs the state a full extra $5,000 to check those from out-of-state). As for the bid prohibition, KinderKids might suggest that a less-discriminatory alternative to accomplishing the state's goal of protecting children would be to require a much more detailed application from *all* bidders, whether in-state or out-of-state (even if that raised the cost for applying for both in-staters and out-of-staters). On balance, I would conclude that both the licensing fee disparity and the bid prohibition would be found to violate the DCC, because there appear to be viable less-discriminatory alternatives.

Next, we would ask if the state measures are facially neutral and discriminatory in impact, but as we have concluded that the fee disparity and bid-prohibition measures are facially discriminatory and hence violate the DCC, we need not repeat the virtually identical analysis, other than to say that both measures would be similarly found to violate the DCC under discriminatory-in-effect analysis.

Next we ask if any aspect of the state law is evenhanded in treating in-staters and out-of-staters alike. Here, the licensing requirement that applicants demonstrate a clean five-year record of experience in the day-care business is evenhanded in its treatment, and in balancing the state benefits against the burdens on interstate commerce it will likely be upheld because the state's purpose is legitimate (making sure day-care operators are qualified), and it does not seem to place any sort of undue burden on interstate commerce.

Finally, we must ask if either of the exceptions to the DCC apply. There is no indication in the facts that Congress has legislated to allow states to discriminate, and with respect to the differing license fee at least, Oblivion is clearly not "participating" in the market (rather, it is regulating the market). With respect to its contract-bidding scheme, however, Oblivion could argue that becauses it actually owns the three day-care centers and operates them solely for the benefit of state employees, it is a "market participant" entitled to favor in-staters at the expense of out-of-staters. KinderKids would argue, on the other hand, that Oblivion is not truly a market participant because it does not actually directly operate the three day-care centers itself, but rather hires someone else to run them. Oblivion's involvement, in other words, is too far "downstream" to qualify under the exception. See *South-Central Timber Development, Inc. v. Wunnicke* (1984). Oblivion could reply that a true market participant may make a decision to outsource the operation of the facility—and that such management decisions themselves constitute "direct" participation, and therefore do not alter one's status as market participant. On balance, it would seem that because Oblivion does actually own the three day-care centers (albeit, as operated through subcontractors), which it runs solely for the benefit of state employees, it is acting as a market participant and may as such favor in-staters over out-of-staters—much as did the state of South Dakota in *Reeves v. Stake* in favoring in-state cement customers over out-of-staters in operating its state-owned cement plant.

In sum, the five-year clean-record-of-experience requirement will likely be upheld under the DCC as an evenhanded measure that does not unduly burden interstate commerce, the licensing fee disparity of $5,000 (discriminatory on its face and in its effect) will likely be struck down because of the availability of less-discriminatory alternatives, and the bid prohibition will likely be upheld under the DCC market-participant exception.

SELF-ASSESSMENT

The Dormant Commerce Clause (DCC) is not, at its root, a difficult concept (i.e., that the U.S. Supreme Court will strike down state/local laws that discriminate economically against out-of-staters), but it becomes difficult in the application due to the U.S. Supreme Court's somewhat opaque jurisprudence in this area. As illustrated in the sample essay, it is a good idea in any DCC question to place the DCC in context of the Commerce Clause in general, which expressly gives Congress the (nonexclusive) power to regulate interstate commerce.

As always, you should state the issue right up front: "You have asked me to discuss the constitutionality of Oblivion's day-care licensing and contract bidding schemes. The issue here involves the so-called Dormant Commerce Clause (DCC)." Then, although not crucial, a brief comment on the criticisms by some that the DCC is an example of Supreme Court overreaching cannot hurt. As for the rule, you should explain that the DCC prohibits intentional discrimination by states against out-of-staters, so there is a heavy presumption against facially discriminatory statutes, whereas for facially neutral statutes, the Court engages in a form of "balancing" of the state's interest against the burdens on interstate commerce caused by the state's action. Facially neutral statutes that discriminate in *effect* will be treated much like facially discriminatory statutes, and presumed to be unconstitutional, whereas those that are evenhanded in effect will be upheld unless they unduly burden interstate commerce.

Although most casebooks and study aids (and the sample essay above) provide a description for the DCC something like that given in the previous paragraph, it is worth noting that the Supreme Court is inconsistent in explaining its doctrinal approach. In particular, the Court has been unclear on how the analysis should distinguish between discriminatory *purpose,* discriminatory *effect,* and *facial* discrimination. A careful examination of the cases, however, shows that if the Court determines that a state has a primary *purpose* of favoring in-staters over out-of-staters, the law will be struck down without any possibility of rebuttal from the state. This is because of the "states-will-sink-or-swim-together" ethos long expressed by the Court. It is one thing for a state to regulate in a way that incidentally discriminates in *effect* against out-of-staters (in which case the Court has said that the law will still be presumed unconstitutional and struck down unless the state meets its burden), but it is another altogether when the state *intentionally* discriminates. This is simply *verboten.* A law that discriminates on its face is very good evidence of discriminatory purpose; therefore, the Court has said that it is virtually per se invalid (i.e., a very heavy presumption of invalidity). However, facial discrimination does not *always* indicate discriminatory purpose. As noted in the sample essay, the quarantine case is a good example of a facially discriminatory law that has an underlying legitimate nondiscriminatory purpose (e.g., to protect the health and safety of a state's citizens or natural resources). The distinctions between discriminatory purpose, facial discrimination, and discrimination in effect are more clearly elucidated in the alternative DCC analytical framework presented in the "Variations on the Theme" selection below.

Also, do not forget to mention the exceptions from the DCC: (1) Congress, because it has the express power to regulate interstate commerce, may itself authorize states to discriminate against out-of-staters in certain commercial areas (in, for example, the regulation of alcohol and tobacco); and (2) the "market participant" exception (as described in the sample essay above). Whether you should discuss policy considerations, as does the sample essay, will vary with the professor. That said, brief mentions of policy are generally harmless.

Finally, please note the "mutually reinforcing relationship" (the Supreme Court's words in *Supreme Court of New Hampshire v. Piper* (1985)) between the DCC and the Article IV Privileges and Immunities Clause at issue in the next hypothetical below. Both promote the Court's core doctrinal principle that, when it comes to the states' treatment of citizens and entities from out-of-state, the Constitution protects the interests of *all* equally, which generally requires states to treat the out-of-staters as if they are their own. There are differences between the DCC and the Privileges and Immunities Clause, though—only "citizens" may bring a claim under Article IV Privileges and Immunities, whereas corporations and aliens *may* sue under the DCC.

VARIATIONS ON THE THEME

Answer the same hypothetical using the framework described below, which consolidates the Supreme Court's various DCC rules and pronouncements into a single coherent linear inquiry that can be used for all DCC questions. (A discussion of this framework is available in "Toward a More Coherent Dormant Commerce Clause: A Proposed Unitary Framework," 21 *Harvard Journal of Law and Public Policy* 471 (1998).).

Stage 1. Discriminatory State Purpose Inquiry: Does the measure have an underlying *purpose* (whether facial or hidden) to discriminate economically against out-of-staters?

- a. if YES, measure is absolutely per se invalid and struck down—inquiry is ended.
- b. if NO, go to Stage 2 Balancing.

Stage 2. Balancing

- a. Inquiry: Is measure discriminatory on its *face*?
    - i. if YES, measure is heavily presumed invalid. (Test: for measure to survive, state has heavy burden of proving the measure is almost certain to achieve its legitimate purpose, and that the purpose cannot be served as well by available less-discriminatory means (similar to "strict scrutiny")).
    - ii. if NO, go to b.
- b. Inquiry: Is the measure discriminatory in *effect*?

i. if YES, measure is presumed invalid. (Test: for measure to survive, state has burden of proving that the measure is likely to achieve its legitimate purpose; challenger then has the burden of either rebutting the state's justification or of showing that the purpose can be served as well by available less-discriminatory alternatives (similar to a cross between "strict scrutiny" and "intermediate scrutiny")).

ii. if NO, go to c.

c. Inquiry: Is the measure *evenhanded* in effect?

i. if YES, measure is presumed valid. (Test: challenger has burden of proving that the measure's burden on interstate commerce is clearly excessive in relation to state benefits (similar to "rational basis")).

d. Inquiry: Is the state a "market participant"?

i. if YES, measure is valid, despite DCC analysis above.

ii. if NO, measure is valid/invalid determined by DCC analysis above.

Problem 3
(30 minutes)

HYPOTHETICAL

Article IV, § 2 of the U.S. Constitution provides: "The Citizens of each State shall be entitled to all Privileges and Immunities of Citizens in the several States." The protections offered under Article IV's Privileges and Immunities Clause doctrine ensure that states cannot punish or deprive citizens from other states of their fundamental rights protected under the Constitution. Historically speaking, the Framers enacted the Privileges and Immunities Clause to ensure domestic tranquility and to facilitate cooperation among the states. Notably, the Privileges and Immunities Clause was intended to prevent discrimination by one state against nonresidents that would lead to discrimination (retributive and otherwise) of the same sort by other states.

The States of Michiana and Indigan have long maintained a healthy commercial and tourist-based relationship. Many residents of Indigan travel north in the summertime to Michiana to visit its many lakes. Many Michiana residents travel south to purchase fireworks, many of which are banned in Michiana, from Indigan vendors. Notwithstanding this relationship, some trouble has begun to brew due to some controversial legislation enacted by the Indigan legislature that Michiana residents claim unfairly discriminates against their fundamental rights as citizens. The Indigan legislation, which is aimed at protecting Indigan fireworks businesses and addresses both fireworks corporations and "mom-and-pop" firework store owners, states:

(a) Any out-of-state firework corporation that opens a fireworks retail outlet in the state of Indigan must pay a $1,000 processing fee and apply for a "Non-Indigan" vendor license.

(b) Indigan banks are not permitted to finance any businesses owned by out-of-state firework store owners. Out-of-state firework businesses must solicit any financing from non-Indigan banks or financiers.

Mark Hooper sells sparklers and other legal fireworks in Michiana (his state of citizenship) in his store called Hot Flash. Seeing the large market for fireworks in Indigan, he wants to open a fireworks store in West Bend, Indigan. Hot Flash is not a corporation, and he is the sole employee of the business. He is troubled with the new Indigan law passed by the Indigan legislature and wants to explore his legal options.

You are a law clerk for a law firm based in Mark's hometown. The attorney handling Mark's case asks you to provide an objective discussion of whether the new Indigan law violates the Article IV Privileges and Immunities Clause. Please provide your discussion.

SAMPLE ESSAY

You have asked me to discuss the constitutionality of the State of Indigan's new law, which imposes fees on out-of-state corporations and restricts the ability of all out-of-state businesses to open fireworks businesses. This issue calls into question whether the law passed by the Indigan legislature violates the Article IV Privileges and Immunities Clause.

The purpose of the Privileges and Immunities Clause is to prevent states from placing unreasonable burdens on noncitizens. For purposes of the Clause, the term "citizens" applies only to individuals who are U.S. citizens—note that it does *not* apply to corporations or other entities. Under the doctrine developed by the Supreme Court, in order to determine whether the Privileges and Immunities Clause of Article IV has been violated, the following two-part inquiry is used.

1. Does the law discriminate against citizens of another state with regard to fundamental constitutional rights or important economic interests? If no, then there is no violation.
2. If yes, the law will be upheld only if (i) there is a substantial reason for the difference in treatment, and (ii) the discrimination practiced against nonresidents bears a substantial relationship to the state's objective.*

*In analyzing item 2(ii), the Court has reasoned that if any less-restrictive means are available, the discrimination is *not* substantially related to the state's objective.

Here, item (a) of the Indigan legislation regulates corporations; therefore, it does not violate the Privileges and Immunities Clause because the clause applies only to *citizens*, not to corporations. Mark Hooper will likely be able to attack the constitutionality of the second prong of Indigan's new law, however.

Regarding item (b) of the legislation, Mr. Hooper would first argue that preventing out-of-state businesses from securing financing from Indigan banks unduly discriminates against the important economic interests of out-of-state owners and potential employees. He will argue that the ability to earn a livelihood has been recognized by the Supreme Court as the sort of economic activity protected by the Privileges and Immunities Clause. Arguably, item (b) of the Indigan law impinges upon this right by making it more difficult for out-of-state firework store owners to secure financing for their new firework stores. If, for example, Mr. Hooper could *only* secure financing from an Indigan bank, the new Indigan law would effectively preclude Mr. Hooper from opening his new fireworks store.

Indigan will argue, on the other hand, that the financing provision does not at all prevent nonresidents such as Mark from opening and operating fireworks stores in the state. Indeed, Mark is free to make a living selling fireworks in Indigan—he just cannot receive financing from Indigan banks. Indigan would emphasize that it is well within its sovereign police power (to regulate for its citizens' health, safety, and welfare) to regulate the banking industry. Mark probably prevails here, however, because the Court has previously held that a state violates the Privileges and Immunities Clause, even when it allows out-of-staters to work, when it charges nonresidents more for a *work* licensing fee than it charges residents. (By contrast, differing fees for in-state and out-of-state residents *are* allowed if the fees do not affect a fundamental constitutional right or important economic activity—such as if the fees are for merely *recreational* activities. See, for example, *Baldwin v. Fish & Game Commission of Montana* (1978).)

On balance, because the financing provision seems to affect an important economic interest (Mark's ability to pursue his livelihood), part 1 of the Privileges and Immunities Clause analysis is satisfied, and we move to part 2. According to part 2 of the analysis, in order to avoid having the provision struck down as a violation of the Privileges and Immunities Clause, the State of Indigan must show that the discrimination is substantially related to the advancement of a substantial state interest. This test (essentially a form of "heightened scrutiny") has been shown in the U.S. Supreme Court to be very difficult to meet, especially as the Court has reasoned that if any less-restrictive alternatives are available, the discrimination is *not* substantially related to the state's objective. Here, Indigan will argue that it has a substantial objective in promoting the economic interests of in-state businesses (which will result in increased tax revenues), and that a law that makes it more difficult for out-of-state businesses to operate in the state is a "substantially related" means toward accomplishing that objective.

Mark, on the other hand, will argue that although promoting in-state businesses and augmenting tax revenue is certainly an important state objective, the discrimination here of prohibiting Indigan banks from *any* financing of out-of-state businesses does *not* bear a substantial relationship to the state's objective, as there are arguably less-restrictive alternatives available. The state could, for example, place a maximum on the amount of Indigan bank financing for out-of-state businesses, but stop short of an outright prohibition; or it could provide subsidies to the affected in-state fireworks businesses, or any number of other less-restrictive alternatives.

In sum, based on all of these circumstances together with the fact that the Supreme Court routinely finds that states fail to meet the rigorous test requiring that the state's law must be the least-restrictive means available to accomplish a substantial state objective, I would conclude that part (b) of Indigan's law prohibiting the financing of out-of state businesses likely violates the Article IV Privileges and Immunities Clause.

SELF-ASSESSMENT

When answering a hypothetical concerning the Article IV Privileges or Immunities (P&I) Clause, it is worth briefly mentioning the purpose of the clause—to prevent discrimination against out-of-staters—after first identifying the issue. Then, the key component of a P&I Clause answer is the two-part test enunciated in the sample answer (stated most clearly in *Supreme Court of New Hampshire v. Piper* (1985)). Simply stating the test in all its parts will likely earn you up to about half the possible points; then, analyzing the facts of the hypothetical in light of the rule and drawing a conclusion will earn you many of the rest.

As noted in the introduction to this chapter, an alleged violation by a state or local government of the Article IV Privileges and Immunities Clause is one of the special circumstances where the Supreme Court has concluded that heightened scrutiny should be applied. Accordingly, for P&I issues the Court applies a form of review that resembles a combination of intermediate scrutiny and strict scrutiny—intermediate because the standard requiring the state to show a "substantial reason for the difference in treatment, and [that] the discrimination practiced against nonresidents bears a substantial relationship to the state's objective" *effectively* requires that the "law/action *substantially advances* an *important* government purpose," and strict scrutiny because in order for the law/action to survive, the Court interprets the standard to require that there be no less-restrictive alternative.

On the facts given in this hypothetical, as always try to argue both sides, unless the question indicates otherwise. (Here, the question asks you to "provide an objective discussion," so it is appropriate to argue both sides.) We first discuss whether harm caused to Mark by the State of Indigan's ban on in-state banks from financing out-of-state businesses is the sort of interest that the Court considers to be covered by the P&I Clause. Then, regardless of what we might conclude, for purposes of analysis we assume that the requirement is met (as we always should in answering any hypothetical), so that we can continue with the analysis. Doing so, we apply the hybrid intermediate/strict standard of review, and argue pro and con whether the state meets its burden.

This hypothetical also touches upon the fact that only "citizens" may bring a claim under Article IV Privileges and Immunities, whereas corporations and aliens *may* sue under the Dormant Commerce Clause (DCC). As noted in the DCC question above, there is a "mutually reinforcing relationship" (the Supreme Court's words) between the Article IV Privileges and Immunities Clause and the DCC. Both promote the Court's core doctrinal principle that, when it comes to the states' treatment of citizens and entities from out of state, the Constitution protects the important interests of *all* equally, which generally requires states to treat the out-of-staters as if they are their own.

VARIATIONS ON THE THEME

Imagine the same facts as provided in the hypothetical above, except that (a) Mark's proposed new business in Indigan will have ten employees, all of whom are citizens and residents of Michiana who will commute daily to their jobs; and (b) the Indigan law contains a third provision:

> 3. Any out-of-state firework business that moves to the state of Indigan to conduct its fireworks operation must employ a workforce comprised, minimally, of 50 percent Indigan residents.

Mark claims that this third provision violates the Privileges and Immunities Clause. Discuss.

D. OPTIONAL READINGS

The following sources present the topics covered in this chapter in more depth than the chapter introduction. The sources are in increasing levels of detail. The first provides an overview, the second provides more detail, and the third and fourth provide the greatest coverage of the material.

MICHAEL C. DORF & TREVOR W. MORRISON, CONSTITUTIONAL LAW (2010), pp. 92–93.
JOHN E. NOWAK & RONALD D. ROTUNDA, PRINCIPLES OF CONSTITUTIONAL LAW (4th ed. 2010), chapters 8, 9.
ERWIN CHEMERINSKY, CONSTITUTIONAL LAW: PRINCIPLES AND POLICIES (4th ed. 2011), Chapter 5.
JOHN E. NOWAK & RONALD D. ROTUNDA, CONSTITUTIONAL LAW (7th ed. 2000), chapters 8, 9.

INCORPORATION, STATE ACTION, AND TAKINGS

5

This chapter covers the topics of incorporation, state action, and takings. Incorporation refers to the U.S. Supreme Court's approach in applying the various Bill of Rights provisions, one at a time, to the states. By its terms, the Bill of Rights applies only to the *federal* government, as recognized by the Supreme Court in *Barron v. Baltimore* (1833). After the Civil War, by which time it had become tragically apparent through the perpetuation of slavery that states were not willing to protect liberty, Congress drafted the Fourteenth Amendment Privileges or Immunities Clause in large part to apply the Bill of Rights to the states. In the *Slaughter-House Cases* (1873), the Supreme Court rejected this interpretation of the Fourteenth Amendment. The process of applying the Bill of Rights to the states was left instead to a gradual process. Beginning in the 1920s, the Court began the task of "selectively incorporating" individual provisions to the states through the Fourteenth Amendment Due Process Clause. (Specifically, the Court asked whether the particular Bill of Rights provision at issue was "the very essence of a scheme of ordered liberty," or was "a fundamental principle of justice rooted in the traditions and conscience of our people," or "basic in our system of jurisprudence." If it was, the right was "incorporated" into the Due Process Clause, which by its terms prohibits states from depriving any person of liberty.) Presently all but four of the twenty-five Bill of Rights provisions—all except the Third Amendment right not to have soldiers quartered within the home, the Fifth Amendment right to grand jury indictment in criminal cases, the Seventh Amendment right to jury trial in a civil case, and the Eighth Amendment right not to have excessive fines imposed—have been incorporated to apply to the states. The hypothetical in this chapter requires you to understand the inquiry undertaken by the Supreme Court as it considered whether to incorporate each individual Bill of Rights provision into the Due Process Clause in order to apply it to the states.

The term "state action" refers to the principle that the Constitution protects only against *governmental* infringements to individual liberty and equal protection. There is one provision where the Constitution's limitations apply to *private* actions: the Thirteenth Amendment's prohibition of slavery and involuntary servitude. Moreover, in some circumstances federal or state laws may impose constitutional requirements on private actors. In addition, in crafting its state action doctrine, the Supreme Court has identified two exceptions where private actors *are* held to be subject to constitutional limitations: when the private actor (1) is performing what is essentially a "public function"; or (2) is so entangled with the government in some way to justify holding it constitutionally accountable. Classic examples of these exceptions are found respectively in *Marsh v. Alabama* (1946) (the private owners of a "company town" must honor the First Amendment free speech rights of speakers on street corners) and *Burton v. Wilmington Parking Authority* (1961) (the private owner of a restaurant located in space leased from the city must observe the Equal Protection Clause in serving its customers). This doctrine was also addressed in the important case of *Shelley v. Kraemer* (1948), where the

Court held that judicial enforcement by a state court of a private contract to discriminate (in a real estate sale) is "state action," thus subjecting the enforcement to the Constitution's Equal Protection Clause.

The state action doctrine is a threshold issue: the Court will not consider the substance of an equal protection or individual liberty claim unless there is state action (or one of the exceptions apply, where the private actor is essentially treated as a state actor). As such, it is ripe territory for writers of exam questions to attempt to test students on whether they understand the doctrine. Accordingly, when answering questions involving equal protection or individual liberty claims, students should get in the habit of asking if the state action requirement is met before moving to the merits. Very often the answer will be obvious—for example, the facts involve a law passed by the legislature—but the question should still be asked and briefly answered.

The final topic in this chapter involves the Fifth Amendment Takings Clause, which states: "nor shall private property be taken for public use without just compensation." Takings is studied in many law schools in the first year Property class instead of Constitutional Law, because the issue is whether and under what circumstances the government may seize and/or otherwise affect the value of private real *property*. We cover it in this Constitutional Law workbook, however, because this question of government propriety is ultimately resolved with a *constitutional* inquiry. As such, the topic of takings is also covered in many Constitutional Law classes and casebooks (under a heading of "economic liberties" or the like).

The Takings Clause acts as a limit on the government sovereign power of "eminent domain": the government's authority to seize private property for its own uses. Nonlawyers are sometimes surprised by eminent domain—that the government actually may legally seize private real property whenever it wants through authorized "condemnation" proceedings, so long as its intended use is public, and so long as just compensation is paid. Many Takings Clause cases involve situations where the government does not actually physically claim possession of the property, but rather where a government *regulation* or other action substantially decreases the value of the property. In such "regulatory taking" cases the owner typically seeks compensation in the amount of the diminution of the property's value. Another issue in takings cases is whether the government's intended use is sufficiently "public" to allow it to take the property. In a very controversial 2005 case, the Supreme Court held in *Kelo v. City of New London* that a city's taking of private property for delivery to a private corporation, for purposes of economic development, *does* satisfy the "public use" requirement.

B. READINGS

Before attempting the problems in this section, you should have read the following material. You may have already read most, if not all, of the cases. Edited versions of the cases contained within casebooks will be adequate for your purposes here.

Barron v. Mayor and City Council of Baltimore, 32 U.S. (7 Pet.) 243 (1833).
Duncan v. Louisiana, 391 U.S. 145 (1968).
McDonald v. City of Chicago, 130 S. Ct. 3020 (2010).
Apodaca v. Oregon, 406 U.S. 404 (1972).
Marsh v. Alabama, 326 U.S. 501 (1946).

Burton v. Wilmington Parking Authority, 365 U.S. 715 (1961).
Shelley v. Kraemer, 334 U.S. 1 (1948).
Moose Lodge No. 107 v. Irvis, 407 U.S. 163 (1972).
Terry v. Adams, 345 U.S. 461 (1953).
Jackson v. Metropolitan Edison Co., 419 U.S. 345 (1974).
Rendell-Baker v. Kohn, 457 U.S. 830 (1982).
Hawaii Housing Authority v. Midkiff, 467 U.S. 229 (1984).
Kelo v. City of New London, 545 U.S. 469 (2005).
Berman v. Parker, 348 U.S. 26 (1954).
Lucas v. South Carolina Coastal Council, 505 U.S. 1003 (1992).

C. PROBLEMS

Problem 1
(45 minutes)

HYPOTHETICAL

Over the past century, most—but not all—of the provisions contained within the Bill of Rights have been held by the U.S. Supreme Court to apply to state and local governments. One of the provisions *not* held to apply to state and local governments is the Third Amendment, which provides:

> *No Soldier shall, in time of peace be quartered in any house, without the consent of the Owner, nor in time of war, but in a manner to be prescribed by law.*

Recently there have been many protests around the world about the inequities between the rich and poor. Angry citizens in many countries have begun to speak out more loudly about an economic system, supported by established governments, that they believe favors a privileged few at the dire expense of the great majority of citizens. Collectively these efforts have been described as the "Reform NOW!" movement.

The city of Yorkville in the State of York is the financial center of the United States. Yorkville has thus been the site of Reform NOW! activists' efforts to bring attention to what they believe is a broken economic system. Along with many peaceful organizations and activities associated with Reform NOW!, several extremist groups that advocate violent property destruction have begun to use the movement as an excuse to loot and pillage in Yorkville. These groups are extremely elusive, and over the course of one year they continue to destroy property, despite efforts by Yorkville city government and York governor Margaret Lindman to subdue the violence. Indeed, the destruction has only worsened over the course of the year.

Governor Lindman is becoming increasingly frustrated with the City's inability to stop the attacks on property. Likewise, Yorkville residents, although they still mostly support the Reform NOW! agenda, are disgusted with the City's ineffectiveness in halting the property damage, and they demand that something be done. In response, Governor Lindman orders one thousand members of the York National Guard to deploy to Yorkville with the instructions to patrol and apprehend anyone observed destroying property.

The most controversial part of the governor's order, however, is the following: "To maximize effectiveness in apprehending those engaged in property destruction, it is necessary for the National Guard soldiers to be integrated into the neighborhoods where the damage is occurring. Accordingly, until such time as the emergency is over, every homeowner with an odd-numbered street address shall provide quartering for one soldier within that house."

Corey Yelson, a resident of Yorkville, thinks there is something terribly wrong with the governor's order, so he calls his friend who recently graduated from law school and inquires if this is constitutional. After a short discussion, Corey decides to bring suit against the governor and State of York for violating his Third Amendment rights.

The governor and State of York respond that they are not subject to the constitutional restrictions because the Third Amendment has never been held to apply to state and local governments—and that the case therefore should be summarily dismissed.

You are the law clerk for the judge hearing the suit. In preparation for the case, the judge asks you to provide an objective discussion of the summary disposition claim made by the governor and State of York. In particular, the judge wants you to discuss, based on precedent, the factors and analysis that should be used to determine whether the Third Amendment should be applied to the governor's action in this case. Please provide your discussion.

SAMPLE ESSAY

You have asked me to discuss the factors and analysis that should be used to determine whether the Third Amendment should be applied to the governor's action. The main issue of this case is whether the Third Amendment governs the actions of the state and local government in its attempt to implement the quartering-of-soldiers mandate. To fully understand this issue, one must investigate the history of the incorporation of the Bill of Rights so it will apply to the state and local government.

The Supreme Court first investigated this issue in *Barron v. Baltimore* in 1833. The Court asked whether the Takings Clause of the Fifth Amendment applied to the state and local government as well as the federal government. The Court stated that "the constitution was ordained and established by the people of the United States for themselves, for their own government, and not for the government of the individual states." Therefore, the Takings Clause as stated in the Fifth Amendment did not apply to the state government.

The Court again examined the issue of whether the Bill of Rights apply to the state and local government in the *Slaughter-House Cases* in 1873, in light of the recently enacted (1868) Fourteenth Amendment. Looking at each of the amendment's provisions—the Privileges and Immunities Clause, the Due Process Clause, and the Equal Protection Clause—the Court held that *none* of them had been intended to incorporate the Bill of Rights (despite substantial evidence in the legislative record that the Privileges and Immunities Clause, in particular, had been intended to incorporate the *entire* Bill of Rights so as to apply to the states).

Eventually the Supreme Court began to find that the term "liberty" in the Fourteenth Amendment's Due Process Clause substantively encompassed certain individual Bill of Rights provisions, thus requiring states to abide by their terms. In undertaking this inquiry, the Court asked whether the specific right is a principle of justice that is "rooted in the tradition and conscience of our people as to be ranked as fundamental and therefore implicit in the concept of ordered liberty."

See, for example, *Palko v. Connecticut* (1937). This process of "selective incorporation" began in the 1920s and continues to this day, to the point where now all but four of the approximately twenty-five individual Bill of Rights provisions have now been incorporated.

In *Duncan v. Louisiana*, for example, the Court in the late 1960s investigated whether the Sixth Amendment right to a jury trial in criminal offenses requires that a state or local government provide a jury trial when the possible punishment for conviction of a particular offense includes up to two years in jail. Reasoning that the right to jury trial for serious offenses leading to possible lengthy incarceration is fundamentally "implicit in the concept of ordered liberty" or "deeply rooted in our nation's history and traditions," the Court answered *yes* and thus incorporated the Sixth Amendment criminal jury trial provision into the Fourteenth Amendment Due Process Clause as applying to the states.

Most recently in 2010, the Supreme Court in *McDonald v. City of Chicago* investigated whether the Second Amendment applies to the state and local government. The Supreme Court affirmed that the right of an individual to keep and bear arms is protected by the Second Amendment (upholding the earlier *District of Columbia v. Heller* case), and then held for the first time that the Second Amendment is incorporated to apply to the state government through the Fourteenth Amendment Due Process Clause. The Court's reasoning was similar to that employed in *Duncan*—that the right to bear arms is so deeply rooted in our nation's traditions, and is so implicit in the concept of liberty, that it must be applied through the Fourteenth Amendment Due Process Clause to state and local governments. Chicago was thus held to be subject to the terms of the Second Amendment; accordingly, the city's handgun ban was found unconstitutional.

With this historical framework, we can examine the Corey Yelson and Yorkville situation. As noted above, there are still four provisions in the Bill of Rights that have not been selectively incorporated to apply to the states, including the Third Amendment right not to have soldiers quartered in one's home during peacetime.

This does *not* mean that Mr. Yelson has no constitutional recourse against the state, however. There have been no major Supreme Court cases concerning the Third Amendment right, so his is a case of "first impression." In order for Mr. Yelson to have his Third Amendment right apply to the state government actions, he must prove that the right to refuse to quarter soldiers in one's home is an "implicit concept of liberty or deeply rooted in our nation's history and traditions." If he is able to prove this, then the amendment most likely will be selectively incorporated to apply to the state government through the Due Process Clause of the Fourteenth Amendment.

In making his case, Yelson can argue that throughout American history, a person's home has been held to be one's "castle," highly protected by law against intrusions by the government and others. In criminal law, for example, the right of self-defense is different whether inside or outside one's home, and there are strict warrant requirements forbidding "unreasonable searches and seizures" (as protected by the Fourth Amendment, which itself *has* been previously incorporated). Also, the idea of being able to exclude another from one's property is a core property law concept that is "deeply rooted in our nation's history and traditions." It follows that a right to restrict who is able to stay in one's home is a fundamental principle and implicit in citizens' concept of liberty and justice. Further support for this conclusion is that since the Constitution was enacted, no government in the United States has ever forced private homeowners to house soldiers. Yelson may conclude, then, that because the ability to exclude a person from one's home is deeply rooted in the history of this nation and an implicit concept of liberty, the right should be selectively incorporated through the Due Process Clause of the Fourteenth Amendment to apply to the state and local government.

The government of York may argue that the Third Amendment is not a right rooted in the conscience and traditions of American society and therefore should not be selectively incorporated to apply to the state government. York may suggest that because state government has the police power (a power that the federal government lacks), the state government is authorized to govern as it sees fit in order to protect the people in the state. It follows that the state government should be able to mandate the housing of soldiers within private homes because this falls within its police power to regulate for the health, safety, and welfare of the people.

On balance, however, the argument by the York government is not persuasive. Rather, Yelson's argument that the right to refuse to quarter soldiers in one's home is implicit in the concept of liberty and deeply rooted in the history and traditions of this nation will likely prevail. Accordingly, the Third Amendment right not to have soldiers quartered in one's home during peacetime would likely be incorporated through the Fourteenth Amendment Due Process Clause to apply to the states, and Governor Lindman's order will probably be found unconstitutional.

SELF-ASSESSMENT

Do not panic when you read toward the beginning of this hypothetical that it involves the Third Amendment—a topic that you almost certainly did not study in law school. The reason you did not study the Third Amendment is because never in the Constitution's 225-year history has a government (federal or state) attempted to require private property owners to quarter soldiers in their homes—so it has not been the subject of a constitutional challenge. Accordingly, there are no cases that discuss the Third Amendment per se.

But keep reading, because toward the end of the hypothetical you receive the information you will need to understand what this hypothetical is driving at (italics added): "The Governor and State of York respond that *they are not subject to the constitutional restrictions since the Third Amendment has never been held to apply to state and local governments* ... the judge wants you to *discuss, based on precedent, the factors and analysis that should be used to determine whether the Third Amendment should be applied to the governor's action* in this case."

This language refers to the doctrine of "selective incorporation"—a topic you likely *have* studied in law school—where the Supreme Court has individually reviewed most of the Bill of Rights provisions (roughly twenty-five, by one count) to determine whether the provision protects a right that falls within the definition of "liberty" (or "property") in the Fourteenth Amendment Due Process Clause ("nor shall any State deprive any Person of life, liberty or property without due process of law"). Once you understand that the issue in the question is one of incorporation, you can proceed in answering the instant question about the unfamiliar Third Amendment based on your knowledge of any one of the incorporation cases, especially those of the 1960s (usually the *Duncan v. Louisiana* (1968) case, in most casebooks) or most recently in 2010 in *McDonald v. Chicago*. In each of these opinions the Court discussed whether the particular right at issue falls within the

Fourteenth Amendment's definition of "liberty"—and its common inquiry is to ask if the right is "implicit in the concept of ordered liberty" or "deeply rooted in our nation's history and traditions." You will then receive the majority of your analysis points by applying these phrases in a pro and con discussion of the right of property owners not to have the government compel them to quarter soldiers in their homes.

It cannot hurt to mention, as does the sample answer, the debate that raged for decades on the Supreme Court and in the scholarly commentary about whether the Fourteenth Amendment was intended to incorporate the entire Bill of Rights in one fell swoop ("total incorporation," through the Privileges or Immunities Clause) or, rather, that the proper approach is to assess each provision one at a time ("selective incorporation," through the Due Process Clause). The latter approach has prevailed through time, most recently in *McDonald v. Chicago* in 2010, where four justices for the plurality adopted the selective incorporation approach in applying the Second Amendment to the states, while one justice (Justice Thomas) stated that the Privileges or Immunities Clause had been intended to apply all of the Bill of Rights to the states. All of that said, unless the question specifically requests discussion of the debate over total versus selective incorporation, it is unnecessary to discuss the debate, but a simple parenthetical demonstrating your knowledge of the nuance can do no harm (e.g., as stated in the sample answer: "(despite substantial evidence in the legislative record that the Privileges and Immunities Clause, in particular, had been intended to incorporate the entire Bill of Rights to apply to the states)").

Finally, although it is beyond the scope of this hypothetical, the Third Amendment is substantively interesting in the sense that it applies a separate condition for the right depending on whether the nation is in a "time of war" as opposed to a "time of peace": whereas in a time of peace no soldier can be quartered in any house without the owner's consent, during a time of war a soldier *may* be quartered in a house without the owner's consent so long as it is done in accordance with the law. Again, this distinction has never been tested, because the Third Amendment has never been adjudicated.

VARIATIONS ON THE THEME

Imagine the following two sets of facts:

1. John Taylor is charged with felony larceny and prosecuted in state court. In accordance with his Sixth Amendment right in a criminal prosecution to "an impartial jury of the State and district wherein the crime shall have been committed" (a right that *has* previously been incorporated to apply to the states), a jury of six individuals is empaneled, and after trial returns a unanimous verdict of *guilty*.

   Taylor argues that the jury's verdict should be thrown out because the six-person jury fails to comply with the twelve-person jury requirement for *federal* criminal trials. Based on U.S. Supreme Court precedent, discuss whether Taylor will succeed in his argument that the six-person state jury is unconstitutional. Would your answer differ if the jury's verdict is *not* unanimous (e.g., if it found him guilty by a 5–1 vote)?
2. John Taylor is charged with felony larceny and prosecuted in state court. In accordance with his Sixth Amendment right in a criminal prosecution to "an

impartial jury of the State and district wherein the crime shall have been committed" (a right which *has* previously been incorporated to apply to the states), a jury of twelve individuals is empaneled, and after trial returns a 10–2 verdict in favor of *guilty*.

Taylor argues that the jury's verdict should be thrown out because the jury failed to convict him by unanimous vote, as is required in *federal* criminal trials. Based on U.S. Supreme Court precedent, discuss whether Taylor will succeed in his argument that the nonunanimous guilty verdict of a twelve-person state jury is unconstitutional.

Problem 2
(45 minutes)

HYPOTHETICAL

Greg Rose lives in Marywille, South Virginia, a city where most of the residents work for Rocks Inc., a large mining company. Rocks Inc. owns almost all of the real property in Marywille, and it leases space to federal and state governmental entities (such as the U.S. Postal Service and Secretary of State) that provide certain specific governmental services. Otherwise, community services are largely provided by private entities who operate under contract with Rocks Inc. For example, the company contracts with a deputized private security company to operate as the Marywille City Police Department; likewise, garbage services, schools, the bus system, and other services typically associated with a public municipality are also operated by Rocks Inc. There are a few South Virginia state troopers who come to Marywille occasionally to check on the city and residents to make sure that the police force is following appropriate protocols; however, they are never present in the area for periods spanning longer than five hours every two weeks.

One day Greg, an African American man, was at home when the Marywille City police knocked on his door. When Greg opened it the officers asked him about a couple documents and valuable items that were taken from the Rocks Inc. home office. When Greg said that he did not know what they were talking about, they forcefully entered his home without a warrant. They tackled Greg to the floor and proceeded to handcuff him to the stairs as they searched the whole house looking unsuccessfully for the documents and valuable items.

The next day, Greg drove to the Longhorn Club, a private restaurant located on land owned by the Club (one of the few parcels of land in Marywille not owned by Rocks Inc.), to purchase a bottle of wine. The Longhorn Club, which has a license from South Virginia to sell liquor on its premises, refused to serve Greg because he is an African American. Aside from paying license fees and taxes, the Club has no further connection with the state. The Longhorn Club is the only state-licensed vendor of liquor in a twenty-five–mile radius around Marywille.

In separate suits, Greg sues the Marywille Police Department and the Longhorn Club, claiming in the first case that the Marywille police force violated his Fourth Amendment rights by performing an illegal search and seizure, and claiming in the second that the Longhorn Club violated his rights under the Equal Protection Clause by refusing on the basis of his race to serve him.

Both the Marywille Police and Longhorn Club have responded in their separate cases with the claim that they are not subject to constitutional restrictions—and that the cases therefore should be summarily dismissed.

You are the law clerk for the judge hearing the suit. In preparation for the case, the judge asks you to provide an objective discussion of the summary disposition claims made by both the Marywille Police and the Longhorn Club. Please provide your discussion.

SAMPLE ESSAY

You have asked me to discuss the summary disposition claims of the Marywille Police and the Longhorn Club arguing that their respective suits should be dismissed. At issue in both of these claims is the "state action" doctrine, which stands for the proposition that only government action is subject to constitutional constraints. The reason for the state action doctrine is that the Constitution is primarily designed to protect against an oppressive government (which has all of the coercive powers of government such as imprisonment, assigning damages, etc.), as opposed to the actions of private actors (who do not have these coercive powers). The actions of a private citizen may be hurtful; however, the danger to liberty posed by the private citizen does not rise to the level of a coercive power as with a state.

The U.S. Supreme Court has recognized, however, that there are some instances when the actions of private actors are subject to constitutional constraints. First, the Thirteenth Amendment (which abolished slavery and involuntary servitude) applies to private and government actors alike. Second, it is possible for properly enacted federal or state law to impose constitutional requirements on private actors. Finally, constitutional constraints apply to private actors who are either: (1) performing an essentially public function (the "public function" exception), and/or (2) substantially entangled with the government (the "entanglement" exception).

Marywille Police Department

The first issue is whether the Marywille Police Department should be considered a state actor. In Marywille, a private company, Rocks Inc., is in control of the city, and it has privately hired the police force. The police department would thus argue that because it is a private entity, under the state action doctrine it does not need to conform with the requirements of the Fourth Amendment.

In response, Greg would argue the public function exception applies here. Under this exception, when a private entity assumes a role that the state normally performs, the private entity must conform to the Constitution. The Supreme Court established this doctrine in *Marsh v. Alabama*, a case where a town was owned by a private company. The company rented out space for a post office; otherwise, the company owned and controlled virtually every other aspect of the town. The Supreme Court held that the Constitution (specifically the First Amendment) does apply to the company's action in attempting to prevent a person from leafleting on a city sidewalk, reasoning that the company was performing the public functions that a state actor would normally perform.

Here, the actions of Marywille Police Department may be analogized to the facts in *Marsh*. In most cities, the police department is run by the city, not by a private entity. Accordingly, when Greg Rose moved to the city, he and probably everyone in the location were under the assumption that they had constitutional rights. Allowing a private company to support its own police department in a privately owned city (which took over the services and performed the role usually provided to citizens by the government) does not give the deputized police officers the right to totally disregard the Fourth Amendment. Because of the public function doctrine exception, the citizens still are protected against illegal searches and seizures by police officers, even if the department was funded by a private company,.

Rocks Inc. could attempt to rebut this argument by stating that there is not a sufficient connection or nexus with the private police department's actions and the services that the government usually provides. There are other circumstances where the government does not provide police presence in quasi-public settings (such as in shopping malls), where visitors understand that the security staff at the mall are not state actors. Rocks Inc. would thus argue that the situation in Marywille is more like the shopping mall, and there is not a sufficient connection between the police in Marywille and the actions usually performed by the government to hold the Marywille Police Department subject to constitutional constraints. Moreover, Rocks Inc. could attempt to argue that this case involving alleged Fourth Amendment rights should be distinguished from *Marsh*, which involved First Amendment speech rights (which are especially well protected under the Court's doctrine).

On balance, Marywille's argument is not persuasive—there is a big difference between a shopping mall and what looks by outside appearances to be a typical downtown municipal sidewalk. Here, the Marywille Police Department is delivering services to the population that are akin to those performed by a governmental municipality. These actions most likely will be seen to fall under the public function exception and cause the police department to be seen as a state actor. Moreover, any distinction between the Fourth Amendment and First Amendment (in *Marsh*) is likely unavailing. Accordingly, the police department must follow the Fourth Amendment, and their actions must conform with the requirements of the Constitution. In this hypothetical, the Marywille Police Depart likely violated Greg Rose's rights by entering and searching his home without a warrant.

Longhorn Club

The issue here is whether the Longhorn Club, a private entity, can be held to constitutional standards (specifically the Equal Protection Clause) for its refusal to sell alcohol to Greg Rose because of his race. Again, the state action doctrine specifies that constitutional restraints apply only to government actors; however, the Supreme Court has established two exceptions (aside from the Thirteenth amendment and federal/state law) where the Constitution does apply to private actors: (1) the public function exception, and (2) the entanglement exception.

Here, the public function doctrine does not apply—the Longhorn Club was not performing a service that is usually provided by the government. However, this situation may fall under the entanglement exception, which provides that if there is a mutually beneficial relationship between the government and a private entity, then the private entity must follow the Constitution. The relationship between the Longhorn Club and the state is one where the private club provides payment to the state in order to obtain a liquor license in return. The Supreme Court considered very similar circumstances in *Moose Lodge v. Irvis*, where a private club that refused to serve African Americans made payments to the Pennsylvania license board in order to obtain a liquor license. In *Moose Lodge* the Court held that absent additional connections, the mere existence of a license relationship between a private entity and the state does not constitute sufficient "entanglement" so as to trigger the entanglement exception to the state action doctrine; therefore, the private entity was not required to abide by the requirements of the Equal Protection Clause.

Greg Rose could argue (much like the dissent did in *Moose Lodge*) that because the state has only issued one liquor license—to the Longhorn Club—within a twenty-five-mile radius around Marywille, the state is effectively "entangled" with the Club in denying him his equal protection rights. Perhaps Greg can distinguish *Moose Lodge* (depending on the facts in that case, as in it there was not such a scarcity of locations from which to purchase liquor as in Greg's case here), and succeed with this argument that the state's active participation in severely limiting his access to a legal product constitutes sufficient "entanglement" between the state and the Longhorn Club. If so, the Longhorn Club would need to comply with the Equal Protection Clause, which would prohibit the Club from refusing on the basis of his race to serve Greg.

For its part, the Longhorn Club would likely argue that the facts here cannot be distinguished from *Moose Lodge*, and that therefore the entanglement exception does not apply—and the Club thus is not subject to the constraints of the Equal Protection Clause.

Unless Greg is able to distinguish the facts in his case from those in *Moose Lodge*, a court will likely hold that Longhorn Club does not fall within the entanglement exception to the state action doctrine, and thus is not bound to observe the requirements of the Equal Protection Clause.

SELF-ASSESSMENT

Because this hypothetical falls under a subheading identifying "state action" as one of its topics, it is fairly obvious what issue the hypothetical involves. If the hypothetical appeared on an exam, however, you would not have that hint, and the issue might not be as clear to you. Specifically, although the hypothetical identifies various actors as "private," the call of the question does not speak directly of "private" versus "public" action: "Both the Marywille Police and Longhorn Club have responded in their separate cases [involving alleged violations of individual rights and equal protection] with the *claim that they are not subject to constitutional restrictions—and that the cases therefore should be summarily dismissed.... Provide an objective discussion of the summary disposition claims ...* " (Incidentally, as you are asked to discuss the summary disposition claims, which involve *constitutional* restrictions, you should not spend time discussing possible *statutory* claims that, for example, the Longhorn Club is required to serve Greg.)

An important point to make is that in any general question regarding the constitutionality of an action alleged to violate individual rights or equal protection, the first issue is whether the actor is in fact even required to comply with the Constitution. The Constitution generally applies only to *government*—not private—action. If we are dealing with a private actor to whom none of the exceptions apply, there simply is no constitutional claim.

So, in self-assessing your own answer to this hypothetical, first ask yourself if you would have identified (without the help of the subheading) that the issue involves state action. Resolve *always* to ask and answer the state action question when dealing with an alleged violation of an individual right or equal protection. The answer is often (usually?) open-and-shut—clearly an act of the legislature or the executive is state action, so you can simply say "state action is satisfied because we're dealing with an act of the legislature/executive," and move on. But if the allegations are directed instead against a *private* actor, there is a major state action issue.

Once you have identified the issue, it is worth spending a sentence or two explaining the rationale for the state action requirement. As explained fairly decently in the sample answer, the reason for the so-called "state action" requirement is that the greatest fear of *We the People* is an oppressive, tyrannical government—with all of the coercive power that such a government can bring to bear. Private oppression and discrimination, as hurtful and harmful as they may be, do not rise to the same level of concern.

When explaining the "rule" for the state action doctrine, note that the *only* constitutional provision that applies to private action is the Thirteenth Amendment, which prohibits slavery and involuntary servitude. (Note also that state/local and federal government may, under some circumstances, pass laws requiring private actors to comply with constitutional constraints—in such cases, the plaintiff brings a *statutory* (not constitutional) claim.) Then, the bulk of your discussion (rule and analysis) will involve the two exceptions to the state action doctrine that have emerged from the Supreme Court's jurisprudence—the "public function" exception and the "entanglement" exception. (Note that some casebooks and study aids speak of a possible new third exception, the "entwinement" exception, but for now it seems doctrinally appropriate still to include entwinement within the entanglement exception.)

In applying the facts to the rule in the analysis, as always check to see that you are making arguments on both sides. This is key, especially in an area such as the state action doctrine where the Supreme Court's jurisprudence has been so internally opaque and seemingly inconsistent (as recognized by the Court itself, which has commented that the "cases deciding when private action might be deemed that of the state have not been a model of consistency"). On the facts of this hypothetical, there are ample arguments on both sides that the private actor is or is not performing a "public function," or that the action is or is not sufficiently "entangled" with the government, such that the exception should or should not apply. In the end, however, because the facts in the hypothetical fairly closely resemble those in *Marsh v. Alabama* (where the Court held that the public function exception does apply) and *Moose Lodge* (holding that the entanglement exception does *not* apply), it is logical to conclude similarly here that the Marywille police department *is* subject to Fourth Amendment constraints, and that the Longhorn Club is *not* subject to Equal Protection Clause limitations. That said, even if you concluded otherwise, the most important part of your answer is the elucidation of the rule and the analysis.

VARIATIONS ON THE THEME

For each of the following fact scenarios, discuss whether the private entity must comply with constitutional restrictions.

1. For decades, a private group, the "Chancellors," comprised (by rule) only of Caucasian members, has conducted a private "straw poll" to decide which political candidates to support in the general election. The Chancellors, which includes among its members many influential business leaders and politicians, is enormously influential in the general election. In fact, most of

the politicians endorsed by the Chancellors run unopposed in the primary election, and nobody other than a person endorsed by the group has been elected to office in more than fifty years.

Randall Wilson, an African-American man, sues, claiming that the Chancellors are violating the Equal Protection Clause by failing to include non-Caucasians as part of its membership. The Chancellors claim they are a private group, and thus not subject to constitutional constraints.

Discuss whether the Equal Protection Clause applies to the Chancellors.

2. For the past year, Stella Baker, a thirty-five–year-old single mother, has been having difficulty paying her bills, including her utility bills. The company that provides her electricity is Standard Power & Light Co., a private company that has been granted a monopoly by the state to provide electricity to customers in Stella's community. After Stella fails to pay her bill for two straight months, and does not answer Standard's phone calls and letters, Standard shuts off her electricity.

Stella sues Standard Power & Light, claiming that the company has deprived her of her Fourteenth Amendment procedural due process rights by failing to provide adequate notice and hearing before shutting off her electricity. Standard claims that it is a private company, and thus is not subject to constitutional constraints.

Discuss whether the Due Process Clause applies to Standard Power & Light.

Problem 3
(45 minutes)

HYPOTHETICAL

The City of Alpine is a small working-class city located in the mountains of the State of Coloyoming. In recent years, the City has suffered an economic downturn, and many of its residents have become unemployed. For the past several months, the Alpine City Council has been pondering ways to improve its public image in order to attract a higher-income residential population as well as create more local jobs. The City Council ultimately decides to redevelop its slope-side area into a ski resort and to create a large upscale outdoor shopping center. The Council hopes that this will attract a more affluent class of individuals to live in Alpine. The Council also thinks that the new shopping mall will create new jobs for Alpine residents.

The Alpine City Economic Development Commission solicits bids from several construction companies to begin the creation of the shopping center. The company ultimately chosen is a private developer, Resort Vacations, Inc., who agrees to construct both the ski resort and the shopping center. Some of the land on which the Alpine Ski Resort Project is to be developed is already owned by the City of Alpine; however, in order to create a resort and shopping center as luxurious as the City desires, three entire blocks of slope-side residences and individually owned parcels of land need to be condemned. On the plus side, the proposed stores and restaurants to be developed by Resort Vacations are projected to create hundreds of jobs for the City's residents.

As the Alpine Ski Resort Project proceeds, the owners of Alpine Mountaineers, a private members-only club, meets with the City Council to discuss dramatically expanding its clubhouse facilities in order to accommodate the increased number of persons who could potentially want to become members. The Council agrees that the Mountaineers' plans would nicely augment the City's development, so the Council amends the redevelopment plan to include an additional one block of property, which will then be sold to the Mountaineers for their clubhouse expansion project.

Shortly thereafter, the City issues a condemnation order (which is done in accordance with state law) for all four blocks of property, which will allow it to take possession within two months.

James Smith, a homeowner whose property is seized in order for the City to transfer the property to Resort Vacations for the development of the ski area and shopping mall, and his cousin, Sarah Smith, a homeowner whose property is seized to accommodate the Alpine Mountaineers' expansion, sue to block the sale of the condemned property. What are James's and Sarah's best arguments and chances of success?

SAMPLE ESSAY

You have asked me to discuss James's and Sarah's best arguments and chances for success in their suits to block the taking of their properties.

James

The Fifth Amendment to the Constitution (which is incorporated so as to apply to state and local governments through the Fourteenth Amendment Due Process Clause) reads: "nor shall private property be taken for public use without just compensation." Accordingly, when a government entity exercises its power of eminent domain to take private property, the taking must be for a public use and the government must provide the owner just compensation for the property. Considering the last element first, assuming there is a taking for public use, the just compensation requirement of the Takings Clause is satisfied where the government pays "fair market value" (as determined before the property was condemned) to the private property owner.

The issue in this instance is not whether there has been a taking—clearly there has been a physical taking of James's and Sarah's properties. Instead, the issue is whether the property was taken for public use. The public use requirement prohibits the government from taking property for private use or benefit. On its face, the term "public use" seems to mean the taken property must be used by the government for some *governmental* function. Accordingly, James would argue that this taking is not in fact for the "public use" because the City is essentially transferring property from one private owner to another (James to Resort Vacations, Inc.).

The City would respond, however, that the U.S. Supreme Court in *Hawaii Housing Authority v. Midkiff*, and again more recently in *Kelo v. New London*, broadly interpreted the "public use" requirement as equivalent to the achievement of a public purpose. Once the City identifies a legitimate state interest or purpose—which can include the motivation to *economically* improve the community—the state has the power to take private property if taking the property is rationally related to the furtherance of the legitimate purpose. The court will not question the City's stated purpose unless it appears to be completely arbitrary and the means appear completely unrelated to the stated purpose.

In this case, the City of Alpine has as its stated purpose the goal to create an upscale environment where members of the Alpine community and other visitors can enjoy the area. Furthermore, the slope-side shopping mall and restaurants have the potential to create numerous jobs for Alpine residents who either lost their jobs in the recent economic downturn or who may be searching for a different job. The City will argue that this taking is "for the public use" both because the public will be able to enjoy the land and also because the development will benefit the community economically through the creation of numerous job opportunities and increased tax base.

The City may add that the Supreme Court concluded in *Hawaii Housing* that the State of Hawaii could condemn land and immediately transfer the land to private citizens to use as private residences. Even though the land would be used by private persons for private uses, the state had a legitimate interest in diversifying land holdings in Hawaii, and condemnation was a legitimate means to accomplish that goal. Similarly, the Court in *Kelo* allowed the transfer of private land to a private corporation, which would then develop the area into an upscale mixed-use area. Similarly, here, although the City is taking land from private individuals to be sold to a private development company, the overall government interest is for the public to benefit from the changed use of the land.

Further support for the City is found in *Berman v. Parker*, where the Supreme Court upheld as a valid "public use" the government's taking and transferring of private properties to private third parties as part of an urban development project of a blighted area of Washington, DC. The Court recognized legitimate state interests in making the community healthy, spacious, aesthetic, clean, sanitary, and well-balanced as well as an interest in alleviating and preventing conditions of unemployment. Taking and transferring the property to private parties was a rational means to advance the legitimate state interest and is a way to strengthen and revitalize the economy of the city.

Thus, although James can argue that the taking of his land is technically being done to transfer the property to another private entity, the Supreme Court has construed the requirement of a "public use" quite broadly. Therefore, the fact that the property is turned over to some private user likely does not prevent the use from being a public one as long as the public can be expected to derive some benefit (e.g., economic development) from the use. Here, that would seem to be the case, and James will likely not prevail on his claim that the taking does not satisfy the "public use" requirement.

Sarah

Sarah, on the other hand, will have a much stronger argument than James in challenging the constitutionality of the condemnation of her land. In her case, the City is seeking to take the property in order to transfer it to the Alpine Mountaineers, a private club that will use the land simply to expand its *private* operations.

Although the Mountaineers may argue that its expanded operation may allow for increased opportunities for the public to join the club, this likely does not rise to the level and nature of "public" use previously accepted by the Supreme Court in cases such as *Kelo, Hawaii Housing,* and *Berman,* as discussed above. In those cases, an important theme was the *economic* benefits that would extend to the community at large. Here there is no meaningful economic benefit to the community; rather, the benefit is virtually only to the private club. Specifically, unlike the taking of James's property, the taking of Sarah's property would offer neither benefits to the general public in being able to visit the club, nor enjoyment of economic benefits in the form of increased employment opportunities and/or substantially enlarged tax base. Therefore, the taking of Sarah's property would likely be found to violate the Takings Clause for failure to satisfy the "public use" requirement.

SELF-ASSESSMENT

There are three questions to ask in any takings problem, which directly track the language of the Fifth Amendment Takings Clause ("nor shall private property be taken for public use without just compensation"): (1) Is there a "taking"?; (2) Is the taking for "public use"?; and (3) What is "just compensation"? Few law school questions will focus on number (3). Although in a practical sense the "just compensation" question is likely the most important for the person whose property is being taken, for analytical purposes this element is fairly straightforward: "just compensation" is whatever was the "fair market value" (FMV) of the property before its condemnation. Accordingly, unless the call of the question asks for a more detailed discussion concerning "just compensation," it should be enough for you to provide the basic rule as stated in the sample answer: "The just compensation requirement of the takings clause is satisfied where the government pays "fair market value" (as determined before the property was condemned) to the private property owner."

The meat of any Takings Clause analysis will be whether the government's action amounts to a "taking," and whether the government's taking meets the "public use" requirement. Our hypothetical focuses on the public use requirement. (As noted in the sample answer, because the facts involve the government's physical acquisition of the property, there is really no issue of whether the property is "taken." See "Variations on the Theme" below for additional practice on the analysis to be used in questions involving whether the government's action amounts to a taking.) The most high-profile recent action in the Supreme Court regarding the Takings Clause involved facts similar to those provided in the hypothetical, whereby a local government would acquire private property and then turn it over to other private companies for "economic redevelopment." As noted in the sample answer, the Supreme Court held in *Kelo v. New London* (2005) that such an action *does* qualify as a "public use," and thus upheld the government's taking. The Court added that states and local government may certainly regulate in order to *narrow* what qualifies as a "public use" in their own jurisdiction, but that for *constitutional* purposes, a goal of public "economic development" satisfies the requirement. Your answer should thus include the Court's reasoning in *Kelo,* but then also argue in the alternative (as did the *Kelo* dissenters as well as many Americans who were outraged by the decision) that the term "public use" requires that the subsequent owner of the property actually be a *public* entity, *not* a private entity that will merely serve the public as part of its business or activities. The hypothetical, in its alternative scenarios for the takings of James's and Sarah's property, explores the nuances of this last point—whether there should be a distinction made between a subsequent private owner who either does (Resort Vacations, Inc.) or does not (Alpine Mountain Club) serve the public—so your answer should discuss this distinction.

VARIATIONS ON THE THEME

1. Consider the following additional facts. In the latest City of Alpine city council election, several council members are elected who ran on a "Preserve Our

Wildlife and Environment" platform. Thereafter the city council takes two dramatic actions: (1) it cancels the entire Alpine Ski Development Project described above (including dropping the legal proceedings to acquire the four-block area that was to be redeveloped); and (2) in order to protect the habitat of a species of owl that has been sighted in the area, which is on the endangered species watch list, it rezones the same four-block area (which had previously been zoned for mixed commercial and residential) so that *no* new construction may occur.

Barry Sandstrom owns a one-acre undeveloped parcel within the four-block area that has been rezoned. He purchased the parcel two years ago for $100,000, with the intention of building a vacation home on it. Now, after the rezoning where he is not allowed to build on his property, the parcel has an appraised value of $5,000. Barry sues, claiming that the city owes him just compensation for the vast diminution in the value of his property. Discuss the merits of Barry's claim.

D. OPTIONAL READINGS

The following sources present the topics covered in this chapter in more depth than the chapter introduction. The sources are in increasing levels of detail. The first provides an overview, the second provides more detail, and the third provides the greatest coverage of the material.

JOHN E. NOWAK & RONALD D. ROTUNDA, PRINCIPLES OF CONSTITUTIONAL LAW (4th ed. 2010), chapters 10 (§§ 10.1–10.5), 11 (§§11.9–11.13); 12.

ERWIN CHEMERINSKY, CONSTITUTIONAL LAW: PRINCIPLES AND POLICIES (3rd ed. 2008), chapter 6; §8.4.

JOHN E. NOWAK & RONALD D. ROTUNDA, CONSTITUTIONAL LAW (7th ed. 2000), chapters 10 (§§ 10.1–10.5), 11 (§§11.10–11.14); 12.

6 MIXED STRUCTURAL PROBLEMS

A. INTRODUCTION

There has been, to this point, a sort of artificiality in the way that the questions you have answered have been presented. The questions have been contained in chapters with identified subject matter. It was clear that a hypothetical in the chapter on federal legislative power involved a federal legislative power issue, for example. Although you had to determine how to conduct the analysis, the constitutional issue had already been identified. On a constitutional law exam you are unlikely to be given similar guidance. You will need to be able to identify, for example, whether the hypothetical raises an issue of the Dormant Commerce Clause or Article IV Privileges and Immunities or, perhaps, both.

Problem 1
(45 minutes)

HYPOTHETICAL

President Hugo Smith was elected as president of the United States in 2008. It was an extremely close presidential race, and during the campaign multiple questions were raised about Mr. Smith's personal life prior to running for president. Many of these personal issues were adroitly averted by Mr. Smith's campaign team; however, as with any good scandal, the media and other outlets refused to forget the issues and continued to report on various allegations.

After being elected, many more of President Smith's personal issues came to light. For example, prior to becoming a politician, Smith worked for an investment bank in New York. Sarah Gold, his secretary when he was at the bank about twenty years ago, recently alleged that Mr. Smith had repeatedly made sexual advances to her at the time. Then another former secretary, Mary Luck, made similar allegations. Recently, five more women have come forward with similar stories. The most recent allegation of sexual harassment is from Amanda Fairfield, who was part of Mr. Smith's campaign staff before he was president and then a legislative aide before quitting last month. She stated that on multiple occasions during the years from 2006 until recently Mr. Smith called her to his hotel rooms and the Oval Office and made sexual advances. She said she rebuffed his advances on every occasion, and that he finally let her leave the room after she broke into tears. Ms. Fairfield brings a sexual harassment suit against President Smith. In response, President Smith asserts presidential immunity from civil suit, at least while he is in office.

Meanwhile, the attorney general of the United States, Maria Conklin, has become increasingly disturbed by the allegations of the president's misconduct, and begins having serious doubts about his fitness to remain in office. Finally, when Ms. Fairfield's allegations become public in 2011, Attorney General Conklin, pursuant to the Ethics in Government Act of 2005 (which renewed in its entirety the previously expired Ethics in Government Act of 1978), decides that further investigation is warranted and therefore calls for the appointment of an independent counsel by a panel of federal court judges to investigate and prosecute any wrongdoing by the president.

Thereafter, the panel of federal judges does appoint an independent counsel, Sam Henderson. After several months and countless hours of interviewing many different women and campaign workers from the president's past, Henderson decides that he has enough information to bring federal criminal charges (related to the sexual harassment) against the president. Before Henderson brings charges, however, to solidify his case he seeks copies of tapes of conversations the president had with several women in the Oval Office (as a matter of practice, President Smith tapes all conversations in the Oval Office). Accordingly, Henderson issues a subpoena for tapes of the relevant conversations. Resisting these efforts, President Smith claims that his inherent power of executive privilege allows him to decline to release the tapes.

Adding to the president's significant problems, yet another individual is not happy with his actions. Robert Vinson, who had been the leading bidder to receive a contract with the U.S. Navy, lost the contract during the final stages of negotiation. Mr. Vinson claims that he lost his contract due to his testimony in a congressional hearing in opposition to a new policy proposed by President Smith. Vinson claims that the president, in retaliation for Vinson's testimony, advised the Navy not to enter into the contract with Vinson (an assertion for which there is some substantial evidence). Vinson seeks money damages from the president. In response, President Smith asserts absolute immunity from suit.

You are the law clerk for President Smith's private attorney, Claire Bowman. Ms. Bowman asks you to discuss the constitutionality of the president's responses to the three issues listed above. Please provide Ms. Bowman with your discussion.

SAMPLE ESSAY ANSWER

You have asked me to provide an objective discussion of the constitutionality of President Smith's responses to a series of three issues posed in the hypothetical. Specifically, President Smith claims that his position as "president" in the constitutional scheme entitles him to: (1) immunity from civil suit (at least while he is in office) for unofficial actions taken before and during his time in office; (2) privilege not to answer a subpoena for evidence in a criminal case; and (3) absolute immunity from civil suit for official actions taken while he is in office.

Supreme Court precedent speaks directly to each of these situations. Regarding his assertion of presidential immunity from civil suit, at least while he is in office, from Ms. Fairfield's claims of sexual harassment, *Clinton v. Jones* is partially on point. In *Clinton,* the Court held that President Bill Clinton could not avoid, or even postpone, defending a lawsuit from a woman (Paula Jones) who claimed he had sexually harassed her before he became president. The Court reasoned that there is no presidential immunity for unofficial conduct engaged in before a president takes office, commenting also that defending the suit would not take much of the president's time (a prediction which, in retrospect, turned out to be highly mistaken). Here, Ms. Fairfield claims President Smith sexually harassed her both before and while he was in office, so the president might argue that this case is distinguishable from *Clinton* by the fact that some of the claimed activity took place *while* he was president, thus giving rise to immunity from suit. Moreover, the president could add that the Court should look at what actually happened after the *Clinton* case was decided—where President Clinton had to spend massive amounts of time and energy defending the suit—in deciding to at least postpone (if not dismiss) the case. Ms. Fairfield could counter that although some of the behavior took place while Smith was president, some of it also happened *before* he was president, which puts the case back within the purview of *Clinton v. Jones*. Moreover, regarding the more recent harassment while Smith was president, Ms. Fairfield may argue that *Clinton* holds that the key component is not so much *when* the action occurred, but whether the president is engaging in *unofficial* conduct. Where, as here, the conduct is "unofficial," she would argue, the president may not avoid or even postpone the suit. (On the other hand, the case of *Nixon v. Fitzgerald*, discussed below, might be read to give absolute immunity to civil suit for money damages for *all* conduct—official and "unofficial"—during the time the president is in office.) On balance, based on the fact that at least some of the conduct occurred *before* President Smith took office, under *Clinton v. Jones,* Ms. Fairfield would seem to have the stronger arguments. A court would likely hold that President Smith does not have immunity, and the court therefore may not dismiss or postpone Ms. Fairfield's suit.

Regarding President Smith's claim of executive privilege not to answer a subpoena from Independent Counsel Henderson for the tapes of conversations the president had with several women in the Oval Office, the president might argue that the Court should look for guidance to the relatively recent case of *Cheney v. U.S. District Court for the District of Columbia*, where Vice-President Richard Cheney invoked executive privilege to avoid complying with a discovery request. The government would reply, however, that *Cheney,* a *civil* case, does not apply to this *criminal* investigation; rather, the government could argue that the case of *United States v. Nixon* is directly on point here. In *Nixon,* the unanimous Court held that President Richard Nixon could not assert executive privilege to avoid complying with a subpoena to turn over potentially incriminating tapes made of conversations in the Oval Office, reasoning that although executive privilege does exist, it is not absolute (e.g., it does not extend to the point where it would interfere with the Court performing its constitutional function in adjudicating a criminal trial). Here, Independent Counsel Henderson will argue that *Nixon* instructs that President Smith cannot assert executive privilege to avoid complying with a subpoena in a criminal investigation. Because the facts here are so close to those in *United States v. Nixon*, President Smith likely has few arguments in his favor, and he will need to turn over the tapes.

President Smith will almost certainly be more successful with his assertion of absolute immunity for civil suit for official actions taken while he was president, however. In *Nixon v. Fitzgerald*, where former president Nixon had played a demonstrable role as president in firing a federal employee who had earlier provided damaging testimony before Congress, the Court held that absolute immunity shielded the former president from suits for money damages for actions taken while he was in office. Similarly, here President Smith is being sued for money damages by Robert Vinson, who alleges that the president retaliated against Vinson's testimony before Congress by playing a role in Vinson's not being awarded a contract with the U.S. Navy. (Although it is beyond the scope of the question, Vinson's suit, if anything, is even weaker than Fitzgerald's was in 1982, because Vinson, unlike Fitzgerald, is not even an employee claiming unlawful termination; rather, he is simply a person who lost out on a contract.) Again, because the facts here are so close to those in *Nixon v. Fitzgerald,* where the president was found to have absolute immunity from suit for money damages for actions taken while he was in office, President Smith very likely will be successful in asserting absolute immunity in Robert Vinson's suit.

SELF-ASSESSMENT

This hypothetical is a bit different than some, in the sense that each of these three issues is directly answered by a specific case decided in the Supreme Court. Accordingly, there is not as much "analysis" that needs to occur; instead, you need to identify that several cases in the area of executive immunity/privilege are directly on point, and be able to apply the holdings of those cases to the hypothetical facts.

These cases involving presidential immunity and executive privilege are available to us courtesy of two presidents in particular, Richard Nixon and Bill Clinton. Prior to their presidencies, these issues were often more-or-less informally asserted by various presidents, but never were they so vigorously asserted in the course of litigation as they were with Presidents Nixon and Clinton. As a result, although the broad parameters of presidential immunity and executive privilege are still quite indistinct, we now have a much better sense for *some* of the contours.

Regarding your answer to President Smith's claim of executive privilege to avoid turning over the tapes, you should, like the sample essay, concentrate on *United States v. Nixon*, because that case is directly on point regarding executive privilege in a *criminal* proceeding. The sample answer refers to the case of *Cheney v. U.S. District Court for the District of Columbia* (2004), which involved a *civil* proceeding, and thus is not on point for the facts of this hypothetical, which involves a subpoena in a criminal investigation. As the *Cheney* Court explained, the "need for information for use in civil cases, while far from negligible, does not share the urgency or significance of the criminal subpoena requests in *Nixon*." *Cheney* nonetheless contains useful information on the topic of executive privilege, with its discussion as to why the judiciary should treat claims of executive privilege with care:

> Executive privilege is an extraordinary assertion of power "not to be lightly invoked." Once executive privilege is asserted, coequal branches of the Government are set on a collision course. The Judiciary is forced into the difficult task of balancing the need for information in a judicial proceeding and the Executive's Article II prerogatives. This inquiry places courts in the awkward position of evaluating the Executive's claims of confidentiality and autonomy, and pushes to the fore difficult questions of separation of powers and checks and balances. These "occasion[s] for constitutional confrontation between the two branches" should be avoided whenever possible.

As demonstrated in the sample essay, the discussion regarding President Smith's assertion of immunity to avoid (or postpone) Ms. Fairfield's civil suit exposes a bit of uncertainty in how executive immunity should be interpreted in cases where the claims focus on *unofficial* action taken *during* the president's term in office. Specifically, although *Clinton v. Jones* holds that the president does not have immunity for unofficial actions taken outside of the term of office, *Nixon v. Fitzgerald* holds that the president has absolute immunity for *official* actions taken during the president's term in office—which leaves unanswered the question of whether the immunity extends to unofficial action taken during the term in office. Accordingly, your answer should briefly discuss this uncertainty and identify the alternative arguments. In the end, the uncertainty in the hypothetical would seem to be resolved by the fact that President Smith is being sued for unofficial actions taken both during *and before* his term in office, thus suggesting that the holding of *Clinton v. Jones* would prevail, and President Smith would likely not be able to assert executive immunity to avoid or postpone Ms. Fairfield's civil suit.

Problem 2
(40 minutes)

HYPOTHETICAL

The town of Sunshine, State of Relaxation, is renowned for its high-quality handmade surfboards, which has resulted in a strong tourist trade that contributes significantly to the local economy. Within the last couple of years, the Sunshine market has been infiltrated by craftspeople from the neighboring village of Hangten and from the adjacent State of Bliss, which has led to a decrease in profits for the local surfboard makers.

Within the past year there have been some reports that the non-Sunshine surfboards have caused severe injuries to a number of people when the boards have split apart in heavy waves, and the entire surfboard industry in Sunshine has suffered as a result. In response, the Sunshine city council enacted the following ordinance to protect customers from the injury caused by splitting surfboards as well as to protect the local economy:

> Any surfboard offered for sale in the town of Sunshine must be certified as having been produced within the town's boundaries by a certified Sunshine resident.

Flanagan, a surfboard craftsman from the adjacent State of Bliss, objects to this restriction, and sues Sunshine in federal court. Please discuss and analyze the major constitutional issues likely to be raised by Flanagan.

SAMPLE ESSAY

You have asked me to analyze the major constitutional issues likely to be raised by Flanagan. The major issues raised in this set of facts involve the Dormant Commerce Clause (DCC) and the Article IV Privileges and Immunities Clause.

When state or local action affects interstate commerce, under the DCC the judiciary determines whether a state or local statute or action violates an implicit limitation of the Commerce Clause that forbids states from economically discriminating against out-of-staters. (Congress has the authority under its commerce power to regulate interstate commerce. However, it is well-settled that Congress's power in this area is not exclusive; states too may regulate interstate commerce—provided that Congress has not preempted the states in the particular area.) Some have criticized the DCC doctrine on separation-of-powers grounds, as an example of the Court's overstepping its authority by reading hidden meaning into a power delegated by the Constitution to another branch of government—Congress. The DCC doctrine is also criticized on federalism grounds: that the federal Court is inappropriately limiting state authority to regulate. On the other hand, supporters of the doctrine maintain that it is a proper exercise of the judiciary's authority to prevent states from placing undue burdens on interstate commerce.

In analyzing DCC cases, the Court first asks whether the state measure "facially" discriminates against out-of-state interests. If so, the measure is presumed to be virtually per se invalid, and will almost always be struck down unless the government is able to rebut this heavy presumption. The reason for this heavy presumption of invalidity is that discrimination on the face of a measure is almost always an indication of discriminatory *purpose*. And if the Constitution means anything at all in the area of interstate relations, it means (in the famous words of Justice Brandeis) that the "states will sink or swim together" economically—which therefore forbids states from purposefully discriminating against out-of-staters. For a facially discriminatory measure to survive, the state must overcome a form of "strict scrutiny" to show that it has a legitimate (i.e., nondiscriminatory) purpose, and that the purpose cannot be accomplished by available less-discriminatory means. (Quarantine-type laws, where states exclude "infected" out-of-state items, are the rare case that will sometimes satisfy this test.)

If the measure is facially neutral, the Court balances the state's interest against the burdens that the measure imposes on interstate commerce, with greater weight against the measure if it discriminates in *effect* against out-of-staters, and greater weight *for* the measure if it affects in-staters and out-of-staters equally. For the former (discriminatory-in-effect laws)—especially those that exclude all or virtually all out-of-staters—the statute is presumed unconstitutional, and will be struck down unless the state proves that there is a legitimate nondiscriminatory purpose to explain the disparate impact, and that the measure is the least-discriminatory means to accomplish the legitimate purpose. (Note that this test for a facially neutral, discriminatory-in-effect state action is very similar to that for facial discrimination, but with a somewhat lower burden for states to overcome the presumption of invalidity.) For the latter (laws that are evenhanded in their effect on in-staters and out-of-staters alike), by contrast, the statute is presumed constitutional and "will be upheld unless the burden imposed on such commerce is clearly excessive in relation to the putative local benefits." See *Pike v. Bruce Church, Inc.* (1970).

There are two important exceptions when states may discriminate against interstate commerce: (1) when Congress, pursuant to its commerce power, authorizes states to discriminate; and (2) when states are acting as market participants, and are thus allowed to operate as would any other private entity in the competitive marketplace—including picking and choosing with whom they will do business.

Applying the DCC framework to this case involving the Sunshine's requirement that "any surfboard offered for sale in the town of Sunshine must be certified as having been produced within the town's boundaries by a certified Sunshine resident," this provision facially discriminates against out-of-staters and is thus virtually per se invalid, and will be struck down unless Sunshine is able to show that it has a legitimate government interest and that there are no less-restrictive alternatives to accomplish its purpose. (Indeed, it does not matter that the law also discriminates against other *in*-staters—under the Court's DCC doctrine, as long as the measure favors *any* in-stater at the expense of out-of-staters, it is said to be virtually per se invalid.) Sunshine could argue that its purpose in requiring the certification is to protect customers from the serious injuries that they have been suffering due to shoddy workmanship. Health and safety regulations are generally considered to be legitimate. And, Sunshine would argue, so long as a substantial part of the town's reason was for health and safety purposes, the fact that "the Sunshine city council enacted the ordinance ... [in part] *to protect the local economy*" should not change this conclusion. Flanagan would argue, on the other hand, that a measure that is intended to favor in-town residents at the expense of out-of-staters is by definition invalid under the Court's DCC doctrine. Even assuming arguendo that Sunshine prevails on this point (which is possible, because courts sometimes give state or local government the "benefit of the doubt" when there is a mixed motivation for a discriminatory statute), it will almost certainly fail on the requirement that there be no less-restrictive alternatives. One less-restrictive alternative, for example, would be for Sunshine to undertake a rigorous inspection program for all out-of-town surfboards sold in the town. Although such an inspection program would still impose some extra burden on out-of-staters (which would subject it to its own DCC analysis), it is certainly less restrictive than the current outright prohibition on the sale of out-of-state surfboards, and as such would serve to invalidate the current ban. An even less-restrictive (indeed, *non*restrictive) alternative would be to undertake a rigorous inspection program for *all* surfboards regardless of origin.

Next we would ask if the Sunshine measure is facially neutral and discriminatory in impact, but because we have already concluded that it is facially discriminatory and hence violates the DCC, we need not repeat the virtually identical analysis, other than to say that the measure would be similarly found to violate the DCC under discriminatory-in-effect analysis. Likewise, as we have determined that the law is discriminatory, we need not work through the "evenhanded-in-effect" analysis.

Finally, it appears that neither of the exceptions to the DCC apply here. Congress has not regulated; and rather than acting as a market *participant*; the Town of Sunshine is simply regulating the market. Therefore the DCC doctrine applies in all of its force.

The second major constitutional argument that Flanagan may raise is that the Town of Sunshine violates the Privileges and Immunities Clause by prohibiting out-of-towners (including out-of-staters) from selling surfboards in the town. The purpose of the Privileges and Immunities Clause is to prevent states from placing unreasonable burdens on noncitizens, and under the doctrine developed by the Supreme Court, in order to determine whether the Privileges and Immunities Clause of Article IV has been violated, the following two-part inquiry is used.

1. Does the law discriminate against citizens of another state in regards to fundamental constitutional rights or important economic interests? If no, there is no violation. If yes, go to 2.
2. If yes, the law will be upheld only if (i) there is a substantial reason for the difference in treatment, and (ii) the discrimination practiced against nonresidents bears a substantial relationship to the State's objective.*

*In analyzing item 2(ii), the Court has reasoned that if any less-restrictive means are available, the discrimination is *not* substantially related to the state's objective.

Here, Flanagan would argue that Sunshine's law *does* infringe on an important economic interest, the right to earn a livelihood—which is a right that the

Supreme Court has regularly found to satisfy this test. Because the law does shut Flanagan completely out of the market, a court would likely find that it does in fact infringe the sort of privilege or immunity that is protected by the clause. Looking then at the second part of the test, the Sunshine law will be struck down unless the town is able to meet a hybrid intermediate/strict scrutiny standard of review to show that there is a substantial reason for the difference in the treatment and that the measure is the least-restrictive means available to accomplish the town's objective. Here the analysis looks much like that in the DCC analysis—Sunshine likely succeeds in its argument that it has a substantial reason (health and safety of surfboard customers), but fails in demonstrating that the law is the least-restrictive alternative (a less-restrictive alternative would be to impose a rigorous inspection program for all out-of-town surfboards, or, for that matter, of *all* surfboards whether from in-town or out-of-town).

SELF-ASSESSMENT

An important point about the Dormant Commerce Clause and the Article IV Privileges and Immunities Clause beyond what was discussed in Chapter 4 is that anytime you see a fact pattern that may give rise to an issue involving either the DCC or Privileges and Immunities Clause, because they are so closely related you should discuss *both*—unless you're instructed to discuss only one or the other. The Supreme Court itself has commented on how the DCC and Privileges and Immunities Clause are intertwined. Both involve restrictions on state and local actions that in some way favor in-staters at the expense of out-of-staters, for example, and, in the end, their analyses are quite similar—especially the requirement that there be "no less-restrictive alternative" for both discriminatory statutes under the DCC and for statutes that affect a constitutionally protected right or important economic interest under the Privileges and Immunities Clause.

Finally, you might note that much of the language in this sample essay is identical to language from the Chapter 4 problems covering the DCC and the Privileges and Immunities Clause. This illustrates the point that there is no reason you cannot prepare certain "canned" language ahead of the time to describe the various constitutional provisions and doctrinal "rules" upon which you expect to be tested, thereby leaving yourself additional time for the all-important analysis.

Problem 3
(40 minutes)

HYPOTHETICAL

Congress, responding to certain actions of the executive branch during the Vietnam War, passed the Foreign Intelligence Surveillance Act of 1978 (FISA), which requires the Federal Bureau of Investigation (FBI) and the National Security Agency (NSA) to obtain search warrants from a special secret court before conducting electronic surveillance of people suspected to be terrorists or spies.

The president, in the wake of a wave of terrorist attacks in the United States, secretly authorizes the FBI and NSA to eavesdrop without a warrant on suspected Americans. The president says he was justified in so acting because he "needed greater agility in investigating terrorism suspects than was possible through the process mandated by FISA."

Andrew Johns, an American citizen who lives in East Lansing, is engaged to a woman who is spending the year in Egypt studying Arabic. Johns and his fiancée stay in frequent contact via Internet telephone. Johns learns that pursuant to the president's authorization, the NSA has been eavesdropping on many of these telephone conversations. The NSA has not obtained warrants for these activities.

Johns sues, claiming the president's authorization of the government to eavesdrop exceeds the executive's constitutional power. You are a law clerk for the court that will hear the case. Based on class readings and discussions, please provide a concise analysis of whether the president's actions are constitutional, discussing arguments both pro and con.

SAMPLE ESSAY

You have asked me to analyze whether the president's actions in authorizing the warrantless eavesdropping on certain American citizens are constitutional.

The first issue on which I will focus is whether Congress had authority to pass the law (this question is not directly asked, but it is relevant to the later analysis of the presidential authority). Two questions should be posed in considering the constitutionality of the Act of Congress: (1) does Congress have the power?, and (2) is there a constitutional limit on this power?

The answer to the first question is *yes*. Congress has constitutional authority in Article I, § 8[1] to create the FISA process in order to "provide for the common Defence and general Welfare of the United States." The creation of such a special process may also be considered "Necessary and Proper" to carry out the common defense and general welfare. Regarding the second question, it seems that there are no constitutional limits (typically found in the Bill of Rights, the Fourteenth Amendment, or the Tenth Amendment) on Congress's power here. It might be argued that FISA infringes the due process or privacy rights of those for whom the special court authorizes eavesdropping warrants, but these interests are possibly outweighed (even under strict scrutiny analysis) by national security interests. In conclusion, Congress had constitutional authority to pass the law, but there are constitutional limits on that authority.

The next issue is the one directly asked: whether the president has the constitutional power to authorize the FBI and NSA to eavesdrop on a suspect without a warrant. This set of facts raises constitutional issues involving the inherent presidential power. As a preliminary matter, executive power arises in three situations; (1) when the power is authorized or given by Congress to the president, (2) when the power is expressly stated as a power of the president in the Constitution, and (3) when a power is implied or inherent to the president. Here, there is neither express authorization by Congress (as discussed above, in FISA Congress authorized eavesdropping only with a warrant) nor express power in the Constitution for the president to authorize warrantless eavesdropping, so if he is to have any power in this situation, it must be pursuant to his inherent power.

In *Youngstown Sheet & Tube v. Sawyer* (1952), the Supreme Court struck down the president's executive order to seize steel mills and keep them operating (in the face of a strike) during the Korean War, reasoning that the president's action was essentially "legislative" in nature. Only *Congress* may legislate; the executive branch may execute—but not make—laws. It may be argued that the president's action here creates a similar scenario: by authorizing warrantless eavesdropping, the president is essentially legislating—and that he may not do.

On the other hand, the president may point out that the greatest impact of the *Youngstown* case has been Justice Jackson's concurring opinion, which spoke of the importance of *Congress* in determining inherent executive power, and identified three categories for classifying inherent presidential power. First, presidential power is at its maximum when the president acts pursuant to an express or implied authorization of Congress. In such situations there is a presumption in favor of authorizing presidential power, which consists of all of the power he has of his own plus all that Congress can delegate. Second, when Congress has neither granted nor denied the president's authority in a particular area, his power is limited to his own independent powers, but there is a kind-of "twilight" zone where he and Congress may have concurrent authority or where the distribution is uncertain. Last, Justice Jackson stated that presidential power is at its lowest ebb when the president takes measures incompatible with the express or implied will of Congress, in which case the president may act only pursuant to his own constitutionally granted power, minus any power of Congress over the matter.

Applying this three-step approach, it seems that here the presidential authority is at its lowest. Congress passed FISA under its constitutional authority and provided the mechanism—obtaining a warrant from a special court—for eavesdropping on suspects. If the president is allowed to arbitrarily ignore laws with impunity, he violates the principle of separation of powers that is crucial for democracy and freedom. Here the president acted in direct contravention of Congress's will, so his power is at its lowest ebb, and he can rely only on his own constitutionally granted power (minus any power of Congress). (On the other hand, it might be argued that Congress has acquiesced in recent years to expansive presidential authority, thus placing the analysis in *Youngstown* category two or even one.)

Accordingly, the next step in the analysis is to determine whether the president has such constitutional authority in the present case. Here the president may argue that his inherent power may be extrapolated through the "Vested" Clause, the "Take Care" Clause, and the "Commander-in-Chief" clause. The "Vested" Clause states that the executive power shall be vested in a president of the United States. Thus, the president has the inherent power to do whatever an "executive" in a system of separated powers would ordinarily do—including, he would argue, protect the nation's security, especially during times of emergency such as in fighting the "war on terror." Indeed, the Supreme Court has stated in *Curtiss Wright* that when it comes to foreign affairs, the president's authority is especially broad, so the president could argue that even while he is ordering the eavesdropping within the United States, because the subject involves foreign affairs, his power is broad. The "Take Care" Clause states that the president shall take care that the laws be faithfully executed. Applying the Take Care Clause, the president may argue that because terrorist activities violate the law, his actions designed to apprehend terrorists are essentially furthering the execution of the law. Finally he may argue that his "Commander-in-Chief" power authorizes the actions, because one of the main targets of terrorists may be military forces, and he is acting to protect them. Moreover, when terrorist attacks occur, the burden falls on the military to respond, and the costs to such response can be very high. Therefore, he would argue, eavesdropping in the United States may be a reasonable and justified decision.

Johns would respond that none of these powers give the president the power to arbitrarily ignore a law with which he disagrees—to allow him to do so would be a serious breach of separation-of-powers principles. As for the president's argument that he has much greater power in foreign relations, Johns could point out that this argument has never been wholeheartedly endorsed by a majority of the

Court since the *Curtiss-Wright* case (1930s) in which it was originally enunciated. Moreover, Johns could argue that the Commander-in-Chief power to which the president refers is limited to his actual authority to command the military, and does not extend to authorizing warrantless searches of civilians. Finally, more recent habeas corpus cases suggest that the president may not resort to extralegal tactics on American soil even when those tactics are in response to the war on terror. See, for example, *Hamdi v. Rumsfeld* (2004), *Hamdan v. Rumsfeld* (2006), and *Boumediene v. Bush* (2008).

In conclusion, on balance it would seem that the stronger arguments favor Johns, and it is more likely than not that the president's authorization of warrantless searches is unconstitutional.

SELF-ASSESSMENT

This hypothetical focuses again on the executive power, which is full of ambiguity (as we previously discussed in Chapter 3)—especially the president's "inherent" authority. In any discussion on executive power, you should enumerate the three sources: (1) express power found in the Constitution, (2) power authorized by Congress, and (3) inherent power. You should state that to the extent it exists, the president's inherent power is in a sense extrapolated from his or her express powers found in, for example, the "Vesting," "Take Care," and "Commander-in-Chief" Clauses. Regarding the scope of that inherent power, we start again with the very important *Youngstown* case, which established the three-part hierarchy tying the president's inherent authority to the degree to which Congress has previously approved of such executive action (either expressly or impliedly).

Finally, a couple of tactical points: First, although it is always good to argue both sides when answering most essay questions, it is especially important to do so when the call of the question gives explicit directions to that end, as in this hypothetical that instructs you to "provide a concise analysis of whether the president's actions are constitutional, *discussing arguments both pro and con.*" Second, although as a general proposition you should not discuss issues beyond the scope of the call of the question, when a particular separate issue is somehow related to the question asked, it cannot hurt to briefly identify and discuss the issue. Here, for example, although the call of the question asks for "a concise analysis of whether the president's actions are constitutional," the sample essay briefly discusses Congress's authority for passing the underlying FISA law that has been ignored by the president. Specifically, the answer lists the two-step inquiry for determining whether an act of Congress is constitutional (i.e., (1) does Congress have the power?, and (2) is there a constitutional limit on this power?), and then does a brief analysis. Because what *Congress* thinks about the president's role in a particular circumstance is such a major factor in the Supreme Court's analysis of the scope of inherent executive authority (*Youngstown*), this particular analysis of Congress's power to enact FISA in the first instance is possibly relevant. Thus, a brief discussion is warranted here.

THE DUE PROCESS CLAUSES AND NON-TEXTUAL RIGHTS

7

A. INTRODUCTION

There are two Due Process Clauses found in the amendments to the U.S. Constitution. The Fifth Amendment protects the individual from the federal government: "No person ... shall be deprived of liberty or property without due process of law." The Fourteenth Amendment provides the same protections from actions by state governments that were taken without due process of law. Because the amendments speak in terms of "process" or procedure, many of the cases that are brought under the clauses insist that the government follow proper or adequate procedure, when an official act is seen as a deprivation.

A plaintiff may challenge an action by the government for lacking procedural due process, but only if the plaintiff first establishes a deprivation of life, liberty, or property. The procedures required, before deprivations of life and some forms of liberty, are the subject of criminal procedure. Constitutional law courses usually include acts that deprive individuals of other forms of liberty, such as the infliction of a stigma that affects an individual's reputation or ability to obtain a job or further education, as well as interests in property.

It is not always easy to recognize an interest in property that matters under the Due Process Clauses. There are the traditional forms of property, such as an automobile, that merit protection by requiring proper procedure before forfeiture. Entitlements, such as welfare and disability benefits, are also considered property for purposes of the Due Process Clauses. One may even have a property interest in one's employment. For example, a non-probationary employee protected under a Civil Service–like program may be discharged only for cause, and the determination of cause requires adequate procedure. These less-traditional property rights arise out of state or federal law, or sources such as employment contracts and manuals, but they are then protected under the Constitution.

Procedural due process challenges assert either that the way a statute is enacted was procedurally inadequate or that the language of the statute or regulation was so vague that one cannot understand the statute's requirements. More commonly, challenges are based on the application of the statute.

When a statute or policy applies only in certain situations, some procedures are required in making the factual determinations necessary for the statute or policy to apply. Procedural due process challenges are the way of contesting the adequacy of those procedures. The interests protected are not solely the product of constitutional law. The Constitution recognizes certain classes of interest that may be protected, but whether that sort of interest exists in a particular case is determined through ordinary law or employee or policy manuals. There must also be intentional or reckless deprivation of property rights. Once those factors are established, the determination of the procedures that are due is a matter of constitutional law, using a test set out in one of the cases you will be asked to read.

In addition to the procedural requirements of the Due Process Clauses, the clauses have been held to provide some protection for substantive rights. Some of those cases are quite controversial.

Among the less-controversial cases are those that identify the individual rights that the Due Process clauses will protect by "incorporating" other parts of the Constitution. For example, the First Amendment provides that Congress shall not infringe on the freedom of expression or establish a religion. It says nothing about the states. It is only through the Fourteenth Amendment Due Process Clause that these limits are imposed on state governments, and it is important to remember that in pleading any violation of a provision of the Bill of Rights by a state, the Fourteenth Amendment Due Process Clause must also be pled.

Most of the incorporations—and not all aspects of the Bill of Rights have been incorporated against the states—are relatively well accepted. For example, the principle that a state should not be able to prohibit political speech with which it simply disagrees seems widely accepted.

Incorporation also works in the opposite direction. The Equal Protection Clause of the Fourteenth Amendment speaks only to state governments in requiring the equal protection of the law for all persons in the jurisdiction. It is this clause that prohibits segregated schools and other forms of discrimination. If that were all there were to it, the federal government would have been able to operate segregated schools in the District of Columbia and to discriminate on the basis of race, gender, or any other characteristic. However, the Fifth Amendment Due Process Clause has been seen as providing against the federal government those rights that the Equal Protection Clause provides against the states. As with incorporation in the opposite direction, any application of equal protection analysis to the federal government must be pled using the Fifth Amendment Due Process Clause, but these cases will arise in a later chapter.

The most controversial applications of the Due Process Clauses are the use of the substantive aspect of the clauses to provide individual protection in areas not specifically set out in other provisions of the Constitution: providing protection for non-textual rights. These applications, however, have a long history ranging from *Calder v. Bull*, 3 U.S. 386 (1798), to the present. They would also seem to be supported by the Ninth Amendment, which says that the existence of the rights contained in the remainder of the Bill of Rights should not be taken "to deny or disparage others retained by the people." This seems to speak to the existence of non-textual rights, and if they are not to be disparaged (i.e., treated unequally), they would seem unenforceable.

There are, of course, those who argue that this sort of judicial role is illegitimate. Courts should not overrule acts of the legislature or executive, unless they violate explicit provisions of the Constitution. That is the issue behind the debate over what is sometimes characterized as an "activist judiciary." But, this can also be seen as a debate over what makes up our constitution. By the lower case "constitution," we mean that which constitutes us as a society. Every government must have such a constitution to have an understanding of where power lies and, perhaps, of limits on governmental power. This is the sense in which the British have a constitution, though a nonwritten one. The United States also has a textual Constitution. The debate over non-textual rights can be seen as a debate over the relationship between that Constitution and the constitution. Those who decry the recognition of non-textual rights would argue that the two are the same. Those who support the recognition believe that the constitution goes beyond the text of the Constitution.

In reading the cases regarding the recognition of non-enumerated fundamental rights, look for the sort of analysis employed by the Court. It is that analysis you will be expected to apply in any case or exam question regarding the recognition of a previously unidentified right. As you will see, the starting place is an examination of precedent to see if the earlier cases encompass the newly claimed right. If precedent does not establish the right, the analysis turns to the nation's history and tradition. In that examination, there is, as you will see, an issue as to how narrowly focused the history or tradition must be.

If there is still no basis for the right, a test based on whether a right is "inherent in the concept of ordered liberty" or is recognized by all governments deserving to be called free may be applied. (It may be that this test works more in conjunction with history and tradition but it was originally presented as independent.) This is not a test favored by judicial conservatives, so the makeup of the Court at any particular time will affect its viability.

If this last test is accepted, it can also serve to explain references to law in other countries. There are cases in which some members of the Court have looked to European law regarding same-sex sexual relations and the juvenile death penalty, although the later example actually speaks to the Eight Amendment ban on cruel and unusual punishment. Although criticized as irrelevant by other members of the Court, these references could be taken as evidence of what rights are protected by governments that are deservedly called free or in countries that have ordered liberty. They may give context to an otherwise fuzzy test, and their rejection is by those who would also find fault with the test itself. Reference to other countries might, alternatively, be seen as an example of looking to emerging consensus, but that would be the adoption of a new test. Speaking to "ordered liberty" would keep the examination within an older tradition, even if one no longer widely adhered to.

The choice might have been made to separate procedural due process and substantive due process into two different chapters. They are, after all, conceptually quite different. They have been treated together in one chapter here because it is important for you to be able to identify the form of due process involved in a question. Had the two been in different chapters, it would have been easy to determine which was at issue. This section requires you to make that determination on your own.

B. READINGS

Before attempting the problems in this section, you should have read the following material. Actually, you have probably already read most, if not all, of the cases. If you have a casebook, the edited copies of the cases contained therein will be adequate. If you do not have a casebook, or if your casebook does not contain one or more of the cases, jump cites are provided to guide you to the relevant material in the full case reports. Although the following list may seem long, the cases can be used for a number of problems. The cases are, to a degree, grouped by more specific subject matter.

1. Procedural Due Process

Board of Regents v. Roth, 408 U.S 564, 566–80 (1972).
Paul v. Davis, 424 U.S. 693, 694–712 (1976).

Castle Rock v. Gonzales, 545 U.S 748, 750–69 (2005).
DeShaney v. Winnebago Co. Department of Social Services, 489 U.S. 189, 191–203 (1989).
Matthews v. Eldridge, 424 U.S. 319, 323–26, 332–49 (1976).
Goss v. Lopez, 419 U.S. 565, 567–84 (1975).
Ingraham v. Wright, 430 U.S. 651, 653–83 (1977).
Board of Curators v. Horowitz, 435 U.S. 78, 79–91 (1978).
Caperton v. A.T. Massey Coal Co., 129 S.Ct. 2252, 2256–67 (2009)

2. Substantive Due Process

Pierce v. Society of Sisters, 268 U. S. 510, 529–35 (1925).
Meyer v. Nebraska, 262 U. S. 390, 396–403 (1923).
Griswold v. Connecticut, 381 U. S. 479, 480–502 (1965).
Roe v. Wade, 410 U. S. 113, 116–22, 129–67 (1973).
Planned Parenthood v. Casey, 505 U. S. 833, 843–53, 869–901, 911–22, 944 (1992).
Gonzales v. Carhart, 550 U. S. 124, 132–68, 169–91 (2007).
Lawrence v. Texas, 539 U. S. 558, 562–79, 586–605 (2003).
Michael H. v. Gerald D., 491 U. S. 110, 113–63 (1989).
Cruzan v. Director, Missouri Department of Health, 497 U. S. 261, 265–87 (1990).
Washington v. Glucksberg, 521 U. S. 702, 705–51 (1997)
Kelley v. Johnson, 425 U. S. 238, 239–40, 244–49 (1976).

C. PROBLEMS

Problem 1

HYPOTHETICAL
(45 MINUTES)

You are counsel for a small state college and have been asked by the dean of students to provide advice on a situation facing her. She has ordered the expulsion of a student because the student allegedly assaulted another student in one of the college dormitories, causing a significant injury. The assault was reported to the resident assistant, who passed the report along to the dean, with his note that he considered the alleged victim reliable. The dean is inclined to accept the report, expel the student, and place a note in the student's record regarding the incident. Additionally, the alleged victim has indicated that he will pursue legal action against the college for the failure to protect him, and that the injury was a deprivation of his liberty.

The student manual provides that, once accepted and enrolled in the college, students have a right to continued enrollment, except that under certain limited circumstances, a student may be dismissed for cause. Among those circumstances are a grade point average falling below certain required levels and actions considered dangerous to other persons. With regard to purportedly dangerous actions, the manual calls for a report to the dean of students, with the dean then deciding the appropriateness of the penalty.

The student accused of assault demands a chance to explain his actions and contest the resident assistant's report before the dean. He has, in fact, asked for a trial-like procedure, under which he would be allowed to confront witnesses testifying against him and call his own witnesses. He argues that this is required by the significance of his penalty, that including the incident in his record will impact his chances of admission to law school and later admission to the bar, and that his reputation among those he knows on campus will be injured.

The dean wants to know what she should do regarding the demands. She also wants to know your thoughts on the potential liability of the college to the victim of the alleged assault.

SAMPLE ESSAY

With regard to the student subject to expulsion, because we are a state college, our actions may be governed by the Due Process Clause of the Fourteenth Amendment. For the Due Process Clause to apply, the student must be intentionally or recklessly deprived of life, liberty, or property. Life is not at issue here, but both liberty and property may be. Turning first to property, what is included as property is not defined constitutionally. It is defined through state law, policy manuals, employee manuals, and most likely student manuals. The issue is whether there is a legitimate expectation of an entitlement to be found there.

In *Goss v. Lopez*, the Supreme Court has recognized a property right to secondary education that can be limited only through due process. The distinction between mandatory education for younger students and the elective nature of college might be argued to distinguish the case, but here the student manual works in favor of the student. The right to continued enrollment seems parallel to employee manual references to non-probationary or permanent employees, whose continued employment is recognized as a property interest. Thus, this interest in continued enrollment may be, in itself, sufficient to implicate the Due Process Clause.

Even if that is not sufficient, there are liberty interests at stake. Inclusion of the expulsion in the student's record would serve to limit his future opportunities to continue his education elsewhere and to be admitted to law school and to the bar. This sort of limitation on future opportunity has been seen as sufficient to invoke the protections of due process. Furthermore, there is an injury to his reputation among those on campus. An injury to reputation alone is not sufficient to require due process, but in conjunction with other deprivations, it has some impact. It can presumably play a role in determining the level of process required.

Because there are sufficient interests to require due process, it must be determined what process is due. The student manual seems to define that process by requiring a report to the dean, who then makes a determination. The problem with that conclusion is that, once a basis for requiring due process is found, the nature of that process is determined not by what is provided in the source of the original protected interest, but rather under a test set out in the case *Matthews v. Eldridge*. That test looks first to the importance of what is at risk to the plaintiff's interests. Here, continuing his education at the college would seem to have significant importance. His liberty interest in his future education and profession are also of importance. Furthermore, although an interest in reputation may not be sufficient, in itself, to invoke due process, once the clause is invoked, the injury to reputation might play a role in assessing importance.

The test then looks at the risk of erroneous deprivation, at the lessening of that risk under alternative procedures, and last at the cost to the state of the alternative procedures. There is certainly a risk of erroneous deprivation in the dean simply acting on the report of the resident assistant, and that risk would seem to be lessened by any additional procedures. *Goss v. Lopez* involved a secondary school suspension and held that the student must be given a chance to receive notice of the grounds for the suspension and be given a chance to respond. Because this penalty is more serious, it would seem that, even given the different settings, this would be the minimum required.

The third factor is the burden on the government. Time and money are the usual burdens. Here, the impact in those terms seems minimal and unlikely to offset the increase in reliability. The closer a proceeding comes to a full trial, the greater the costs to the state and the less likelihood that a court would require the procedure.

The Court has indicated that the Due Process Clause may require less procedure for the academic dismissal of a student, but this is a disciplinary matter. Thus, it may be best to provide even more procedure than what might turn out to be the minimum required, thus avoiding eventual liability. An opportunity to explain his actions in person and even an opportunity to present witnesses seem to be costs worth bearing. Even confrontation might be afforded. By providing as much procedure as can reasonably be afforded, the college may limit its constitutional liability. But, if there is a disinclination to provide a hearing, there should at least be an opportunity to respond. The costs are minimal, and it would bring the college into line with the procedures imposed on school systems.

With regard to the student who was allegedly injured, there would seem not to be a valid due process claim. The Supreme Court, in *DeShaney v. Winnebag Co. Deptartment of Social Services* refused to recognize such a claim when a social welfare department failed to provide adequate protection for a child for which it had some responsibility. It is not the college that allegedly deprived the victim of his liberty, and the Court has seemed unwilling to include a positive right to protection. There may be situations, involving a more custodial relationship, in which such a positive right exists, but the college seems not to be in such a relationship with the student. Without an intention or reckless deprivation by the college itself, there would not seem to be liability under the Due Process Clause.

SELF-ASSESSMENT

The first thing to do, assuming you have identified the question as one raising a due process issue, is to determine what sort of due process is involved. A substantive claim would argue that the statute or provision is unconstitutional, because it violates individual rights to do or refrain from doing something. That is, the statute cannot address the issue or situation under consideration. That is not the argument here. The claim is not that anyone must be allowed to enter the university or that no one may be expelled. Rather, the claim is that, accepting the fact a student may, for a variety of reasons, be expelled, there has been an inadequacy in the procedures for determining whether one of those reasons is present. That is the crux of procedural due process.

It is important, before addressing the issue of what procedure should be required, to determine whether there is a liberty or property interest to be protected. Although reversing the order of the two considerations could still include all the issues to be addressed, considering the existence of the protected interest first demonstrates an understanding of how the clause works.

In discussing whether an interest is protected, remember that it is not a matter of importance but of entitlement. Identify the source of the interest to be protected. Here, it was in the student manual. Also, discuss any cases that provide a basis for claiming entitlement for the interest. It could also be important, once you have found a single interest sufficient to invoke the Due Process Clause, not to end the consideration of interests. Because part of the test that determines what procedure is required turns on the importance of the interests involved, the cumulative importance of interests might play a role.

Once the interest is identified, the Supreme Court's test does not, in itself, provide a great deal of guidance in terms of the procedure that is due. The test does tell us what factors are to be examined. First, you should consider how the different aspects of the test apply to the facts. Having done so, there is no formula for adding up scores to determine outcome. Here, the best approach is to think about any cases you may know that have any similarity to the facts and look at the procedure that was required in those cases. As is generally the case, however, be careful not to overgeneralize the application of a case. For example, in *Horowitz*, the Court said that less procedure may be required in dismissal from a university, but the issue there was seen as involving an academic dismissal. It should not be generalized to encompass all dismissals.

The analysis in the sample essay on the failure of the procedure in the student manual to set the requirements for due process is adequate. However, your professor may have taken the time to present the history of what is sometimes known as the "bitter with the sweet" approach. That approach, to which the Court adhered for a period of time, said that the property interest in a job (the sweet), is accompanied by limitations in the document or law setting out that property interest (the bitter). Although the approach was later rejected, if your professor covered the area, there may be points to be gained from a brief discussion of the now-rejected approach. But, be sure to acknowledge that rejection.

With regard to the claim by the alleged victim of the assault, the physical injury that has an impact on his liberty was not brought about by the government. The deprivation was allegedly by the student who might be expelled. Although the discussion was short, the issue was presented to see if you understand the case or cases limiting the government's liability.

VARIATIONS ON THE THEME

1. Suppose that the student manual, instead of providing a right to continued enrollment, states that a student may be dis-enrolled, with repayment of tuition for the uncompleted term, or denied enrollment at the sole discretion of the college.
2. Suppose, instead, that the dean does not expel the student but simply places a record of the incident in the student's file.
3. Suppose the only action is the publication of a notice to the student body that the incident occurred, naming the student as the actor.

Problem 2
(30 minutes)

HYPOTHETICAL

You are a legislative aide to a state senator. The senator chairs a committee considering a bill to regulate abortion. A number of senators have suggested provisions, and the senator has asked you to report on the constitutionality of each of the suggestions. The suggested regulations include the following.

1. Any woman seeking an abortion must give her informed consent. Consent will be considered informed only if the woman is told the stage of development of the fetus, of the availability of adoption services, and of the availability of assistance in obtaining child support from the father.
2. Any woman seeking an abortion must be given, at a preliminary visit with the provider, a publication to be developed by the state health department explaining fetal development. She must then wait one week and pass a state-developed test on her understanding of the material.
3. All facilities providing abortion services must report monthly to the state health department the number of procedures performed, indicating the number for each type of procedure. Any complications must also be reported, with those reports to include the age of the patient, the gestational age of the fetus, and the procedure employed.
4. Facilities performing abortions must provide to the state health service department a report on each abortion performed. The reports are to include the age of the patient, her county and city or township of residence, number of children, and prior abortions. Also required in the report are the procedure employed and any complications.

How do you respond to the senator's request?

SAMPLE ESSAY

The current test for regulations regarding abortion is the "undue burden" test. A regulation is an undue burden when it has the purpose or effect of standing in the way of women seeking abortions. Lesser regulations, those that simply provide an orderly process, are not undue burdens. When a regulation is not an undue burden, it is not a deprivation of liberty that requires the state to meet strict scrutiny. Of course, even if a regulation is an undue burden, in the sense that it severely limits or prohibits abortion, it may still be valid, as long as it can meet strict scrutiny. Thus, a ban on abortions after viability, except where necessary to protect the life or health of the mother, is valid as necessary to protect the state's compelling interest in the life of the viable fetus. (An alternative analysis would suggest that the undue burden test applies only to previability abortions, with post-viability abortions subject to bans as well as lesser restrictions.)

If we turn to the suggested provisions and apply the undue burden test, provision one would not seem to present a constitutional problem. Informed consent is required for any medical procedure, and this provision simply adds detail as to the information that must be provided for consent to be informed. It seems similar to a provision approved in *Casey*. It is common to discuss other possible treatments, and although this provision includes information on alternatives that might not be considered treatments (adoption or child support), they seem not that different in kind from regularly provided information. The information provided might be seen as an effort to dissuade, but that would depend on its content. If it is simply informative, it would seem acceptable. Indeed, the Court has recognized that the state can express its preference for childbirth over abortion, as long as it does not impose an undue burden. If the material constitutes a tract of moral condemnation regarding women who abort, that might possibly be seen as an undue burden.

Provision two would seem to go too far. Requiring a week to study the material would seem to indicate that the content is far in excess of what would be required to make an informed decision. The ability to pass the state's test, depending on the content of the instrument, might bar some individuals from receiving abortions, even though they are competent to make their own decisions. The week-long period in itself may present a problem. A woman who has to travel any great distance to obtain an abortion will be put to an expense far beyond that brought about by a short, say twenty-four hour, period to examine the material provided. She will either have to make the trip twice or incur a week's hotel costs. The provision may represent an undue burden in that it would stand in the way of a substantial number of women seeking to obtain an abortion.

Further, a week delay at a crucial time might require a change in the procedure employed to one that is more dangerous to maternal health. The delay could, under those circumstances, be an undue burden. The week delay might also push the procedure past the point of viability, at which time the abortion could be barred. Although *Casey* approved a twenty-four–hour waiting period, this may simply be too long a delay.

Provision three would not seem to present a problem. The requirements address only reporting statistics regarding the practice of the clinic or office, and such a requirement was approved in *Casey*. There seems to be no burden on the individual seeking an abortion. In the extreme, if reporting became such an onus that providers went out of business or had to increase their charges so much that abortion became unaffordable, that could be a problem, but there is no indication of that here. It does not seem likely that this provision will stand in the way of women seeking an abortion; it is not an undue burden.

Provision four may be an undue burden. The reporting of procedures and complications, like the reporting in provision three, in not problematic. However, reporting the combination of county and city or township of residence, age and number of children and/or prior abortions might be sufficient, in a small county and city or township, to allow the identification of the patient. Anyone who did not want to be identified might well be deterred, and that could well be a substantial percentage. The requirement seems to present an undue burden.

SELF-ASSESSMENT

First, this is a substantive due process question. That is obvious from the fact that it is an abortion question, and abortion cases are substantive due process cases. Nonetheless, it is instructive to see why this is substantive due process and not procedural due process. The potential challenge is to the statute itself. The issue is not whether there has been an adequate determination of facts on which application of the statute depends. The question is thus substantive rather than procedural.

A fairly common mistake on questions regarding substantive due process is to turn them into questions on procedural due process. It is not common to ignore the substantive issue completely; instead, after the discussion of substantive due process, the student launches into an analysis of procedural due process with an application of the test from *Matthews v. Eldridge*. This is, at a minimum, a waste of time.

The question itself calls for a relatively straightforward application of the "undue burden" test. As long as the test is applied well to the facts, the conclusions are usually less important than the analysis. An exception would be where one of the provisions has been clearly held by the Supreme Court either to be or not to be an undue burden. Be sure to state the test and, where there is guidance to be drawn from a case, show your knowledge by referencing that case.

Here, there was guidance to be drawn from *Casey*. Compare the provisions in the hypothetical with those considered in *Casey*. Argue that the case makes the application of the undue burden test clear, or explain the difference between the provision in the hypothetical and the provision considered in the case.

VARIATIONS ON THE THEME

1. Suppose provision two contained the one-week wait but did not require passing a test but only being given a chance to ask any questions the patient has regarding what she was given. What about forty-eight hours, instead of a week?
2. Suppose that, in provision two, the materials could be provided by mail a week before the procedure is scheduled.
3. Suppose provision four did not include in the report the township or city, but only the county of residence of the patient.

Problem 3
(45 minutes)

You are a staff attorney for an organization involved in family planning and birth control. The organization also provides referrals for abortion services and provides legal assistance for individuals seeking an abortion. A seventeen-year-old female has come to your office for such assistance. The state law provides that, for a minor to obtain an abortion, she must have the permission of one parent. There is also a provision that, if the minor cannot or does not wish to seek the permission of a parent, she may go before the local county attorney for the county in which she lives, not the county in which the abortion would be performed, if different. She is to be given the opportunity to show that either she is mature enough to make the decision for herself or that an abortion would be in her best interests.

You filed the papers for her asking for a bypass determination by the relevant county attorney. You included in the request the fact that your client has graduated from high school and has a scholarship to attend the local university. You also included a statement from the client that, if she had to care for a child, she is unlikely to be able to go to college. The county attorney, without ever meeting with you or your client, denied the request to authorize the abortion.

After a discussion with your client, you agree that the only option is to go to federal court, claiming a violation of your client's constitutional rights. What arguments do you offer in federal court?

SAMPLE ESSAY

When a minor wishes to obtain an abortion, a state may require the permission of one of her parents, but the law must allow a judicial bypass for a minor unable to obtain or unwilling to seek such permission. Here, state law provides for a bypass, but it is not a judicial bypass. Instead, she must seek a determination by an administrative official. The central question to put before the court here is whether such review provides the protection for her rights required by the Constitution.

The Supreme Court, in requiring judicial bypass, has recognized the right of minors of sufficient maturity to make their own decisions regarding abortion. Even when a minor is not sufficiently mature, she has a right to a judicial decision regarding her best interests. The minor's rights are not left solely to the discretion of her parent or parents.

The requirement of judicial bypass would seem to assure the minor of a neutral, and presumably confidential, decision maker. The local county attorney would seem an inadequate replacement. Here the county attorney is a member of the executive, rather than the judicial, branch of government. The executive branch is seen as more inherently political, and a decision rendered by the county attorney may be seen as more likely affected by political influences than that of a judge. Even if state judges are elected, there is an assumption that they are guided by law rather than by politics.

With judges there is also a stronger perception of confidentiality. If a person believes the county attorney is less likely to maintain confidentiality, she will be less willing to pursue this form of bypass. This would seem especially true where the requirement is that the permission be by the county attorney for the county in which the minor resides. This requirement assures that someone in her locale knows that she has obtained, or at least sought, an abortion. This requirement could stand in the way of a substantial number of minors seeking abortions. Although the "undue burden" test has been applied in the context of adults, rather than minors, this requirement would seem an undue burden on the minor's more limited rights. The court should declare the bypass procedure unconstitutional and require that your client be given an opportunity to go before a judge for the determination required by the Constitution.

If the court refuses to invalidate the bypass procedure provided, on the grounds that bypass must be judicial, there is also a procedural issue to be addressed. The right of a minor to obtain an abortion on a showing of adequate maturity to make the decision herself or that the abortion is in her best interest is not simply an expectation: it is a constitutionally protected interest to which she has a right. This would be properly classified as a protected liberty interest. If she is to be deprived of that right, it can only be through proper procedure. The procedure that is due is not necessarily that set out in the statute; it is determined under the test from *Matthews v. Eldridge*.

The first question, under that test, is the importance of the plaintiff's interest. In this case, her interest is constitutionally protected. She has a right to obtain the abortion upon an adequate showing. There can hardly be a more important interest than one that is constitutionally protected. The test also examines the risk of erroneous deprivation under the procedure provided and how much the risk is reduced by the procedure requested. Here, the request is for a meeting in person between the plaintiff and the decision maker. Without such a meeting—and none was in fact afforded—there is no adequate opportunity to assess the minor's maturity. An opportunity to talk with the minor would have to reduce the likelihood of error here. The last factor is the cost to the state of the additional procedure requested. Although the interview would take some period of time, it is far short of the costs of a trial and seems worth the increased protection it would afford.

An additional issue here is that the hearing, or even the initial petition, should be before or addressed to an impartial decision maker. The summary nature of the first rejection, given the evidence of maturity demonstrated by age and educational achievement, and the evidence of best interest, would seem to demand a better examination. Even if the court should decide that judicial bypass is not necessary and that bypass through a county attorney is adequate, the court should order that the decision maker be one whose predetermination is not so easily demonstrated.

SELF-ASSESSMENT

The major point to be made here is that there are cases in which it is reasonable to raise both substantive and procedural due process claims. This is in contrast to the previous problem in which a discussion of procedural due process would have been irrelevant. In both problems there is a substantive issue as to whether the statute involved violated constitutional rights. The difference between the two problems is that in this problem there was also a factual issue to be determined: the maturity of the plaintiff or her best interests. The former problem involved no such determinations. The factual issues raised in the case of the minor seeking an abortion will necessarily be resolved under some sort of procedure. This raises the issues of whether the procedure provided is adequate, whether there is a constitutional mandate for adequate procedure, and what that adequate procedure might be. Thus the discussion of procedural due process is relevant.

With regard to substance, it is important not to be thrown offtrack simply by the word "bypass." The case law, including *Planned Parenthood v. Casey*, requires not just that there be a bypass but that it be a judicial bypass. Because this bypass was not judicial, that might be sufficient to invalidate the statute. On the other hand, the Court has not really spoken on the issue of some other form of bypass, except perhaps by negative inference from its requirement of the judicial bypass. Rather than simply draw that negative inference, it would seem wiser to engage in at least a short discussion of the role of the bypass and why a bypass to the county attorney is inadequate to protect the minor's interests.

The facts specifically said that the determination be made by the county attorney in the minor's county of residence. Think about the relevance of the facts presented. Here, the facts lead to a consideration of confidentiality.

Additionally, the fact given that the original request was denied without much consideration should have raised procedural concerns. That leads into a discussion of procedural due process and signals the need to discuss the nature of the interest involved as sufficient to require adequate procedure. It will then lead to an application of the test from *Matthews v. Eldridge*.

VARIATIONS ON THE THEME

1. Suppose that the statute provided for a judicial bypass but also required an assessment of maturity by a psychologist and that the assessment be given strong consideration by the judge.
2. Suppose instead that the statute, as in the hypothetical, provided for a decision by the county attorney but with the submission of a psychologist's report. What bearing would the existence of the report have on the procedural issues, if there still was no interview of the minor by the county attorney?

3. Suppose the statute included an irrebuttable presumption of a lack of maturity for a minor under the age of sixteen with only the best interest determination being considered by a judge.
4. What if the statute required the permission of both parents, with the option of a judicial bypass, but the minor client has the permission of only one parent? Is the permission of that one parent sufficient; that is, is the requirement of the permission of both parents unconstitutional?

Problem 4
(25 minutes)

You have recently been employed as a staff member for the state senate judiciary committee and have been given your first assignment. The committee chair has been engaged in a long-term project examining the state's criminal code to determine whether any of the particular provisions present constitutional problems. Her attention has turned to the provisions addressing consensual, noncommercial sexual conduct. Prior to the Supreme Court's decision in *Lawrence v. Texas*, the code had contained a prohibition against sodomy. After the Court's decision, the legislature removed that provision, but the chair is concerned about what remains. Specifically, she has read Justice Scalia's dissent in *Lawrence* in which he suggests that the majority opinion leads to the invalidation of a variety of laws regarding sexual activities.

Your assignment is to examine the remaining provisions in this section addressing consensual, noncommercial sexual conduct to determine whether any of them would also be held unconstitutional under the reasoning in *Lawrence*, so that the committee can consider removing or changing the provisions. The sections to be addressed are as follows:

Consensual, Noncommercial Sexual Activity

1. Fornication, sexual intercourse between a male and female not married to each other, is punishable as a misdemeanor.
2. Bestiality, any sexual interaction between a human being and a nonhuman animal, is punishable as a felony.

Existing case law and definitions provided elsewhere in the statute make all the terms involved in the provisions sufficiently definite that you have been directed not to consider any issue regarding vagueness.

What advice do you provide the committee chair?

SAMPLE ESSAY

I have been asked to analyze the constitutionality of two provisions of the criminal code section on consensual, noncommercial sexual activity in light of the Supreme Court's decision in *Lawrence v. Texas*. Before beginning an analysis of each of the provisions, it should be stressed that it is not clear exactly what the Court did in that case. The immediate result is clear: the Court declared unconstitutional a Texas statute criminalizing intimate sexual conduct between persons of the same sex. What is not clear is the theoretical basis for that decision.

As Justice Scalia's dissent points out, the majority never says that there is a fundamental right for members of the same sex to engage in sodomy. Nor, says Justice Scalia, does the majority apply the scrutiny test that would be appropriate, had it concluded that a fundamental right had been infringed by the Texas statute.

Justice Scalia is correct in noting that such language and the reference to strict scrutiny are missing, but there is language in the majority opinion that might be taken to indicate that a fundamental right is involved. The majority says that intimate sexual relationships among people can be an element of an enduring personal bond and that the liberty protected by the Constitution allows individuals the right to make this choice. The majority also says elsewhere that the liberty protected by the Due Process Clause provides a right to engage in this activity. Although never using the language "fundamental right," the analysis might be read as the recognition of such a right.

It is also true that the majority opinion does not read in terms of strict scrutiny. Instead, it concludes that the Texas law does not further any legitimate state interest. This sounds like the language of rational basis, and Justice Scalia argues that if no rational basis can be found for this statute, the decision puts an end to all morality-based legislation.

As we turn to the provisions at issue, it would seem likely that the fornication provision would have to be found unconstitutional. Just as intimate sexual relationships between members of the same sex can be part of the enduring personal bond that the majority found to be a liberty protected by the Constitution, intimate sexual relationships between members of the opposite sex would seem to enjoy the same protection. If the Texas statute furthered no legitimate state interest, neither would this provision.

The bestiality statute should probably, despite Justice Scalia's concern, be held constitutional. Even if he is correct in concluding that morality-based statutes are now called into question, this provision differs from the Texas statute. Although the Texas statute, and the fornication provision examined here, are examples of victimless crimes, the animal involved in an act of bestiality may be seen as a victim. Thus, the statute can be argued to be more than purely moral based. Furthermore, the majority spoke specifically of sexual relations between people. That would distinguish the case involving sexual activity between a person and animal.

SELF-ASSESSMENT

Although this is clearly a substantive due process issue, it is a difficult question. It required a careful analysis of the Supreme Court opinion that may be less than fully clear. There are several errors that could lead you away from the careful analysis required. The first would be simply to conclude that *Lawrence* did not concern fornication or bestiality, so there is no guidance to be drawn from the case. Instead, the reasoning present in the case may provide the guidance sought and should be explained and applied. When there is no case law exactly on point, pick the closest cases and analogize from them.

A second sort of error would be to note that the Supreme Court has never found a fundamental right to engage in either fornication or bestiality, so there is no fundamental right. If the Supreme Court has never said that there is no such right, the question would seem to be asking for an analysis of whether the Court would find such a right to exist. Never assume that an essay question can be answered simply by saying that the Court has not recognized a right.

A third caution relevant here is that you should be careful not to accept at face value an explanation given in a dissent, or sometimes even in a concurrence, as to what the majority held or said. Analyze the majority's position yourself.

The dissent may be trying to undermine the majority decision, and even a concurrence in the result may involve an attempt to undermine the majority's reasoning.

The time provided may also be an indication of what is expected of you. Although twenty-five minutes is relatively short, it is far more than what would be required to say that, because *Lawrence* protects sodomy, fornication should also be protected and that animals are not consenting adults. When you have more time available, think about what else is expected of you and what you can do to demonstrate your knowledge of the subject. Here a discussion of what *Lawrence* determined shows your understanding of the case.

VARIATIONS ON THE THEME

1. Consider a statute that prohibits incest between persons who are second cousins or more closely related than second cousins, as applied to adults who are second cousins.
2. Consider a statute that prohibits sexual relations involving those under the age of sixteen as applied to the case of two fifteen-year-olds found to have engaged in sexual intercourse.

Problem 5

HYPOTHETICAL

(45 MINUTES)

You are interning for a state trial court judge, who has jurisdiction over issues regarding children and families. The state department dealing with families and child services has filed a request with the judge for an order directed to a parent. The parent has a wasting condition that will eventually cause his death. There are three children, and the other parent has already passed away. The condition of the living parent has worsened to the point where the department has had to take temporary custody of the children. The department is concerned that, if the condition goes untreated, the children will lose their one remaining parent and will become wards of the state. The department expresses concern over the psychological health of the children as well as the fiscal impact on the state.

There is, fortunately, a treatment for the condition. It requires a single injection in any fleshy part of the body. That single injection will permanently reverse the course of the disease. The agent injected has been used over a long period of time with no record of any side effects or complications. The parent, however, has refused the injection. The drug involved is manufactured by injecting an animal with the disease-causing pathogen and extracting antibodies from the animal's blood. The parent has nonreligious, philosophical objections to the injection of any animal products. He has said that he will acquiesce and receive the injection, if so ordered by a court, but will not do so without such an order.

State law provides the judge with the authority to order that the parent receive the injection. The parent, however, claims that such an order would be in violation of his rights under the U.S. Constitution, although again he is not claiming a violation of the Constitution's religion clauses. The judge has sought your advice on the issue. How do you respond?

SAMPLE ESSAY

The parent in this case is asserting the existence of a non-textual constitutional right to refuse to submit to medical treatment. The analysis involved in determining the existence of a non-textual right looks first to precedent. Here, two cases seem relevant. First, in the *Glucksberg* case, the Supreme Court considered a claim that there is a constitutional right to assisted suicide. The Court rejected the claim, even when put forth by a physician for a terminally ill patient. The case, however, is not dispositive, because it involved taking action causing death, rather than refusing treatment without which death will result.

Second, and closer in its facts is *Cruzan*, a case involving a person who was in a persistent vegetative state as the result of an automobile accident. Her parents claimed that she would not want to live under such circumstances and asked that hydration and nutrition be withdrawn. The Supreme Court resolved the case under the assumption that there was a right to refuse medical care, including hydration and nutrition, but held that the state could require clear and convincing evidence of the patient's wishes. Although the case may be seen to support the parent's position, here the Court only assumed the existence of the right to refuse medical care, without so holding.

If *Cruzan* is not taken as establishing a right and thus precedent is not clear, the next step is to look to history and tradition. If asked the general question of whether there is a history and tradition of allowing patients to refuse medical care, the answer would seem to be in the affirmative. However, the Court has said, in a parental rights case involving a biological father of a child born to a woman married to another man that it will look to specific, rather than general, tradition. Under that approach, it is not clear how to define that specificity and what the result will be. If the tradition involved painful or dangerous treatment, or treatment that would merely prolong the course of the disease, rather than reversing its course, those cases might not speak to whether there is a history and tradition involving facts such as those in this case. Similarly, if the tradition did not involve minor children who would be orphaned and become wards of the state, they may not count as being tradition under these facts.

There are also cases in which the Court seems not to have drawn this general/specific distinction and has looked at the more general history or tradition. The Court in the assisted suicide case looked at suicide generally, rather than at suicide by terminally ill patients. And in the same-sex sodomy case, the Court did look to the protection of sexual intimacy more generally in finding same sex acts protected as well. If the court were to look to a general tradition, the right to refuse would seem to stand.

If neither precedent nor history and tradition provide guidance, there can be an inquiry into whether a right to refuse medical care in these circumstances is inherent in the concept of ordered liberty, assuming this court will consider that test. That may not provide much guidance. It would not seem that a statute requiring parents to provide care for their children would be inconsistent with ordered liberty, and this is at least somewhat similar. Although this clearly would limit the parent's individual freedom to make his or her own decision, it seems a stretch to say that a country in which such an order could issue would lack ordered liberty.

In summation, the Supreme Court case law does not flatly state that there is a right to refuse medical care, but the Court may be seen to have leaned in that direction. This case may, at this point, require more research into the cases and statutes allowing such a right, to determine how closely on point they are.

If the analysis leads to the conclusion that there is a fundamental right to refuse medical care, there would still be the issue of whether the state can meet strict scrutiny. Is there a compelling governmental interest as to which the court order for the injection would be necessary? The Supreme Court, in its case, did find sufficient interests to at least impose procedural requirements on the exercise of the right. Here, the state has at least a strong, if not compelling, interest in the psychological and fiscal well-being of the children. If that interest is compelling, the injection would seem necessary to the interest.

If there is no fundamental right, then only rational basis will apply. The plaintiff must demonstrate that there is no permissible governmental interest to which a court order and the statute under which it is issued would be rationally related. The concerns over the surviving children and the fiscal concerns are permissible interests, and the treatment order is rationally related.

SELF-ASSESSMENT

Although the issue here is an order directed to an individual, there do not appear to be any facts at issue. There are, then, no procedural issues tied to the resolution of facts. The question is not one of procedural due process. Rather, the claim is that the parent has an individual right to refuse the injection: the question involves substantive due process.

The easiest place to go astray here is by reading *Cruzan* too strongly. It might be tempting to read the cases as having established a constitutional right to refuse medical care. However, the Court did not really so decide. It did not have to, because even if such a fundamental right existed, the Court could still rule in favor of the state regarding the procedure it had demanded. Thus, it only assumed that such a right existed. This hypothetical requires an actual resolution of the issue.

The examination follows the route set out by the Court. After discussing precedent, it proceeds to history and tradition and shows an understanding of the general/specific issue. Even though the "inherent in the concept of ordered liberty" test may not be in vogue, it is worth stating and briefly discussing.

Another bit of advice, one that is given in a variety of contexts, is "don't fight the hypothetical." There may well be no such wasting disease so easily and permanently treatable with a single injection. Discussing that issue, however, does not demonstrate any legal knowledge and would be a waste of time.

Once the existence or not of a fundamental right has been examined, do not forget the possibility of the state statute passing strict scrutiny. State and then apply the test. Also, consider the alternative. Even if you believe that there is a fundamental right, consider the test to be applied if there is no fundamental right, and discuss its application.

VARIATIONS ON THE THEME

1. Suppose it is a child who has the easily treatable wasting disease. The parent expresses the same philosophical, nonreligious views and refuses to allow the injection for the child. The department seeks a court order mandating the injection. What advice do you give?
2. Suppose that the treatment is extremely painful but not dangerous and has only a 50 percent chance of success.
3. What if the procedure has a 30 percent chance of causing the death of the patient?

Problem 6

HYPOTHETICAL

(45 MINUTES)

Flora Flowerchild, a twenty-three-year old woman, has come to you seeking legal advice and representation. She has, over the past several years, gotten a number of small tattoos, all of them of flowers. She decided to add to her collection with a small tulip on her left shoulder. When she went to the tattoo parlor that had done her previous work, she discovered they were in the process of closing down. The tattoo artist informed her that the state had recently passed a law banning the practice of tattooing.

You have researched the law and have discovered that there is, in fact, a newly passed statute that completely bars the practice of tattooing. When you read the legislative history, you found that the bill sponsors were motivated by a concern over blood-borne diseases that might be spread through tattooing. The bill's sponsor admitted that tattoo parlors seemed to be adhering to health regulations in using only sterilized needles. But, ink is expensive, and a number of parlors had been using the same ink from customer to customer.

You also asked Flora if there was any meaning behind the tattoo she wished to obtain. She was quite adamant that there was not, asking pointedly "Why does everything have to have a meaning?" She said she just liked the way the tattoos looked. You have explained that there might be a free expression right, even if there is no message, but she refuses to accept that; for her, a tattoo is not any form of expression.

She wants a court to order that she be allowed to obtain her tattoo and to hold that the enforcement of the statute is invalid under the U.S. Constitution. What advice do you give?

SAMPLE ESSAY

Although she cannot be anywhere near certain of victory, you can advise her that her case is not hopeless. She seems to be looking for a court to recognize a fundamental right with regard to this sort of decision concerning her own appearance. There is no constitutional text directly establishing such a right, but the Court has recognized non-textual fundamental rights. Although the Supreme Court has not recognized the existence of this particular right, it has also not clearly denied the possibility of such a right. The Court, in its more recent cases, has also provided a framework for analysis when examining the possibility of recognizing a non-textual fundamental right.

The first step in the analysis is to examine precedent to see if such a right can be found there. When we look at those precedents, we find the cases establishing non-textual fundamental rights have tended to be in the area of family relations and procreation. The cases, however, arguably go beyond that, because *Griswold v. Connecticut* seems to establish a right to have non-procreative sex. *Lawrence v. Texas*, although perhaps lacking clarity in its analysis, also recognized some sort of right to engage in same-sex sexual activities. These cases, then, go beyond family and procreation, but they may say little about a right to personal appearance.

The Supreme Court, in *Kelley v. Johnson*, refused to strike down a regulation regarding hair length and facial hair. That case, however, involved a police department and applied only to police officers. The Court said that, in that context, there was no right to make one's own decisions regarding personal appearance. It did not, however, decide whether the ordinary citizen has a right to make such decisions free of government interference; rather it specifically set aside that question.

If precedent cannot be said to establish a particular right, the second step is to look at history and tradition. In doing so, one must be careful to recognize the difference between general and specific traditions. The more general tradition would be a recognition that individuals have a broad right to make decisions regarding their personal appearance. The more specific tradition would be one that has recognized a right to obtain tattoos. As is often the case, the more general tradition is more likely to be found. Although fashion may make it seem that at times everyone dresses alike, we have not had a history of sanctions for those who are out of fashion. People have generally been able to choose their mode of dress. There may have been requirements, in certain specific situations, with regard to things such as hair length or dress in schools or in the police department, but the average citizen with a different sense of fashion has been free to go his or her own way.

It is likely more difficult to establish a history or tradition with regard to the freedom to obtain a tattoo. Certainly, until the recent past, tattoos do not seem to have been a mainstream acquisition but have been common in some subpopulations. A simple lack of concern over those who put themselves out of the mainstream may not speak to a recognition of any right to obtain a tattoo. There is, nonetheless, some chance that a court would recognize that history and tradition protects this claim to a right.

If unsuccessful in this argument, it is possible that an appeal to the old "inherent in the concept of ordered liberty" language of Justice Harlan may provide some help. Some members of the Court have been willing to look to law in other countries in recognizing fundamental rights. If countries in which there is "ordered liberty" recognize a right to personal appearance, that might be seen as at least correlated to, if not inherent in, the concept of ordered liberty. Regimentation of appearance seems more the product of a totalitarian state than one in which the citizens enjoy liberty. This would seem to speak in Flora's favor, although it is not clear that a ban on tattoos would qualify as a regimentation of appearance.

If, after applying these tests, the court determines that there is no right to obtain a tattoo, then the rational basis test will apply. Flora will have to show that the tattoo ban is not rationally related to any permissible governmental interest. That, as usual, seems to be a test unlikely to be passed. The state's concern about health is clearly a permissible governmental interest. Because tattooing can spread blood-borne disease, the ban would further that interest and is hence rationally related to it.

If the court determines that there is a fundamental right for Flora to obtain the tattoo, strict scrutiny will apply. The state will have to show that it has a compelling governmental interest to which the ban is necessary. An interest in public health is likely to be seen as compelling, but the necessity of the ban is more questionable. If blood-borne diseases could be spread through tattooing only if needles are not sterile or the same ink is used from one customer to another, more stringently enforced regulations in those areas would be adequate to prevent disease. The complete ban would not be necessary, and Flora should be allowed to obtain the tattoo.

In sum, Flora should be advised that there is no clear right to obtain a tattoo but that there is at least some, even if slight, possibility that a court will recognize a non-textual right and that she will be able to get her tattoo.

SELF-ASSESSMENT

The most important fact in the hypothetical is Flora's reaction to the question regarding whether the tattoo had any meaning. Had the tattoo been intended to communicate a message of some sort, the analysis would have gone off in a different direction, involving issues of free expression. But, Flora was clear that there was no message. Asking Flora to testify otherwise, in order to have a different route for the challenge, would raise ethical concerns.

Once you recognize this as a non-textual fundamental rights issue, the most likely source of error would be in assuming too much from one of the cases you've read. *Kelley v. Johnson* did consider the issue of a fundamental right to determine one's own appearance and, in its specific context, rejected that right. But, the case involved a police officer. The Court, in refusing to recognize a right for police officers, did say that it could assume that the citizenry at large had a right to make decisions regarding personal appearance, while still ruling against the police officer.

If you had concluded that *Kelley v. Johnson* completely resolved this issue then you would not have had that much to write about. In a single paragraph, you could have said that no such right exists, so rational basis then applies, and that test is easily met. The very limited length of such an answer should have been a hint that the question was, perhaps, more complicated than you had first thought. Taking *Kelley*'s assumption as establishing that civilians do have such a right would have led to a similarly short, and incomplete, answer in the other direction.

You should then have applied the test for recognizing fundamental rights. Having done so, your coming quickly to a solution would have been another error. Unless an answer is completely clear, it is better to go forward considering both alternative answers. If you had concluded that there was no possibility of a fundamental right, you would not have considered applying strict scrutiny. Similarly, if you had concluded that there clearly was a fundamental right, you would not have applied rational basis. In either case, you could have missed available points. When applying the tests, state the elements of the test, and then discuss its application.

A common mistake on this sort of question is to waste time discussing procedural due process. Procedure becomes necessary when there is some fact at issue. Here the outcome does not depend on the resolution of some issue about Flora. She may have the right to have her case heard, but there is no real issue presented regarding procedure, and application of a test for adequate procedure under the Due Process Clause would have been a waste of time.

There is a little bit of history that would speak against the right that Flora seeks to establish. There were, at one time, sumptuary laws that limited dress. They were aimed at extravagance generally but included limits on luxury dress. The laws had only the slightest impact on even early colonial America, so the answer given should remain the same. The sumptuary laws were not even mentioned in the sample essay because of the slim likelihood that someone answering the question would have any familiarity with them. If, however, you did recognize the existence of these laws, there could be a rather brief mention in the discussion of history and tradition.

VARIATIONS ON THE THEME

1. Suppose that instead of citing health concerns, the state's concern was over people who obtain tattoos only later to regret the decision. Although tattoos may be removable, it is an expensive and painful process. The state has, for

that reason, passed a law requiring a twenty-four–hour waiting period before obtaining a tattoo. A person seeking a tattoo must register with the tattoo artist in advance and then return at least twenty-four–hours later to obtain the actual tattoo. The statute is challenged by a tattoo artist and a customer. Assuming that a fundamental right to obtain a tattoo has been established, what is the result?

2. Suppose instead that the state focuses its preventive efforts on minors. Its law requires that a minor who wishes to obtain a tattoo must obtain the written permission of one parent. The law is challenged by a minor and a tattoo artist. Again assuming a fundamental right, what result?
3. Assuming a right for adults, what about a complete ban on tattoos for minors, if challenged by a minor and his or her parent, who wants the child tattooed?

D. OPTIONAL READINGS

Procedural Due Process

The following sources present the topics covered in this chapter in more depth than the chapter introduction. The sources are in increasing levels of detail. The first provides an overview with some detail, and the second and third greater coverage of the material.

ERWIN CHEMERINSKY, CONSTITUTIONAL LAW: PRINCIPLES AND POLICIES (4th ed. 2011), chapter 7.
JOHN E. NOWAK & RONALD D. ROTUNDA, PRINCIPLES OF CONSTITUTIONAL LAW (4th ed. 2010), chapter 13.
JOHN E. NOWAK & RONALD D. ROTUNDA, CONSTITUTIONAL LAW (7th ed. 2000), chapter 13.

Non-Textual Rights

The following sources present the topics covered in this chapter in more depth than the chapter introduction. The sources are in increasing levels of detail. The first provides an overview, the second provides more detail, and the third and fourth provide the greatest coverage of the material. .

MICHAEL C. DORF & TREVOR W. MORRISON, CONSTITUTIONAL LAW (2010), chapter 8.
ERWIN CHEMERINSKY, CONSTITUTIONAL LAW: PRINCIPLES AND POLICIES (4th ed. 2011), chapter 10.
JOHN E. NOWAK & RONALD D. ROTUNDA, PRINCIPLES OF CONSTITUTIONAL LAW (4th ed. 2010), chapter 11, §§ 1–4.
JOHN E. NOWAK & RONALD D. ROTUNDA, CONSTITUTIONAL LAW (7th ed. 2000), chapter 11, §§ 1–4.

8 EQUAL PROTECTION

A. INTRODUCTION

The Equal Protection Clause is found in the Fourteenth Amendment to the U.S. Constitution. It provides that "no state ... shall deny to any person within its jurisdiction the equal protection of the law." As it speaks of states, it does not apply directly to the federal government. However, it has been held that the guarantee provided by the Equal Protection Clause is among the rights protected by the Due Process Clause of the Fifth Amendment, which applies to the federal government. Thus, Equal Protection analysis may apply when the federal government acts, but the basis must be stated as the Due Process Clause of the Fifth Amendment.

A potential violation of the Equal Protection Clause occurs when people, or even corporate persons, are separated into two or more classes, and the classes are treated differently. There must be intent for there to be a violation of Equal Protection. If a law simply has a greater impact on, for example, a particular ethnic group, that is not necessarily a violation of equal protection. It takes more than this disparate impact: there must be the intent to discriminate.

Furthermore, not all intentional unequal treatments are treated alike. If there is no reason to suspect legislative bias in establishing a classification, as for example with a law that distinguishes between opticians and optometrists, the statute may only need to satisfy the rational basis test. It must be rationally related to a permissible governmental purpose. This is an extremely easy test to meet, particularly because the burden is on the party challenging the statute or policy to show that there is no such permissible governmental purpose to which the statute or policy is rationally related.

If there is good reason to believe that the government is biased, the classification is considered suspect and the law or policy is tested under strict scrutiny. The burden is on the government to show that it has a compelling governmental interest to which the classification is necessary. There is also an intermediate level of scrutiny, when a classification is seen as quasi-suspect. That intermediate scrutiny demands that the government demonstrate an important governmental interest to which the classification is substantially related, a standard not terribly well-defined but lying somewhere between "rationally related to" and "necessary to."

There are said to be two prongs to the Equal Protection Clause, the suspect class prong and the fundamental rights prong. What this really means is that there are two ways through which the level of scrutiny may be raised from rational basis to one of the levels of heightened scrutiny. As with most constitutional issues, the level of scrutiny and the resultant test often determine the outcome. That, however, is not always the case. There are cases in which the Supreme Court said that it would apply the rational basis test but still found a violation of equal protection. And, there are cases where the Court applied strict scrutiny but upheld the governmental action.

Suspect class analysis is employed when people (or even corporations) are put into two or more classes, and the classes are treated differently. Many statutes and policies involve this separation of individuals into classes with differing treatment. Convicted felons, even after their release from prison, may be prohibited from carrying firearms. Children under a certain age are required, when riding in an automobile, to be in a safety seat. And, during World War II, Americans of Japanese descent were required to leave certain areas of the West Coast of the United States. The issue, when examining these sorts of classes or classifications, is to determine whether they are suspect, quasi-suspect, or not suspect at all. How much reason is there to suspect the legislature, or whatever part of the government is involved? Note that motive and intent are not the same. To even raise an equal protection issue, there must be intent: a purpose to bring about the result. Motive has to do with the origins of that intent.

In determining how suspect the class or classification is, several factors are examined. One factor is whether the group discriminated against is a "discrete and insular minority." The "discrete" aspect of that factor asks whether group membership is defined on a yes-or-no basis or describes a place on a spectrum or continuum. For example, membership in a minority group might be seen as a yes-or-no issue. This is in contrast with a categorization based, for example, on being good looking, which is not a yes-or-no characteristic. The first is discrete; the second is not.

It is also true that the characteristics that are generally taken as being discrete are not, in fact, actually discrete. Many people are of mixed race, so it would seem that racial classification is not truly discrete. That is, membership in a racial or ethnic class may not be a yes-or-no situation but a case of yes and no. But, in large part people feel that we are able to identify most individuals as members of a particular racial group, and the classes are considered discrete. Similarly, for some individuals, at least the physical characteristics generally associated with gender may be ambiguous, and sexual orientation may not have a singular direction. So for these classifications as well, the answer may not truly be yes or no.

"Insular," derived from Latin for island, means living separately, as, for example, within an ethnically identifiable neighborhood. "Minority" presents no definitional problems, although there may be an issue as to how small the population must be to be a minority for this purpose.

A second factor is whether there is a history of discrimination against the group. It is not completely clear how recent the history must be, but for groups receiving heightened scrutiny it would seem likely that discrimination should have, even if in a somewhat lessened way, continued to the present. The third factor is whether the group lacks political power. Although the clearest case is a denial of the vote, underrepresentation in the legislative body would also likely indicate a lack of political power. Last, the test asks whether the classification is based on an immutable (i.e., unchangeable) characteristic not related to ability or merit.

Once these questions are answered, it is not clear how the individual answers ought to be summed up in coming to a conclusion regarding how suspect the class is. For purposes of exam questions, once the factors are examined, it is best not to be certain how suspect the class is or what level of scrutiny applies. Instead, conclude when the Court has not ruled on a particular classification that the class might be suspect, if that is a possible result, and apply strict scrutiny. Then, go on to consider the possibility that a court would conclude that the class is quasi-suspect and apply the intermediate scrutiny test. Finally, turn to the possibility that a court would consider the class not to be suspect at all and apply the rational basis test.

Interestingly, once the Court has come to the conclusion that a class is suspect or quasi-suspect, the law quickly moves from suspect class to suspect classification. If the test is applied to many racial or ethnic minorities, it becomes apparent that those minorities are suspect classes. Any law or policy that intentionally discriminated against members of those classes would be subject to strict scrutiny. It turns out, however, that it is not just discrimination against a minority that is subject to strict scrutiny. Discrimination against a non-minority population, despite the lack of a history of discrimination against that population and the presence of political power, is also tested using strict scrutiny. It is now the very classification, without regard to who is harmed, that is suspect.

Some of the cases listed below will indicate the conclusions of the Supreme Court as to the suspect character of certain classifications. Where the Court has clearly held that a class is suspect, quasi-suspect, or not suspect, you should generally not reargue the conclusion, as it would be a waste of time. But, be careful: the Court may not have spoken as clearly as you think, and may not have actually answered the question. For example, if a statute cannot even pass the rational basis test, there is no need to determine whether there should be heightened scrutiny. That does not mean that, in another context, a court would not consider and find reason for increased scrutiny.

In summation, for a problem to raise an Equal Protection issue, there must be two or more groups with intentional unequal treatment between or among the groups. If that is the case, consider the possibility of suspect class analysis. Is the classification based on some difference in characteristics between the individuals in the differing groups? If so, and if the Court has already ruled on whether the class is suspect, quasi-suspect, or not at all suspect, apply the test that matches the Court's ruling. If the Court has not ruled on the suspectness of the class, proceed through the analysis for determining whether the class is suspect, quasi-suspect, or not suspect, and then apply the appropriate test. Where there is any question at all as to how suspect the class is, state all three outcomes, and apply all the relevant tests.

The second part of equal protection, the fundamental rights prong is, for most students, a bit more challenging. The analysis of the fundamental rights prong presented here should help, but it is not drawn directly from any opinions of the Court. It would thus be a mistake to categorize the analysis as presenting rules. The analysis is provided solely to help you understand how these cases may be seen as presenting equal protection challenges.

The situation is complicated, in part, because there are two ways a statute or policy can implicate the fundamental rights prong. One way is where a statute or policy treats persons differently, but not because of the characteristics (e.g., race or gender) of the people involved. Rather the classification is based on the individuals having exercised a fundamental right. So, as you will see in the cases, refusing welfare or even non-vital medical care to people who have moved into the state in the recent past violates equal protection. This is not because the people refused the benefit share a characteristic that would implicate suspect class analysis. Nor is it because welfare and non-vital medical care are fundamental rights; though they may be important, a state would not violate the Constitution, if it failed to provide such benefits. The equal protection problem is instead the result of the basis for drawing the line between who does, and who does not, receive the benefits. If the line is drawn on the basis of the exercise of a fundamental right, here the right to move from one state to another, then the state will have to demonstrate that its classification meets strict scrutiny.

A difficulty with this approach is drawing a line between the deprivation of the fundamental right and using its exercise to draw a line, with a benefit being denied to those having exercised the right. If the penalty for having exercised the right is too heavy, that would seem to involve a deprivation. For example, a statute that those moving into a state must pay the state government an entry fee would be seen as a violation of the right to move from state to state. The denial of welfare for a year is not a deprivation of the right to move, but it is, once again, a line drawn based on the exercise of the right. Where to draw the line between the two may, however, not be clear. Where it is not clear whether a classification with unequal treatment or a deprivation is involved, a question may call for both equal protection analysis and an analysis based on the deprivation of a textual or non-textual right.

The other aspect of the fundamental rights prong involves benefits that are not really fundamental rights but are, in a sense, close to being fundamental. A number of cases involve issues surrounding criminal appeals. There is a constitutional right to a trial in a criminal case, but there is no similar right to an appeal. Nonetheless, every state provides for a right to appeal under its own constitution or statutes. This right is not simply important to the individual convicted at trial—it is important to the system. The right to a trial should mean the right to a trial relatively free from error; in that sense the appeal is tied to the constitutional right to trial. Although appeals are not constitutionally mandated, they are sufficiently tied to a fundamental right that, if they are granted as of right to some, they must also be provided to others. Treating people differently, for example by not providing a trial transcript or an attorney, must be justified under strict scrutiny.

So, if the classification is based on the exercise of a fundamental right, apply strict scrutiny. If it is not based on having exercised a fundamental right but involves differing treatment with regard to a right that is closely tied to a fundamental right, again apply strict scrutiny. Remember that it is also possible for a classification to raise an equal protection problem in more than one way. For example, a fact scenario might include differing treatment based on a characteristic of the individuals involved, where that differing treatment is with regard to a right closely tied to a fundamental right. In that sort of scenario, go through both varieties of analysis.

Finally, note that the Equal Protection Clause speaks only to the states, although it also applies to lower levels of state government, such as cities and counties, and entities such as state universities. It does not apply directly to the federal government. If a question or case involved discrimination at the federal level, the Due Process Clause of the Fifth Amendment, which has been held to incorporate the rights contained in the Equal Protection Clause and to make it applicable to the federal government, must also be pled. Once pled, the analysis is the same.

B. READINGS

Before attempting the problems in this section, you should have read the following material. You may have already read most, if not all, of the cases. If you have a casebook, the edited copies of the cases contained therein will be adequate. If you do not have a casebook, or if your casebook does not contain one or more of the cases, jump cites are provided to guide you to the relevant material in the full case reports. Although the following list may seem long, the cases are used for a number of problems.

Railway Express Agency v. New York, 336 U.S. 106, 107–10 (1949).
Korematsu v. United States, 323 U.S. 214, 215–20 (1944).
Brown v. Board of Education (Brown I), 347 U.S. 483, 486–96 (1954).
Brown v. Board of Education (Brown II), 349 U.S. 294, 298–301 (1955).
Loving v. Virginia, 388 U.S. 1, 2–12 (1967).
Washington v. Davis, 426 U.S. 229, 232–52 (1976).
Grutter v. Bollinger, 539 U.S. 306, 311–95 (2003).
Gratz v. Bollinger, 539 U.S. 244, 249–61, 267–83, 291, 293–305 (2003).
Adarand Constructors, Inc. v. Pena, 515 U.S. 200, 204–10, 212–76 (1995).
Craig v. Boren, 429 U.S. 190, 191–92, 197–204 (1976).
United States v. Virginia, 518 U.S. 515, 519–603 (1996).
Clark v. Jeter. 486 U.S. 456, 457–65 (1988).
Cleburne v. Cleburne Living Center, 473 U.S. 432, 435–50 (1985).
Romer v. Evans, 517 U.S. 620, 623–53 (1996).
Ambach v. Norwick, 441 U.S. 68, 69–82 (1979).
Kramer v. Union Free School District, 395 U.S. 621, 622–33 (1969).
Reynolds v. Sims, 377 U.S. 533, 536–87 (1964).
Saenz v. Roe, 526 U.S. 489, 492–511 (1999).
Memorial Hospital v. Maricopa County, 415 U.S. 250, 251–70 (1974).

C. PROBLEMS

Problem 1

HYPOTHETICAL
(30 MINUTES)

Note: As this volume was going into production, the Supreme Court was in the process of reconsidering the issue of affirmative action. As a result, the following problem may or may not have any continued relevance. You will, undoubtedly, have seen the Court's opinion from the 2012 term. If it upholds affirmative action, do the problem. If it bans affirmative action, simply skip the problem. If it changes the dimensions of affirmative action, the problem may still be interesting, but the model answer may no longer be a good answer.

You work in the office of university counsel for Pacifica State University. The university has long employed an affirmative action program that serves to ensure the admission of a critical mass of students from populations underrepresented in the student body. The program, which takes into account race or ethnicity, among a number of other diversity factors, has had the desired effect. Although the target populations are still underrepresented, the percentages and numbers of students from those populations have increased significantly.

Recently, members of a particular minority population have come to dominate the population of students admitted using neutral criteria such as high school grade point averages and admission test scores. The number of members of the underrepresented minority groups has remained constant, but the increase in members of this now–no longer underrepresented minority, in conjunction with the affirmative action program, has led to what the administration sees as an underrepresentation of students of European descent. Although the population of the state, as a whole, is 67 percent of European extraction, the last four classes admitted to the university have had an average of 43 percent students of European origin.

The admissions office has come to you for advice. They want to know if they can adopt a policy of allowing diversity points for European ethnicities. If they cannot do that, they want to know if there are other things they can do to increase the admissions of students of European ethnicities. What advice do you give?

SAMPLE ESSAY

Because Pacifica State University is a state university, and thus a state actor, it is subject to the Equal Protection Clause of the Fourteenth Amendment. A state may not deny any person the equal protection of the law, and this would apply to unequal treatment under state university policies. There must be an actual intent to provide this unequal treatment, but that would be present, given the desire of the administration to add diversity points.

The Supreme Court applies strict scrutiny whenever a classification is drawn on the basis of race or ethnicity. The proposed program would involve such a classification and is intended to have a differential impact on that basis, so the program must meet strict scrutiny. Although that test is usually fatal, the Court has approved certain affirmative action plans in the higher education setting. Assuring diversity in universities is a compelling governmental interest, and a consideration of race and ethnicity seems necessary to that goal. The critical mass approach has been approved (*Grutter v. Bollinger*) as necessary to assure a range of views in minority populations and to engender an atmosphere in which such comments are welcome and willingly offered.

Here, the percentage of students of European descent has dropped significantly below the percentage in the general population. In that sense, European Americans have become underrepresented. But, simply trying to assure that the student body and the population have the same ethnic mix would not be constitutional. That would seem to be an approach based on quotas, and there must be a better justification for such practices.

Again, diversity of viewpoints is the compelling governmental interest in the university setting. That diversity not only requires the presence of minority voices, but the Court has held that a university may attempt to enroll enough members of minority groups to assure that the contributions of the groups are active and perhaps themselves diverse.

Applying this critical mass approach to a population of European descent requires a consideration of the demographics of the university. A historically African-American college or university might well rely on the need for a critical mass of students of European descent to assure diversity in the academic exchange there. Here, however, the percentage of students of European descent is far above the percentages that justified affirmative action programs aimed at helping admit underrepresented minority groups. Although now, in a sense, students of European descent are a minority in the student body, the fact they still comprise 43 percent of the student body would mean that there is already a critical mass. There seems little likelihood that the European-American view on the issues under discussion would go unrepresented when such students still make up such a large part of the student body.

There are other things that might be done, but that should be on a race- or ethnicity-neutral basis. Certainly, the university can, for example, offer entrance test preparation classes, open to all, that might serve to improve test scores generally and perhaps specifically in populations not already obtaining admission. The university can also engage in recruitment activities designed to increase the applicant pool. That might serve to bring more applications generally, but might also specifically increase the pool of more talented European ethnicity students, who may now be applying elsewhere. That might increase the number of such students admitted based on race- and ethnicity-neutral factors. The university can also, given the original affirmative action plan was voluntarily adopted, drop affirmative action altogether. That, however, would not seem to fit with the university's goals.

SELF-ASSESSMENT

The fact that the proposed policy concerns classes of people and treating those classes differently should lead you to treat the question as raising an equal protection issue. (Of course, the chapter title also should lead you to equal protection analysis, but on an exam you are not likely to be given such a strong clue.) The classification is based on the characteristic of ethnicity or race, so the equal protection analysis would involve suspect class analysis.

One place where a great deal of time (and ink) is wasted in answering a question such as this is in considering the suspect class status of the European-American population. The Supreme Court has already concluded that all classifications based on race or ethnicity are suspect. Strict scrutiny applies, whether a minority or a majority population is the beneficiary of, or is negatively affected by, a classification. Any effort other than stating that fact and turning directly toward applying the test is wasted. If, on the other hand, a question directly asked whether the strict scrutiny should apply, when the majority population is the subject of what might be seen as discrimination, that might be taken as a call to apply the factors for determining the level of scrutiny. You would then state what the Court has said about racial classifications before going on to apply the factors.

What the question really calls for is the application of the strict scrutiny test. Does the justification the Court accepted as justifying affirmative action programs aimed at underrepresented minorities apply here? It is, then, important to understand the Court's rationale in its university affirmative action cases. Although Justice Ginsburg, concurring in *Grutter v. Bollinger,* explained her position in terms of economic and educational disadvantage, factors that might well not apply in the hypothetical, the majority position was based on the value of diversity. That should be the focus of the essay. You need to explain why the interest in diversity led to the Court's decisions and discuss whether that interest is present here.

VARIATIONS ON THE THEME

1. Suppose that the population of students of European descent has dropped to 10 percent. Would there be any difference in result?
2. Suppose the issue was not one of ethnicity but of gender. Because of better grades and test scores, the university population has become 60 percent female. Can there be an affirmative action program that favors male applicants by awarding diversity points to be taken into account along with other diversity factors?
3. Suppose the female population has increased to 93 percent of the student body. What result then?

Problem 2

HYPOTHETICAL

(45 MINUTES)

The State of Ozarka has regularly allowed single parents to petition a court to approve the adoption of their children by their significant others. The courts have made their decisions under a "best interests of the child" standard but have generally deferred to the wishes of the child's parent. In cases where the single parent has been living with the significant other for more than one year, adoption has almost always been granted. Over the past few years, the state's family court judges have applied the same standards and reached the same result when the significant other is of the same sex as the parent.

The state legislature of Ozarka passed a statute banning any adoption that would result in same-sex parenting. The legislative history stated concerns over the psychological health of such adopted children, and that the homes provided by same-sex couples would be less stable than those of opposite-sex couples. There was also concern expressed over the development of sexual identity among children raised by same-sex couples. Finally, there was concern that children raised in gay or lesbian households would face taunting by other children.

Ann Archer and Betty Bartle are a lesbian couple who have lived together for three years. They decided they wanted to have a child and that Ann should be the biological mother. Ann has now given birth to a child conceived through artificial insemination, and is recognized under state law to be both the biological and legal mother of the child. Ann and Betty want the child also to be adopted by Betty, so that both Ann and Betty would have parental status. They come to you for legal advice. What advice would you give as a theory to challenge the constitutionality of the state law and as to their likelihood of success?

SAMPLE ESSAY

There is a reasonable chance of success here. The case will be based on a claim that there is a violation of the protection afforded by the Equal Protection Clause. The provision complained of is contained in a state statute, and is therefore state action, and it is intended to discriminate. The major, and first, issue will be the test under which to examine the statute. That is, what level of scrutiny applies? The Supreme Court has considered equal protection and same-sex orientation in the context of a Colorado constitutional initiative. The Court, however, did not need to resolve the question of the level of scrutiny because it found the state unable to meet even the lowest level of scrutiny.

One factor in determining whether a suspect or quasi-suspect class is involved and the level of scrutiny to be applied is whether the classification involves a discrete and insular minority. Here, those with same-sex orientation are a minority. "Discrete" has to do with whether or not a characteristic is of a yes-or-no variety. That would not seem true of same-sex versus opposite-sex orientation, because there are also people who are bisexual. But, perhaps "discrete" does apply here, because a person who is bisexual has a same-sex attraction as well as an opposite-sex attraction. The only way in which there is insularity is in the fact that there are cities and neighborhoods that draw a population of those with same-sex orientation. But, there is also likely to be a number of residents of opposite-sex orientation, so there is not the isolation found in at least some ethnic neighborhoods.

A second factor is a history of discrimination. There can hardly be any question that there has been such a history, and it is a history that continues to the present. A third factor is a lack or political power. Although there are members of state legislatures and Congress who are openly gay or lesbian, the existence of laws limiting marriage to heterosexual couples, despite efforts to change those laws, indicates some lack of political power, as well as a continuing practice of discrimination.

The last factor is that the classification be based on an immutable characteristic unrelated to ability. There is some debate here. There are those who believe that a course of "therapy" can lead one to change from a same-sex to an opposite-sex orientation. Others, seemingly including most scientists, believe that sexual orientation is more deeply ingrained and not subject to change.

Adding up the factors, there is a case to be made for the classification being suspect. If a court so concludes, then strict scrutiny will apply: the state will have to demonstrate a compelling governmental interest to which the classification is necessary. Although the psychological well-being of children is likely to be seen as a compelling interest, it may be difficult to show that being raised by a heterosexual couple is necessary to that interest. There seems to be no reason to conclude that a same-sex couple cannot raise a psychologically healthy child. An opposite conclusion would seem to require a court to hold both that heterosexual identity is necessary to psychological well-being and that, if so, being raised by a same-sex couple would necessarily lead to a same-sex orientation. Avoidance of taunting would also fail to justify the statute, because this would reduce equal protection to protecting what is popular.

If a court does not find the classification suspect, there is still the possibility that it could be held quasi-suspect. There would be a nice fit here, in that classifications based on gender are quasi-suspect, and there is at least a tie to gender here. If the classification is quasi-suspect, intermediate scrutiny will apply. The state must put forward an important interest to which the classification is substantially related. Intermediate scrutiny is easier to meet, and the compelling interest already suggested will also be an important interest. Again, to hold that the statute meets intermediate scrutiny, the court would have to conclude that psychological health rests on a heterosexual orientation. The court would also have to conclude that, even if having heterosexual parents is not necessary to that orientation, it is at least substantially related. The response to the issue of taunting would be the same as it was under strict scrutiny analysis.

If the classification is not considered at all suspect, then rational basis will apply. The plaintiffs will have to show that there is no permissible state interest to which the classification and ban are rationally related. It is usually very easy for a state to survive this test. Here, the interest would be permissible. Under a true rational basis test, the connection would likely be seen as rational, because historically only a rather weak connection is required. There are cases, however, including *Romer v. Evans* (1996), that rest on the premise that simple dislike for a group is not a permissible reason for a discriminatory classification. If the court can be persuaded that the distinction here is based on such a dislike, rather than a concern for children, or that the purported concern for children is itself the product of a dislike for same-sex couples, this stronger version of rational basis may lead to the statute's invalidation.

Although the outcome may not be completely clear, there is at least a reasonable likelihood of a successful attack on the statute.

SELF-ASSESSMENT

Here, the fact that people are being treated differently indicates that this is an equal protection question. The fact that the classification is based on a characteristic of the persons discriminated against indicates that suspect class analysis is the proper approach. State action and intent are clear, so any extended discussion would be a waste of time. A simple mention, however, may be worthwhile.

The major mistake likely to be made here is simply to state that the Supreme Court has never held that discrimination based on sexual orientation is subject to strict scrutiny. That is, in fact, true, but simply stating the fact and going on to apply a rational basis test will miss much of what this hypothetical is about. The issue is complicated by the fact that the Court did examine a discriminatory state constitutional provision aimed at sexual orientation. When the Court did so, it used only rational basis, even if in a somewhat stronger form. However, the Court did not conclude that heightened scrutiny would never be proper in the case of such discrimination. Rather, the Court needed only rational basis to strike down the provision. There was no need to examine whether there should be heightened scrutiny. Thus, an examination of that issue is appropriate.

Where answers are not clear, it is best to hedge your bets. For example, you may believe that discrimination on the basis of sexual orientation should surely be subject to strict scrutiny. But, if you so conclude and do not consider other possible outcomes, you will miss parts of the discussion that might have been important. For example, here you would not have discussed the application of the intermediate scrutiny and rational basis tests.

Where there is an alternative test, or there are a number of possible tests, take the time to apply all of them. If the question were simply what level of scrutiny applies to classifications based on sexual orientation, the answer (and the question) would have been shorter. The facts are there for a reason, and often that reason is for purposes of applying a test. Here, you were given the concerns raised in the legislative history. Although a given fact may sometimes be a red herring, you need to at least consider each fact to see if it raises an issue or suggests a direction for the analysis. The stated concerns raise the issue of whether they are adequate or even permissible. That certainly should have led you to a discussion of whether the tests are satisfied.

VARIATIONS ON THE THEME

1. Suppose that the client was, instead, an attorney in the office of the state attorney general. The attorney general had run a campaign that spoke

strongly against what he called the "homosexual agenda." On taking office and learning that your client is gay, a fact about which your client has been quite open, the attorney general fired your client. Your client wants to challenge the firing in federal court.

2. Suppose your client is a gay male who was denied a job as a guard in a federal prison for men. The warden explained the decision as being based on a belief that he would be in greater danger of rape by the prisoners.

Problem 3

HYPOTHETICAL

(60 MINUTES)

You have recently been hired as an associate at a law firm with a litigation practice. One of the partners has heard that you have an interest in constitutional litigation, her specialty area, and has asked you to write a memo regarding strategy regarding a new case. She has told you that she has been unable to find any law speaking directly to the issues raised and has encouraged you to be creative in suggesting a theory.

The client is a woman in her mid-thirties who has been unable to have her own biological child and would like to adopt. She meets all the requirements usually imposed on potential adoptive parents, but she has been denied adoption, as the result of a state law passed two years earlier. That statute bars adoption, either as a single parent or a member of a couple, by any person who has had an abortion. The client had an abortion when she was twenty. Although she is confident that any records of the abortion are confidential, the adoption application asked whether she had ever obtained an abortion, and the application also noted that any knowingly false answers would be considered perjury. She responded that she had once obtained an abortion, and that led to her disqualification.

The law has already been challenged twice in federal courts. The first challenge argued that the restriction on adoption was a limitation on the fundamental right to choose an abortion. The second argued that the statute constituted unconstitutional discrimination on the basis of gender. In both cases, the federal court ruled that there was no constitutional violation.

The partner needs a novel approach. What can you suggest?

SAMPLE ESSAY

Given the failure of the first two challenges, the best strategy remaining open may be to argue that there is an equal protection violation in the line that is drawn between those who have had abortions and those who have not. There is certainly a classification involved, and the state has intentionally discriminated.

One approach to equal protection would be to try to establish that those who have obtained an abortion are a suspect class. Those who have obtained abortions are, presumably, a minority, and the class is discrete, given the yes-or-no nature of the classification. There would seem to be no insularity here. With regard to a history of discrimination, the discreetness of the class, in the sense that membership is not obvious, would limit the effectiveness of any discriminatory animus. The same may be true with regard to a lack of political power. To the degree that there is underrepresentation, it is probably due to any underrepresentation with regard to women more generally. The characteristic of having obtained an abortion is immutable, once the abortion has been performed, but it is not the sort of characteristic that is usually the basis for suspect class analysis, especially as there was a choice involved in the decision to have the abortion. Those characteristics have tended to be something about the person, rather than the person's actions. Thus, suspect class analysis may not be the best approach.

That leaves the fundamental rights prong of equal protection, and there are two lines of cases that should be considered. One of these lines involves cases where important rights that are not fundamental, and are thus not constitutionally required to be granted, are granted to some but not to all. The best examples of this sort of case are found in decisions regarding appeals of criminal convictions. Although there is no U.S. constitutional provision that requires states to allow appeals of criminal convictions, the Supreme Court has said that, where a state has granted a right to appeal, it must grant that right equally. Thus, a transcript and counsel must be provided to an indigent appellant.

This approach would seem not to work particularly well for this case. The right to seek an abortion is fundamental, but the courts have already ruled that the statute does not infringe that right. The only other approach that might fit this theory is to argue that the right to adopt is constitutionally similar to the right to an appeal. Perhaps neither has to be granted, but if granted, people must be treated equally. However, although the right to adopt may be important to the individual, it is not clear that it may be important to the constitutional system. Whereas criminal appeals are linked to a constitution provision guaranteeing a criminal trial, the link between adoption and an explicit constitutional value is less clear. The best tie might be to the Supreme Court cases regarding procreation, but it seems unlikely that courts would want to require that all adoption regulations meet strict scrutiny.

The best match, under the fundamental rights prong, might be found in the cases that involved restrictions on obtaining welfare or free nonemergency medical care until a potential recipient had been resident in the state for at least one year. The plaintiffs in these cases had exercised the fundamental right to move from one state to another and had been denied benefits based upon the exercise of that right. That seems to be what has happened here. The client, and similarly situated women, have exercised the fundamental right to seek an abortion. Based on the exercise of that right, they are being denied the opportunity to adopt a child. That would seem to be a violation of the fundamental rights prong of equal protection.

If any of these approaches holds up, that is, if the class is suspect or there is a violation of either variety of the fundamental rights prong of equal protection, the statute would be tested under strict scrutiny. The state would have to demonstrate that the classification is necessary to a compelling governmental interest. Although the state clearly has a compelling interest in the well-being of youth, including those who would be adopted, it would seem difficult to impossible for the state to establish that prohibiting adoption by anyone who has obtained an abortion at any time in the past is necessary to that interest.

If a court were to proceed along the suspect class prong of equal protection but find that the class was only quasi-suspect, then intermediate scrutiny would apply. The state would have to demonstrate that the classification was substantially related to an important governmental objective. The compelling interest in the well-being of youth is also an important interest, but it would seem that the ban would fail to meet the substantial relationship requirement.

If a court rejects all three approaches to equal protection, the statute must meet only rational basis. The burden will be on the plaintiff to show that there is no permissible governmental interest to which the classification is rationally related. Although the rational basis standard has, historically, been very easily met, there are cases involving mental retardation and sexual orientation in which the Supreme Court has found a lack of rational basis. The Court's basis for that conclusion is that expressing dislike for a group is not a permissible governmental purpose. That may be applicable here, if the court is convinced that the classification is based on an animus against those who obtained abortions.

There may be some question as to why this rational basis approach would not have been successful in the earlier cases, but it may simply be that the approach was not applicable in those cases. The fundamental rights case would not have been a challenge to classification, so animus against the class would not have been an issue. The first equal protection case was a claim based on discrimination against women, and the statute may simply have been seen as not expressing a general animus against women. The question as to whether it expresses an animus against those who have sought an abortion would remain open and may make a challenge successful even under rational basis.

SELF-ASSESSMENT

This is a difficult question. It requires a relatively sophisticated understanding of the workings of the Equal Protection Clause. That being said, it is worth noting that the more difficult or sophisticated a question is, the less close one has to come to a model answer to do well in comparison to others taking the exam. There was a specific goal to be creative in answering this question, so a discussion of theory and the novel approaches that may result from that consideration is important. The time provided (one hour) also indicates that there is an expectation of some depth to the analysis. If you finish your answer quickly, consider the possibility that you either missed an issue or did not address an issue in sufficient depth.

There is always an issue of the allocation of time or effort when there is more than one issue or more than one approach to the question. Here, there was suspect class analysis and two possible approaches to fundamental rights prong analysis. The consideration in too much depth of any one of the three approaches could have led to inadequate consideration of the others. The best approach may well then be to consider with some brevity all three and then return for analysis in greater depth to the approach or approaches that are the most interesting.

It would have been a mistake to spend any time on the issue of the statute interfering with the fundamental right to seek an abortion or the issue of gender discrimination. You may wonder how the courts could have upheld the statute against those challenges, but the facts state that they did. Remember the advice not to fight the hypothetical.

Note how the explanation of the fundamental rights prong presented in the introduction played into answering this question. The introduction suggested that there were two types of cases subsumed under the fundamental rights prong. One type involved what were described as quasi-fundamental rights, rights that are not actually fundamental but are sufficiently important to the system as to require that, if granted, people must be treated equally. The other involved cases where the exercise of a fundamental right was the basis for the classification. Because this analysis has not been explicitly adopted by the Supreme Court, the answer was not presented in those terms. The suggested approach did, however, lead to the selection of the most-relevant cases, and the cases were the basis for the discussion.

Also note that the facts may remove some issues from consideration. It would not be uncommon for a student answering a question like this to argue that, because only women can obtain an abortion, this could be seen as a gender discrimination issue. But the facts said that the gender approach had already been raised unsuccessfully, and asked for an alternative approach. Discussing gender-based discrimination would not have been responsive and would simply have been a waste of your time.

Having analyzed the level of scrutiny to apply, do not forget actually to state and apply the tests.

VARIATIONS ON THE THEME

1. Assuming you have already read the chapter on the Due Process Clauses, discuss the court's likely basis for concluding that the statute was not a violation of the fundamental right to seek an abortion.
2. What must have been the earlier court's analysis in its conclusion that the statute was not a violation of equal protection guarantees to women?

Problem 4

HYPOTHETICAL

(40 MINUTES)

High school sports in the state of Lincoln are governed by the Lincoln State High School Activities Association ("the Association"). The Association schedules playoffs and championship tournaments for all high school sports in the state. It also approves regular-season schedules, adopts rules under which the sports are played, and determines rules for student-athlete participation. All the state's high schools are members of the Association, and roughly 95 percent of them are public schools. Although much of the work of the Association is done by a professional staff, rules are adopted only upon a vote by a majority of the member schools.

There have been recent controversies over two sports. In soccer, a public school in a city with a large population of immigrant families has begun completely to dominate play in the state. The families are legal residents of the United States, but a number of them have children who were in their teen years at the time of their immigration. Those children, having learned to play soccer in their home countries, have skill levels far beyond those who grew up in Lincoln.

The other issue involves volleyball. The Association has sponsored a state tournament in the sport and has limited participation to females. Although in many sports the Association sponsors championships and tournaments for both boys' and girls' teams, there is no tournament for boys' volleyball, and as a result, no schools sponsor boys' teams. A boy at Todd High School has asked to be allowed to play on the girls' team, and the school, citing Association rules, has denied the request.

A significant number of schools have come together to introduce a rule for potential adoption by the Association that would bar aliens from playing high school sports. The parents of several resident-alien soccer players have indicated that, if such a rule is adopted, they will bring suit alleging a violation of their children's constitutional rights. Additionally, the parents of the boy who wishes to play volleyball have threatened to file a suit against the Association, alleging violations of his constitutional rights. The Association executive director has come to you, as general counsel for the Association, to inquire as to potential liability. What advice do you give?

SAMPLE ESSAY

First, for the Association to be liable for the violation of anyone's constitutional rights, the Association would have to be determined to be a state actor. The Constitution speaks to the structure of government and the relationship between government and individuals. Although an individual may violate another individual's statutory rights, only the government can violate an individual's constitutional rights. That being said, a violation does not have to be by the federal government, the state itself, or a governmental subdivision of the state itself. Certain individuals or entities that are not actually governmental units may be seen as acting on behalf of or as sufficiently in conjunction with government as to come within the limits imposed by the Constitution. Those who are tied closely enough to the government are considered state actors.

The Association will most likely be considered a state actor. Its membership is made up almost entirely of public schools. Certainly the voting strength of the public schools within the membership is sufficient for all Association rules to be seen as having been adopted by the joint action of the public schools. The public schools have effectively turned over their scheduling authority and rulemaking regarding participation to the Association. The public schools involved would not be allowed, individually, to violate students' constitutional rights, and they are not likely to be allowed to do so through group action. The Association is, thus, likely be held subject to the provisions of the Fourteenth Amendment's Equal Protection Clause.

We turn first to the soccer situation, in which the proposed rule classifies on the basis of alienage and intentionally discriminates against aliens. Determining the test to be employed in examining discrimination against aliens involves asking whether the position from which aliens are barred is one that has a political function. If there is a political function, the rule must meet only the rational basis test: it must be rationally related to a permissible governmental objective. If there is no political function, the rule must meet strict scrutiny: it must be necessary to a compelling governmental objective. Although school teachers, at least under certain circumstances, have been held to fill a political function, the case would seem completely inapplicable to students. This would seem even more so with regard to student involvement in extracurricular activities. The proposed rule would have to meet strict scrutiny and would fail that test. Giving students raised in Lincoln the opportunity to play soccer against weaker competition would seem unlikely to be held a compelling governmental objective.

We turn next to volleyball, in which the participation rule draws a line based on gender: boys are not allowed to play on the girls' team, and there is no separate team for boys. The equal protection test for gender-based discrimination has been intermediate scrutiny: the rule would have to be shown to be substantially related to an important governmental objective. More recently, in *United States v. Virginia*, 518 U.S. 515 (1996), although not adopted by the court as a new test, it has been suggested that there must be an exceedingly persuasive justification for any gender discrimination. In terms of intermediate scrutiny, the important objective in limiting volleyball to girls would be providing athletic opportunities for girls. If there were not volleyball teams limited to girls, height differences between boys and girls of high school age might well lead to the boys dominating the sport in which height is such an asset. Thus, the ban on boys is substantially related to the provision of athletic opportunities for girls. It is not clear exactly what the language of "exceedingly persuasive justification" is meant to do. If it were taken as an indication that gender classifications are to be tested under strict scrutiny, the ban may not stand up, but again, the Court has stuck with intermediate scrutiny, and banning boys from playing girls' volleyball would seem to stand that test.

SELF-ASSESSMENT

This is clearly an equal protection question, and the classes and level of scrutiny are easily identified. The major discussion should have been the application of the tests. The time allocation would suggest that at least some depth of discussion in the application of the tests is warranted. Indeed, if you did not discuss application, you would most probably have finished well before the forty minutes allocated had passed. When that happens, you should consider the possibility that you missed an issue or did not discuss an issue in the depth expected.

It is sometimes suggested that all constitutional questions involving individual rights be answered by first considering the question of state action. This often causes students to waste a lot of time on the issue. If a question involves action by the U.S. Army, spending time discussing whether the Army is a state actor is an unwise allocation of effort. The Army is the ultimate state actor, and simply to state that there is no state action problem should be sufficient. Sometimes, however, as here, there may be a legitimate question of state action. When the question is legitimate, it needs to be addressed. There are two cases that might have been brought into the discussion here, *Brentwood Academy v. Tennessee Secondary Schools Athletics Ass'n*, 531 U.S. 288 (2001), and *National Collegiate Athletic Ass'n v. Tarkanian*, 488 U.S. 179 (1988), if they were part of the readings for your course. If they were not, the discussion in the sample essay would have been adequate. If they were, their relevance should have been discussed. *Brentwood*, because it involved a high school activities association, seems more relevant. *Tarkanian*, involving the National Collegiate Athletics Association in an enforcement context, is less relevant. A discussion involving the two cases should lead to the same result.

Another place in which you might waste time would be the application of the factors to determine the level of scrutiny for the two classifications involved. The Court has spoken clearly on the level of scrutiny and the test to be applied for both the classifications at issue. This is a situation in which those conclusions should simply be stated and the tests applied.

With regard to gender discrimination, the discussion of the "exceedingly persuasive justification" language may not have been necessary. The test is intermediate scrutiny, and you could simply have applied it. The discussion of "exceedingly persuasive justification," however, demonstrates more depth of understanding of the issues and may be worth some points.

VARIATIONS ON THE THEME

1. Suppose that instead of banning resident aliens, the ban addressed only illegal aliens and prohibited them from playing high school sports.
2. Suppose that in addition to prohibiting boys from playing on the girls' volleyball team, Association rules prohibited girls from playing on boys' high

school football teams. What if the parents of a female student, who wishes to play football, file suit over that rule?

3. Suppose that the Association sponsors state tournaments in both boys' and girls' tennis. A girl, who won the state girls' tournaments in both her freshman and sophomore years, has asked to be allowed to participate on the boys' team, including in the state boys' tournament. If she is refused permission and her parents file suit, what is the result?

Problem 5

HYPOTHETICAL
(45 MINUTES)

The Sixth Amendment to the U.S. Constitution guarantees the right to a jury trial for all serious criminal offenses. Offenses that are punishable by fewer than six months imprisonment are considered petty, and jury trials have not been required. The State of Hoover has, however, provided a broader right for criminal trials in its state courts. A person charged with a petty offense may request a jury trial. The request will be granted if the defendant posts a $1000 bond. If the defendant is convicted, the bond is forfeited; if the defendant is acquitted, the bond is refunded. Because $1000 falls far short of covering the increased cost of a jury trial, the state has limited the right to request a jury trial in petty cases to those who have been resident in the state for at least one year.

You are a public defender with a client charged with a petty offense. The client moved to the state three months ago. He, therefore, does not have the statutory right to request a jury trial. He also cannot afford the $1000 bond. He has asked you if he can demand a jury trial, despite the circumstances. What arguments, based on the U.S. Constitution, can you offer on his behalf?

SAMPLE ESSAY

As the Sixth Amendment does not provide a right to a jury trial in this sort of case, any constitutional argument will have to be based elsewhere. The argument that the client has a right to a jury trial will be based on the fundamental rights prong of the Equal Protection Clause. There are, in fact, two different arguments that could be offered based on the fundamental rights prong: one based on the residency requirement, and the other based on the required $1000 bond.

With regard to durational residency requirements, the Court has struck down state regulations denying welfare to people who have not been residents of the state for at least one year. The Court also held unconstitutional a rule that limited welfare payments to the same amount as received in the prior state of residency, until the new state resident had lived there for one year. Additionally, the Court threw out a one-year residency requirement for state-funded indigent medical care, even in nonemergency situations. There have also been decisions throwing out durational residency requirements on voting, at least when longer than necessary for preparation of voter lists. The Court also banned the state of Alaska from distributing its oil revenue based on how long residents had lived in the state. On the other hand, the Court has allowed durational residency requirements for divorce and for attending state universities at in-state tuition rates.

Overall, the Court has looked with disfavor on state regulations that create classes of citizenship. The Fourteenth Amendment provides that all those born in or naturalized in the United States are U.S. citizens and citizens of the states within which they reside. That would not appear to allow for distinctions based on how long the residency has been. It may not be clear why tuition is treated differently, whereas divorce may be explained by the state wanting to have acquired jurisdiction over the res of the marriage. Even with these exceptions, it would seem that the jury trial issue should fit with the majority of the cases, and the state would not be able to limit the right to request a jury to those who had been resident for a year.

As to the $1000 bond, the argument is slightly different. It might at first seem that there could be a suspect class analysis based on poverty. There are, however, two problems with that approach. First, although the impoverished are unable to pay the bond and thus are denied the right, this might be argued not to be intentional discrimination against the class. It is based on the need to cover the extra expense, and although the impact is disparate, it might not be held to be intentional. More important, the Court has said that the poor are not a suspect class.

The better argument regarding the bond is that the right to a jury trial in petty criminal cases, although not a fundamental right under the Sixth Amendment, is sufficiently important to require that, if the state grants the right to some, it must treat people equally. This would put the result on the same track as cases requiring that defendant-appellants receive trial transcripts and counsel for an appeal as of right. Although there is no U.S. constitutional right to appeal a criminal conviction, appeals are sufficiently important that, if they are granted as of right to some, others must be treated equally. It is not just importance to the individual but importance to actual fundamental rights that requires the provision of a jury trial, without bond, if the petty criminal defendant so requests. Here, the recognition of the importance of juries might lead a court to conclude that, even when not required by the Constitution, they must be provided equally, when they are provided to some.

Having found a violation, the state would have to meet strict scrutiny. It would have to demonstrate a compelling governmental interest to which the classification was necessary. The state's interests seem to be fiscal. Such interests seem unlikely to be compelling, as demonstrated by the welfare cases.

SELF-ASSESSMENT

The analysis of the fundamental rights prong of equal protection presented in the introduction guides the approach taken here, even though the analysis is not actually presented. This is because the analysis in the introduction does not represent what the Court has said but is more a matter of organizing the decided cases and finding arguments available from those cases.

It is wise first to consider the possibility of suspect class analysis before going on to the fundamental rights prong. There may be situations in which arguments under both prongs are available, and it would be unwise to neglect the suspect class argument. Here, however, there is no suspect class involved. If you had not recognized that the Court has rejected the possibility of poverty as a suspect class, you might have discussed the factors involved in determining the level of suspectness, but with the Court's decision that would be a waste of time.

Again, the sample essay did not explicitly rely on the analysis in the introduction, but that analysis led to an understanding of what cases were relevant. Once those cases were identified, the analysis proceeded from those results.

As the essay moved to discussion of the fundamental rights prong, it was suggested that there are two types of cases. First, there can be a violation when a classification is drawn based on the exercise of a fundamental right. There is a fundamental right to migrate from state to state, and recent exercise of that right is the basis for the denial of a jury trial. That opens up one line of cases to consider.

There can also be a violation when a right is not really fundamental but is sufficiently tied to actual fundamental rights as to demand equal treatment; if it is granted to some, it must be equally granted to others. That recognition opens up the other line of inquiry. Again, in both approaches, the analysis in the introduction is not presented directly. Rather, it guides the reasoning and suggests relevant cases on which to base the arguments.

It is also always important, even when a constitutional violation is found, to consider the possibility that the state can justify its infringement. Even if the possibility is dismissed in a few lines, as it was here, it is worth considering.

VARIATIONS ON THE THEME

1. Suppose that the refusal to provide a jury trial for petty cases applies only to aliens. What then?
2. What about application only to illegal aliens?
3. Suppose the state denies to those who have not been residents for at least one year discretionary appeals to the state supreme court of criminal convictions affirmed by the intermediate court of appeals. What then?

Problem 6

HYPOTHETICAL

(45 MINUTES)

Sandra Smith is a thirty-year-old female college graduate. In the eight years since she left school, she has worked for a bank, starting as a teller and working her way up to branch manager. Despite her success and consistently excellent performance reviews, she was unhappy because she always wanted to be a police officer. She decided to leave her job and apply for admission to the City of Moronia police academy.

As a part of the admissions process, Smith was given a battery of physical and mental tests, and her background was checked. Her age was within the acceptable range. Her background check disclosed no problems. She was among the top candidates on the physical tests and showed no emotional or other psychological problems. On an intelligence test, given as part of the test battery, she scored at the top of the group of candidates and, in fact, in the top 1 percent of the general population. Despite these results she was denied admission.

Smith sued, arguing discrimination. Based on the composition of entering classes to the police academy over a period of several years, there is no evidence of gender, ethnic, or racial discrimination in the department or in the admissions process. When pressed as to why Smith was rejected, the police chief said that Smith's score on the intelligence test was too high. He said that, in his experience, people who were too intelligent did not do well as police officers because they could not tolerate the boring aspects of the position, and they often quit shortly after becoming officers. After that explanation, Smith's attorneys put in evidence other statements by the chief to the effect that he did not get along with high-scoring police cadets and officers because they were "smart alecks" and "know-it-alls." The chief admitted that he felt threatened by college graduates and that, because he had made it with no degree and what he conceded was only slightly above-average intelligence, he wanted the same qualities in his officers.

Discuss the likelihood of Smith's success in a non-ethnic, non-gender–based discrimination suit under the Equal Protection Clause.

SAMPLE ESSAY

The police department is certainly a state actor, and there is clearly intentional discrimination here, because the chief admits that Smith was been denied admission to the police academy because of her intelligence. As this is a characteristic of the individual, an analysis to determine whether the class is suspect or quasi-suspect is called for.

The first issue will be just how suspect, if at all, a classification based on intelligence may be. In that regard, the first factor is whether the intelligent are a discrete and insular minority. Minority status would seem to exist, as having significantly above-average intelligence means, mathematically, that one is in a relatively small portion of the population. Whether this minority is discrete is an interesting question. Whether one is intelligent is not a yes-or-no question. However, educational testing has, by definition, made this somewhat discrete. At least in the school context, there is a point at which one's IQ score defines one as intellectually gifted, as well as a point at which one's IQ score may define one as developmentally delayed. As to insularity, if there are neighborhoods for those of above-average intelligence, it would most likely have to do with any correlation between intelligence and earning capacity and the choice of more-intelligent individuals to live in more expensive neighborhoods.

A second factor is a history of discrimination. This would seem difficult to establish. Those with above-average intelligence would seem to be, on average, both successful and free from societal discrimination. There would also seem not to be a lack of political power. Presumably, most of those involved in government would be of at least above-average intellectual ability. Finally, there is the issue of whether intelligence is an immutable characteristic unrelated to ability. There may be some debate over how fixed intelligence is, but by the time one is an adult there is perhaps little likelihood of change. In terms of relationship to ability, in many circumstances intelligence would indicate an above-average ability. The police chief, however, has indicated a belief that intelligence may be negatively correlated with ability in the position for which Smith has applied. He stated that, in his experience, those of above-average intelligence become bored with the job and quit. This may well be stereotyping, and certainly Smith's track record in banking shows no indication that she would become bored and leave.

It is not clear how to add these factors up. If they did add up to the intelligent being a suspect class, the police department would have to meet strict liability. It would have to demonstrate a compelling governmental interest to which the classification and discrimination were necessary. The police chief's concerns and impressions would seem to fall short. If the intelligent are a quasi-suspect class, the department would have to meet intermediate scrutiny. It would have to demonstrate that the classification and discrimination were substantially related to an important governmental objective. Here, too, the police chief's concerns would likely fall short.

It seems most likely that classifications based on intelligence would be seen as non-suspect. This conclusion would lead to a symmetry in the treatment of those at both ends of the distribution on intelligence tests. The Supreme Court has held that the developmentally delayed are not a suspect class, so it would seem odd to conclude that those at the opposite end of the distribution are suspect. The conclusion as to being a discrete and insular minority would be the same for intellectually gifted and for the developmentally delayed, although there may have been, historically, an insularity in terms of institutionalization and segregated classes for the developmentally delayed that was not present for the intellectually gifted. The developmentally delayed are far more likely to have been the subject of discrimination and to lack political power. Immutability would seem to apply equally, although the characteristic's relationship to ability may be stronger in the case of the developmentally delayed.

Given the similarity in analysis of the Court's unwillingness to consider the developmentally delayed a suspect class, it seems very likely that a court would conclude that there was a lack of suspectness here and that rational basis should apply. Ms. Smith would have to demonstrate that there was no permissible governmental objective to which the classification and discrimination were rationally related. Although this test is historically very easily met, the Supreme Court's handling of its case involving the developmentally delayed may provide some guidance here, as it did with regard to the level of suspectness. There, the Court saw the justifications offered as being based on a dislike for the targeted group, and concluded that dislike for a group could not constitute a permissible governmental objective. That ought to apply here as well. The police chief's comments about more intelligent officers becoming bored and leaving are stereotypes. Even more telling, the chief's comments about intelligent police officers being "smart alecks" and "know-it-alls" are strongly demonstrative of a dislike for the group, and again, that cannot be the foundation for meeting the rational basis test.

Ms. Smith's likelihood of success seems reasonably positive.

SELF-ASSESSMENT

This is clearly an equal protection question, because a group, the intelligent, is being singled out for unequal treatment. As the treatment is based on a characteristic, the suspect class prong is indicated.

There is a strategy choice to be made in answering this question. Instead of applying the factors used to determine whether a classification should be considered suspect, an alternative approach would have been simply to compare the classifications in this case and in the case involving the developmentally delayed. That is, the answer could have begun by arguing that, if the developmentally delayed are not a suspect or quasi-suspect class, then neither should be the intellectually gifted. If that were the approach taken, it would, nonetheless, be important not simply to state that conclusion but also to offer an analysis demonstrating the position. That analysis would seem to require a comparison of the two groups regarding the relevant factors. So, although the organization of the answer might differ, the substantive content of the discussion would remain the same.

It is also important not simply to state that, because the Supreme Court has never held the intellectually gifted to be a suspect or quasi-suspect class, the class lacks suspectness. When the Supreme Court has not ruled either way on the issue raised, that should be seen as an invitation to apply the kind of analysis the Court employs in the area to the new situation.

Once you have decided on the test to apply, there are points to be earned in the application. In fact, if it is not clear what test is the best, there may be points in applying each of the alternatives.

VARIATIONS ON THE THEME

1. Suppose Smith had not been a college graduate with a successful career and had been denied admission because of an exceptionally low score on the intelligence test. In his testimony, the police chief stated that no one with a score that low had successfully graduated from the police academy.
2. Suppose the testing disclosed an emotional disorder of Smith's that included an inability to control her temper.

D. OPTIONAL READINGS

The following sources present the topics covered in this chapter in more depth than the chapter introduction. The sources are in increasing levels of detail. The first provides an overview, the second provides more detail, and the third and fourth provide the greatest coverage of the material.

MICHAEL C. DORF & TREVOR W. MORRISON, CONSTITUTIONAL LAW (2010), chapter 6.
ERWIN CHEMERINSKY, CONSTITUTIONAL LAW: PRINCIPLES AND POLICIES (4th ed. 2011), chapter 9.
JOHN E. NOWAK & RONALD D. ROTUNDA, PRINCIPLES OF CONSTITUTIONAL LAW (4th ed. 2010), chapter 14.
JOHN E. NOWAK & RONALD D. ROTUNDA, CONSTITUTIONAL LAW (7th ed. 2000), chapter 14.

9 FREE EXPRESSION

A. INTRODUCTION

Free expression is protected by the Speech and Press Clauses of the First Amendment. Although the First Amendment says only that Congress may make no law that abridges the freedoms of speech or of the press, the provisions are applicable to the states through the Due Process Clause of the Fourteenth Amendment. The original intent behind the Free Expression Clauses seems, at most, to have been the protection of political speech. It may even have been intended to do less: to protect only against requirements that the government approve expression prior to its distribution, with later punishment still permissible. Whatever the original intent, the First Amendment has come to protect even entertainment on the grounds that it is too difficult to draw lines between that which only entertains and that which informs. Now, the default position is that expression is protected, unless the expression fits into one of a number of recognized exceptions to the First Amendment.

When expression is protected, any limitations will have to meet a special version of the strict scrutiny test. If speech, even speech that might be considered political, raises a "clear and present danger," it may be suppressed. Speech presents a clear and present danger when it is intended to bring about imminent lawless action and is likely to do so. The application of that test will be seen in some of the cases listed below.

The existence of the clear and present danger test should not be taken to mean that there is only one way to meet strict scrutiny in the context of expression. Any other demonstration that there is a compelling governmental interest to which the restriction is necessary will suffice. So, for example, courts have held that an interest in the well-being of youth is sufficiently compelling to meet strict scrutiny, but they have found that certain limits imposed for that purpose (for example, bans on violent video games) are not necessary to the interest.

As mentioned, there are types of expression that are unprotected by the First Amendment. Where expression falls outside the protection of the First Amendment, limits need only meet the rational basis test. Unprotected speech includes obscene depictions and fighting words, which you will see defined in some of the cases. Read the cases carefully to develop an understanding of the distinctions between the protected and the unprotected.

It has commonly been said that libel is also unprotected, but as the cases will show, defamatory expression enjoys some level of protection. Although defamatory expression may not be valuable in itself, there needs to be breathing space to allow for political and social criticism that would be choked off if it were too easy to recover for defamation. This potential limit on valuable speech is what is known as a chilling effect. Be sure, in reading the cases, to come to an understanding of the "actual malice" test and the protection it provides. Also be sure to understand when the test applies. That requires an understanding of differences among public officials, public figures, and private figures. For private figures, the test also has relevance as to the sorts of damages available.

Free expression is also an area of the law that sometimes employs an intermediate scrutiny test. This may be because of the method employed in communication; thus, conduct intended to convey a message may, when the governmental concern is over the conduct and not the message, be tested with the lower level of scrutiny. The same is true when the governmental concern is not with the message but with the time, place, and manner of conveying that message. A third such situation is dependent upon the subject matter of the speech. Commercial speech is not as fully protected as, for example, political speech.

It is also important to note that the protection afforded speech may vary with the place in which the expression is offered. Expression in a public park or on a sidewalk is considered to be in a public forum. It is subject to time, place, and manner regulation, and under that test, intermediate scrutiny is employed, so long as the restriction is not based on the message. If it is, instead, in a non-forum, restrictions then need only be reasonable. Recognizing the differences between places that are public fora and those that are not is important.

There are also different rules when the government regulates speech in schools and in the broadcast media. The cases below will present some of these different situations. But, it is particularly worth repeating for this chapter that the treatment of the subject matters included in this book is far from exhaustive. There are a great many topics that could be included in the free expression section of a Constitutional Law course that are not included in the selection of cases or hypotheticals in this chapter. If your course included topics such as the government regulation of the speech of its employees, the First Amendment and campaign contributions, media reports and the criminal trial, or any of a variety of other topics, do not take the exclusion of those topics here as an indication that the topic will not show up on your exam. There were only so many hypotheticals that could be included, and the readings selected were aimed at those that are included.

B. READINGS

Before attempting the problems in this section, read the following cases. Actually, you may well have already read at least most of them. Edited casebook versions of them will be adequate. If you do not have a casebook version of one or more of the cases, the jump cites will guide you to the relevant material in the unedited case reports. Although the list may seem long, the cases can be used for a number of problems. The cases are, to a degree, grouped by more specific subject matter.

New York Times Co. v. United States, 403 U.S. 713, 714–20, 752–59 (1971).
Brandenburg v. Ohio, 395 U.S. 444, 444–49 (1969).
Miller v. California, 413 U.S. 15, 16–37 (1973).
Stanley v. Georgia, 394 U.S. 557, 558–68 (1969).
Mishkin v. New York, 383 U.S. 502, 503–11 (1966).
Ginsberg v. New York, 390 U.S. 629, 631–37 (1968),
Ginzburg v. United States, 383 U.S. 463, 464–76 (1966).
Kingsley Books, Inc. v. Brown, 354 U.S. 436, 437–45 (1957).
Feiner v. New York, 340 U.S. 315, 316–21 (1951).
New York Times Co. v. Sullivan, 376 U.S. 254, 256–92 (1964).

Curtis Pub. Co. v. Butts, 388 U.S. 130, 133–40, 146–55, 162–65 (1967).
Gertz v. Robert Welch Co., 418 U.S. 323, 325–33, 339–53 (1974).
Hustler Magazine v. Falwell, 485 U.S. 46, 47–57 (1988).
Cohen v. California, 403 U.S. 15, 15–26 (1971).
New York v. Ferber, 458 U.S. 747, 749–53, 756–74 (1982).
Ashcroft v. American Civil Liberties Union, 535 U.S. 234, 239–59 (2002).
Brown v. Entertainment Merchants Ass'n, 131 S.Ct. 2729, 2732–42 (2011).
R.A.V. v. St Paul, 505 U.S. 377, 379–96 (1992).
Virginia v. Black, 538 U.S. 343, 347–400 (2003).
United States v. O'Brien, 391 U.S. 367, 369–86 (1968).
Texas v. Johnson, 491 U.S. 397, 399–420 (1989).
Clark v. Community for Creative Non-Violence, 468 U.S. 288, 289–99 (1984).
Renton v. Playtime Theatres, 475 U.S. 41, 43–55 (1986).
Central Hudson Gas & Elec. Corp. v. Public Serv. Commission, 447 U.S. 557, 563–66 (1980).
Lorillard Tobacco Co. v. Reilly, 533 U.S. 525, 532–40, 553–71 (2001).
Tinker v. Des Moines School District, 393 U.S. 503, 504–14 (1969).
Bethel School District v. Fraser, 478 U.S. 675 (1986).
Hazelwood School District v. Kuhlmeier, 484 U.S. 260 (1988).
Morse v. Frederick, 551 U.S. 393, 396–410, 422–25 (2007).
F.C.C. v. Pacifica Foundation, 438 U.S. 726, 729–51, 755–62 (1978).
Ashcroft v. American Civil Liberties Union, 542 U.S. 656, 659–73 (2004).
Ward v. Rock against Racism, 491 U.S. 781, 784–803 (1981).
International Society for Krishna Consciousness v. Lee, 505 U.S. 672, 674–85 (1992).
Hill v. Colorado, 530 U.S. 703, 707–10, 714–18, 725–32 (2000).

C. PROBLEMS

Problem 1

HYPOTHETICAL
(30 MINUTES)

In the aftermath of a major terrorist attack on the United States, the federal government became concerned that there would be future attacks. One part the government's concern focused on was video recordings sent by the leadership of the organization that conducted the initial attacks to television networks in the United States. The concern was twofold. First, something said by the speaker could be code directing the initiation of a second attack. Second, the recording as a whole could have an embedded message, which would be generally unrecognizable but could, using a computer program, be extracted and provide guidance to the terrorist movement.

The government asked the networks not to air the videos. When the networks refused to comply voluntarily, the government sought and received an order in federal district court prohibiting the airing. The order did not bar coverage of the statements contained in the videos, but the videos themselves could not be shown, and the networks would have to paraphrase the statements instead of quoting them word for word. The networks have appealed the order, and you have been asked by the judge for whom you are clerking to draft a memo discussing the issues likely to be raised in that appeal.

SAMPLE ESSAY

This case raises at least two issues. The first is whether the speech under discussion may be limited in a manner consistent with the First Amendment. Generally, speech is protected, unless it falls within an exception to First Amendment protection. This speech would not seem to fall into an exception, and the limitation would probably be characterized as content-based. Thus the limitation will be tested under strict scrutiny. In this context, *Brandenburg*'s clear-and-present-danger test would seem relevant.

The clear-and-present-danger test allows restrictions on speech when the speech is intended to bring about imminent lawless action and is likely to have that result. The test does not allow the suppression of speech that is merely abstract advocacy or even the advocacy of some future action. Here, the government fears that the speech may contain an order directing terrorist activities or even more complex plans embedded within the videos. If so, and if the order is for imminent action, that would seem to satisfy the test. The problem here, however, is that, although the tests would justify the suppression of the terrorist's speech, the order is directed at the networks. Presumably, the networks do not possess an intent that there be imminent lawless action, so it is questionable whether the clear-and-present-danger test applies to them.

If the clear-and-present-danger test is not the applicable test, there may be other ways to meet strict scrutiny. What is required is a compelling governmental objective and that the restriction be necessary to that objective. National defense would generally be considered a compelling governmental interest. The question would be the necessity to that objective of barring the broadcasts. The government asserts that necessity by suggesting the potential for an order or an embedded message in the video, but it is not clear whether this is simply speculation or whether there is some evidence for this concern. An issue for the court to consider is how much deference on this subject should be given to the executive branch. It is also important to recognize, in this regard, that the order is seemingly fairly narrowly tailored. It does not prohibit coverage of the statements or even a paraphrased report of the content of the statements. It prohibits only broadcasting the videos or directly quoting from the videos. If there is necessity, the order does not seem to be overly broad.

The second major issue has to do with the propriety of a prior restraint, the order prohibiting the broadcast before it has aired. Prior restraints are of particular concern in First Amendment jurisprudence, and there is a particularly heavy burden on the government to justify them. The cases do seem to be willing to allow such prior restraints in some circumstances. Standard examples include publishing the sailing dates of troop ships in an era in which troops ships were used. This would indicate that information that would disclose vulnerabilities and, by so doing, endanger the national defense may be subject to prior restraint. The conveyance of enemy orders would seem to be a similar danger, but here again, there is the question of how speculative this danger is and what deference should be given to the executive.

Finally, there is no citation to a statute that authorizes the executive to seek this court order. There needs to be some inquiry into the basis of the order and, if it is not a statutory basis, whether the authority of the executive branch regarding national defense in an emergency situation can be sufficient, on its own, to justify the order.

SELF-ASSESSMENT

As this is an action by the federal government, there is no need to plead the Fourteenth Amendment Due Process Clause, and doing so would be an error.

There might be a temptation to go directly into an analysis of prior restraints. That would not be in error, unless it caused you not to address the other issues. With regard to the prior restraint, the *Pentagon Papers* case, *New York Times v. United States*, probably provides the most guidance. But the information at issue in the *Pentagon Papers* case was not only less dangerous than the videos here might be but also was not directed toward urging anyone to take violent action against the United States. The greater potential damage here leads to the possibility of a different result regarding a prior restraint. The assertion that the videos may contain an order is what raises the issues surrounding the clear-and-present-danger test.

The *Pentagon Papers* case also seems not to spend much of any effort on an analysis of strict scrutiny. That might have led you not to provide that analysis here. Perhaps, most of the Court there thought it unlikely that any such showing could be made. The dissent did raise issues that it thought should have been resolved, and some of those issues may have been directed at addressing the possibility of meeting strict scrutiny. Here there seems to be a much more real likelihood that strict scrutiny could be met, and the issue merits discussion. It might not have seemed necessary here, given the availability of the clear-and-present-danger test, but if the intent of the media was to be required for that test, that intent seems lacking. Some other form of strict scrutiny argument would be required. Thus, the compelling interest is national defense. and the necessity of the ban to that interest was considered.

VARIATIONS ON THE THEME

1. Suppose that the court order to the networks was that they not provide any coverage at all for the videos, based on the government assertion that it was vital not to give credibility to the terrorists, and that the public airing would provoke public concern or even panic What result then?
2. Suppose that the government admits that it sees no likelihood of imminent action and that its only concern is the conveyance, as embedded messages, of detailed plans for terrorist acts scheduled to occur several months later.
3. Suppose that the government makes no assertions with regard to cues or embedded messages. The government's concern is that the charismatic leader of the terrorist movement will attract adherents who may hear and see the videos.

Problem 2

HYPOTHETICAL

(45 MINUTES)

Simon Publishing had, in the past, published a book titled *Fifty Ways to Love Your Lover*. The book contained photographs of a variety of explicit sexual acts, accompanied by text that described the acts in great detail and described the participants' reactions, using language generally considered lewd. The book was marketed through a Web site that guaranteed that the book would "arouse your interest." It was also available in adult bookstores. The county attorney for the County of Samuel in the State of Adams brought charges of obscenity, based on the availability of the book for sale in the county. After a jury trial, the book was held to be obscene, and the decision was upheld on appeal.

Lewis Publishing had, also in the past, published a book titled *In Front of the Looking Glass*. The book contained dozens of photographs of females between the ages of eight and sixteen posing naked in front of a mirror. The book contained only the photographs and no text. Finding it, too, available in the county, the same county attorney brought charges for violating the state's child pornography law and obtained a conviction that was upheld on appeal.

Both books have been republished. *Fifty Ways to Love Your Lover* has been republished as *Human Sexuality*. The photographs are exactly the same, but the text has been changed so that the language is that of medicine and psychology, using a variety of technical terms. The republished book is marketed in a magazine aimed at psychologists and suggests that the content can help psychologists working with those experiencing sexual problems. *In Front of the Looking Glass* has been republished as *Child Models in the Arts*. All previous photos remain, but reproductions of a number of classical paintings of nude females of the same age range and photos of similar sculptures have been added. There is also added text that discusses the history of such depictions.

The county attorney has discovered that *Child Models in the Arts* is available for sale in the county. She has also been told that a local mainstream bookstore intends to offer *Human Sexuality* for sale. She has asked you, a recently employed attorney in her office, to draft a memo regarding the possibility of seeking an injunction against the sale of *Human Sexuality* and whether she is likely to be successful in bringing child pornography charges regarding the sale of *Child Models in the Arts*. What advice do you give?

SAMPLE ESSAY

Although an injunction, a form of prior restraint, will seldom be issued against expression, obscenity provides an exception. Where a work has been held by the courts to be obscene, its distribution may be enjoined. The issue regarding the injunction here turns on whether *Human Sexuality* has been held to be obscene. On that issue, the analysis will turn on the *Miller* test for obscenity that was held to have been met for *Fifty Ways to Love Your Lover* and whether that holding carries over to the new book.

The first part of the *Miller* test requires that the work, taken as a whole, appeals to the prurient interest in sex. The earlier version of the book must have, given the outcome of the earlier case, been held to have met this test. Although the new version contains the same photographs, it may not be clear that there is the same appeal to the prurient interest. The photos in the first book were accompanied by text that most likely enhanced their appeal to the prurient interest. The medical/psychological text in the second version might detract from that appeal. Thus, it is not clear that the finding in the first version applies to the second version.

The second part of the *Miller* test requires that the work be offensive, under contemporary community standards, and that statutory language adequately describe the depictions addressed. Presumably, the statutory language does not present a problem. The depictions are the same in the two versions, and if the statute was held adequate in the earlier trial, it would appear adequate here as well. Offensiveness under contemporary community standards may present more difficulty. Presumably, any offense contained in the pictures has not changed, but the change in language may be sufficient to negate the earlier findings of offensiveness.

The third requirement of *Miller*, that the material lacks serious literary artistic, political, or scientific value, raises even more difficulty. The change in language appears to have been aimed at lending a serious scientific value to the work. Although simply including some short snippet of serious value may not serve to save a work that would otherwise be obscene (because it would have little effect on the work taken as a whole), the inclusion of scientific language throughout may provide serious value to the work taken as a whole.

There is an additional factor that needs to be considered. The Supreme Court has held that, with regard to prurient interest, that interest is to be judged based on the audience to which the work is marketed or made available. In that case, the Court said that material marketed to a population with a deviant sexual interest need not appeal to the prurient interest of the population as a whole but only to those with that interest. And, when material is sold to juveniles, prurient interest is judged based on the appeal to that group. Here, the new version of the book is being marketed to psychologists, and the prurient interest appealed to by the earlier version in the general population may not be the same as the prurient appeal (if any) this book would have to psychologists.

All in all, it would not seem that the prior holding that *Fifty Ways to Love Your Lover* was obscene should carry over to the republished *Human Sexuality*.

With regard to *Child Models in the Arts*, there appears to have been an effort also to provide the earlier *In Front of the Looking Glass* with serious value. In its child pornography cases, the Supreme Court has said that the failure to include a savings clause for material with serious value does not require that a state statute be held unconstitutional. So, if the state statute does not exempt material with serious value, a child pornography conviction might be obtained.

The concern in the child pornography cases was over the exploitation and sexual abuse of children. Possession and distribution of child pornography could be banned in order to limit the market that would drive production and to eliminate the more or less permanent record of the abuse of the children involved. Here, the addition of reproductions and photos does not mitigate those concerns. The exploitation of children that led to the first book also provides the basis for the second version. The same market forces are in play, and there is the same permanency of the record.

The reproductions and photos of sculptures might not themselves be child pornography, because the Supreme Court has held that virtual child pornography is protected by the First Amendment. However, the inclusion of work that might not be child pornography does not negate a holding that the photos from the earlier version were child pornography, and any addition of serious value does not constitutionally require that the material now be protected. If it is to be protected, this may depend on whether state law limits child pornography to material that lacks serious value. It is also true, however, that some members of the Supreme Court, in the child pornography decision, did say that there should still be room for an as-applied challenge based on serious value. This may be such a case.

SELF-ASSESSMENT

The most obvious error here would be to proceed directly from the holding that the first version of *Fifty Ways to Love Your Lover* is obscene and the recognition that obscene works may be enjoined to a conclusion that the later version could be enjoined. In reading the facts of the hypothetical, assume that they are intended to make a difference and that the answer is not as easy as it might be thought. The *Miller* test had to be applied to the second version. In applying that test, you could simply speculate or leave a lot of unanswered questions, but the first part of the hypothetical should have led you to realize that there is some relevance to the earlier holding of obscenity. Using what must have been the basis of that holding provides more clarity in answering the question you have been asked. It was important to address all three parts of the *Miller* test because the revision had an impact on each. It would have been easy to miss the impact of audience, but again here, the inclusion in the facts that the audience was different should have led you to consider whether there would be any impact on the result.

With regard to the second book, it was most important to recognize that serious value does not necessarily keep a set of photographs from being considered child pornography. Having recognized that and having assumed that the reproductions and sculptural photographs were included in an attempt to lend serious value, you may have tried to answer the question in relatively short order. Having used that fact, you may not have seen the relevance of any discussion of virtual child pornography. Although that discussion would probably not be worth a large share of the points available in an exam question, some points may be missed by failing to recognize that a short set of facts may be intended to raise more than one issue.

VARIATIONS ON THE THEME

1. Suppose that, instead of changing *Fifty Ways to Love Your Lover* in the ways indicated it had simply been republished with the photographs changed to drawings.
2. Suppose that in *Child Models in the Art* the photos that were present in *In Front of the Looking Glass* were altered, using a computer, to make them appear to be oil paintings. Would the second version still be considered child pornography?

Problem 3

HYPOTHETICAL

(45 MINUTES)

The *Capital City Gazette*, a newspaper with circulation throughout the State of Jackson, published a story exposing what it said was bribery involving a member of the Jackson delegation to the U.S. House of Representatives. The story alleged that two brothers, who were very successful business persons and who had also run a Political Action Committee (PAC) championing political causes, this time went beyond sponsoring ideological television advertisements and making campaign contributions. The story said that, at a meeting with the congressman, they offered a direct personal financial inducement to the congressman to vote for a bill they favored, and that the congressman had accepted the money offered. The story also implicated the star quarterback of the professional football team playing in the capital city as being at the meeting and providing additional money for the congressman. Furthermore, a local schoolteacher was identified as having served as a go-between in arranging the meeting.

The story was factually incorrect: no such bribe was offered or accepted. The reporter who wrote the story had based it on a tip from a person who, although anonymous, had provided accurate tips in the past. The tip contained a good bit of detail, and the reporter checked a significant percentage of the details offered with stories in the newspaper files, and he found that the new story did not conflict with any of the file stories he read. This conformity was not surprising, as it turned out that the source, who had made up the story, based the details in the story on items that had appeared in the paper. Finding his initial check of the facts provided confirmation, the reporter did not dig any deeper. He did not check the travel records of either the congressman or the two brothers. Had he done so, he would have found that they were in different places at the time of the alleged meeting. The quarterback, in fact, had been playing in an away game at the time. The schoolteacher had played no role, but he had the same name as an aide to the congressman. Having discovered someone with that name on the congressman's staff, the reporter went no further.

It appears that the reporter has failed to adhere to practices that are the standard within the news industry. Reporters generally would check travel schedules to be sure that a meeting could have occurred. They would also generally allow those targeted in a story an opportunity to respond, and the response would have shown the impossibility of the meeting. A reporter would also usually check to be sure that the schoolteacher who was identified actually had some connection to the congressman, the brothers, or the quarterback.

The newspaper has been sued for libel by the congressman, the brothers, the quarterback, and the schoolteacher. The paper has come to you for an analysis of its liability and all of the types of damages it may have to pay. What advice do you give?

SAMPLE ESSAY

Although this is a libel action, and although the Supreme Court has said in the past that libel is among the varieties of speech not protected by the First Amendment, the First Amendment, as applied to the states through the Fourteenth Amendment Due Process Clause, does place limits on the ability of states to allow recovery for defamation. At least with regard to some plaintiffs, leeway must be allowed in order to shield the sort of debate necessary to consideration of issues of public interest. Otherwise, there would be a "chilling effect" on speech—speech that is important in a democratic society.

Liability and damages will turn on the status of the plaintiffs involved. Public officials and public figures face a different burden of proof in a libel case than that required of private individuals. According to the case *New York Times v. Sullivan*, to recover any damages, public officials must demonstrate "actual malice" on the part of the newspaper. That is, public officials must show that the paper knew that the story was false or had a reckless disregard for truth or falsity. Later cases, one of them involving a football coach and athletic director, made it clear that public figures, individuals who are not public officials but who have attained a general notoriety or who have become publicly involved in the specific issue, must meet the same burden. Private individuals, as demonstrated in *Gertz*, need not show actual malice in order to recover their actual damages. If, however, they seek punitive damages, they too must demonstrate actual malice.

As we turn to the burdens of proof in this case, it is clear that a member of the U.S. House of Representatives is a public official. In order to be a basis for libel, any statements made regarding such an elected official will have to be shown to have been made with actual malice.

The brothers and the quarterback are not public officials, but they may be public figures. Public figures come in two varieties. General-purpose public figures are those who have sufficient fame or notoriety as to be considered public figures for all purposes. They are constantly in the public eye. The capital city football team's star quarterback may well be such a general-purpose public figure. Thus, he too may have to demonstrate actual malice. If the two brothers are not generally in the public spotlight, they may not be general-purpose public figures. They may still, however, be limited-purpose public figures. Limited-purpose public figures have put themselves in the forefront regarding particular issues. The brothers, given their record of campaigning regarding ideological issues and supporting the election of candidates in agreement with their positions, might be seen as public figures on all issues touching on politics and elections. This would seem to be such a political issue, so they too may have to demonstrate actual malice. Of course, if either the quarterback or the brothers are not held to be public figures, they will be treated in the same way as the schoolteacher discussed below.

The schoolteacher would certainly seem to be a private individual. Even if he is a teacher in a public school and might, for that reason, be thought a public official, the allegations have nothing to do with his role as a schoolteacher and do not touch on his capability as a teacher or his relationship with children. He may well not have to demonstrate actual malice in order to recover any actual damages. The Court has said, however, that recovery may not be allowed without some showing of fault. Although he cannot be awarded damages on a no-fault basis, negligence is sufficient fault to allow recovery of actual damages. Negligence will suffice for actual damages, unless state law is found to require more. In order to recover any punitive damages, however, the Court has said that the schoolteacher will have to demonstrate actual malice.

We now turn to the level of culpability on the part of the newspaper, where it appears unlikely that actual malice can be established. Neither the newspaper nor the reporter seems to have known that the story was false. Neither the newspaper nor the reporter seems to harbor doubts with regard to the story that could establish a recklessness with regard to truth or falsity. The reporter relied on the past accuracy of the anonymous informant, and the details that he did check out were confirmed. It would seem that the congressman, the quarterback, and the brothers are not likely to prevail in their libel action.

The schoolteacher is another matter. If he is in fact a private individual, he can recover on a showing of negligence. The reporter may have been negligent, as it appears he did not adhere to standards within the news industry. There are facts he should have checked and individuals with whom he should have talked before the story was published. The schoolteacher may be able to recover damages, but it will only be actual damages. If the schoolteacher seeks punitive damages, he too would seem to be unable to establish actual malice and likely will not be able to recover punitive damages.

SELF-ASSESSMENT

It should be explained why the First Amendment is relevant here. This is not the case of the state directly imposing limits or sanctions on speech, but allowing others to recover damages for speech may also be damaging to the sort of interests protected by the First Amendment. For that reason, the First Amendment and its incorporation under the Fourteenth Amendment Due Process Clause place a limit on libel actions. It cannot hurt to mention the important term "chilling effect" when describing the effect of the restrictions on the speech.

This is a question that required both a discussion of the rule of law and the distinctions to be drawn under that law as well as a consideration of the facts given in order to apply those distinctions. Simply stating that, if the brothers and the quarterback are public figures, they will have to demonstrate actual malice, would be a correct statement of the law. It would, however, not demonstrate a knowledge of the cases regarding determining whether a person is a public figure. Never pass up an opportunity to demonstrate an understanding of the law, at least when that area of the law is relevant to the question, as it clearly is here.

This is also a question for which, at least under the answer provided above, there would not be a cost in coming to a firm conclusion. That is because the conclusions were either clear or were with regard to the final issues to be considered. The place where too-definite a conclusion can lead to a weaker essay is where that conclusion is at an intermediate point. Where there are two or more potential answers and only one is considered, any points that would be available following up on discussion of the other answer or answers are missed. Here the conclusions were either sufficiently clear or came late enough in the analysis so as not to cut off further inquiry.

There is a possibility that you believed that all the plaintiffs could establish actual malice. Although the subjective lack of knowledge or doubt speaks against that conclusion, you would probably still obtain a significant percentage of the points available on this question with this approach. The analysis is usually more important than the actual answer. As long as you distinguished where actual malice was required and provided a statement of that test, your conclusion is likely to be seen as less important.

VARIATIONS ON THE THEME

1. Suppose the reporter, in submitting the story to the editor, had said that there were other sources he should have checked but that he was concerned that a political blog was about to release the story and that he thought the newspaper should try to beat that release.
2. Suppose that the schoolteacher had been a regular contributor to the newspaper's letters-to-the-editor column and that the contributions had been critical of the congressman.
3. Suppose that the source was not anonymous, and the reporter knew that the source was a long-time opponent of the congressman.

Problem 4

HYPOTHETICAL

(60 MINUTES)

The City of Alexander, for a period of several years, saw large reductions in retail sales in its downtown shopping district, which led to a reduction in sales tax revenue. Instead of coming downtown to shop, shoppers were increasingly going to suburban malls. The city, to re-attract shoppers, purchased a large abandoned factory adjacent to the downtown area. Interior walls were built in each of the factory's floors. As a result, each floor contained a central area extending from one end of the factory to the other to accommodate pedestrian movement and smaller 400–1000 square-foot areas to serve as small shops. The city leased the shop spaces to small businesses, with preference given to those businesses selling goods with an artistic quality.

The plan worked. Shoppers were drawn to the artistic shops in the renovated factory, and many would do their more ordinary shopping in the adjacent downtown area. The success of the project also made it a focal point for demonstrations and protests. There were several instances in which large crowds of demonstrators gathered both on the sidewalk outside the factory and in the interior pedestrian areas. Some of the demonstrators were carrying signs attached to sticks. Others carried signs written on cardboard but with no sticks, and still others participated without carrying any signs but handed out leaflets. Several times, persons attempting to cross the sidewalk and enter the renovated factory were hit, either accidentally or intentionally, with sticks holding signs. Furthermore, artists/merchants who leased the shop space complained that, with all the signs, potential customers could not see the stores' own signs or window displays.

In response, the city is considering an ordinance prohibiting the carrying of signs on any form of rigid support either on the sidewalk outside the complex or in the interior pedestrian spaces. The ordinance would also prohibit any signs larger than 1' x 1', whether on rigid supports or not, in the interior pedestrian spaces. Leafleting is not to be addressed by the ordinance. You, as municipal attorney, have been asked for an opinion with regard to the constitutionality of the proposed ordinance. What advice do you give?

SAMPLE ESSAY

The constitutionality of limits on expression varies with the nature of the geographical area in which the restrictions are imposed. In an area that is considered a public forum, the city may impose what are known as time, place, and manner regulations, even when those regulations have an impact on expression. Time, place, and manner regulations must be content independent. That is, they cannot address expression only with regard to particular messages. If the restriction is, instead, content dependent, it will be tested under strict scrutiny: the regulation must be justified as being narrowly tailored to a compelling governmental interest. If the regulation is content neutral, the remainder of the time, place, and manner test requires that the governmental interest be significant, that the restriction be narrowly tailored to the interest, and that there be ample alternate channels of communication. If an area is not a public forum, the test is weaker, but any regulations must still be reasonable.

With regard to the areas at issue here, the sidewalks outside the factory will almost assuredly be held to be a traditional public forum. The test is whether, from time immemorial, the area in question has been one that has been used for expression purposes. The sidewalks and public parks are prime examples of traditional public fora. Applying the time, place, and manner test, the limit on all signs carried on sticks is neutral with regard to the message. The limit is motivated by concern for public safety, growing out of a series of incidents, and that interest is likely to be considered significant. Taking sticks out of the hands of those who might, intentionally or accidentally, injure those attempting to enter the building would seem to be narrowly tailored to that interest. On the other hand, given the impact this would have on picketing generally, a court might not see this as a sufficiently significant public interest or as sufficiently narrowly tailored. There may be an issue as to whether there are ample alternate channels of communications. The ordinance would seem to allow signs not attached to a rigid support, and that might be held to leave open ample alternative channels. Out of concern that a court might not agree, the city might decide to limit signs carried on supports only within a limited distance from the entrance. The increased visibility of the sign on a support, even if a short distance from the entrance, could be seen as increasing communicative possibilities. Limiting the restriction to an area close to the entrance would also bring the regulation in line with a Supreme Court case, *Hill v. Colorado*, upholding restrictions close to the entrance to healthcare facilities.

The public forum status of the interior pedestrian areas is more questionable. Such areas would not seem to be the traditional public fora that parks and sidewalks are. It is possible, however, that a court will consider them to be the equivalent of parks and sidewalks and, as a result, public fora. The Supreme Court has considered the public forum status of the shopping area at an airport and concluded that that area was not a public forum. Airports have not existed long enough to be traditional public fora, and the Court considered the analogy to other transportation nodes to be inapposite, because those nodes were privately owned, and because the issue was airports not transportation nodes. Here the equivalent analogy would be to a downtown shopping area. Both the factory shopping area and the downtown district are publicly owned, so the analogy is stronger, but a court might be persuaded that the issue is not downtown sidewalks but pedestrian areas in publicly constructed shopping buildings.

If the court holds that the pedestrian areas are not traditional public fora, they could still be designated public fora. This will depend on the city's intent in opening the area. The city's position will have to be that it did not intend to open the area with any intent other than for individuals to be able to move freely from store to store. This rationale, along with moving from plane to plane, served to justify limits in the airport case. Even if an area is a designated public forum, it may be a limited-purpose public forum, but the regulations here are not purpose dependent, so that distinction seems irrelevant.

If the court holds the pedestrian areas to be either traditional or designated public fora, the test for the restrictions will be the time, place, and manner analysis discussed above. The analysis for the signs carried on supports will be the same. With regard to the requirement that the signs not on supports be smaller than one foot by one foot (1' x 1'), the intent behind the regulation may be seen as content neutral. The purpose of this regulation is not public safety but visual clutter and distraction from the signs in the stores. Although this might be seen as favoring the commercial messages of the stores over political messages, a conclusion that would lead to strict scrutiny, it seems to apply to all signs, including signs belonging to the stores themselves, if displayed in the pedestrian area, rather than in or on the stores. It should probably be seen as content neutral. If it is content neutral, the next issue is how significant the government's interest is. Given the commercial nature of the venture in response to a downturn in retail sales, it might be seen as a significant interest that potential customers be able to see the window displays of the shops. If so, this regulation will be seen as narrowly tailored to the interests. If this economic interest is not seen as sufficiently significant, the regulation will fail.

The result may come down to whether allowing leafleting provides ample alternate channels of communication. Leafleting is probably not as effective a form of communication, because someone who would see a sign may refuse to accept a leaflet or, having accepted it, may simply discard it without reading it. On the other hand, adequate alternate channels would seem to require consideration of all channels, not just those within the pedestrian area. The Court, in the airport case, noted that people could still receive the communication as they crossed the sidewalk to enter the airport. The same would be true here.

If the interior pedestrian spaces are not held to be public fora, regulations need only be reasonable. The city's purposes and the relation of the regulations to those purposes would seem to meet that test.

There is also some possibility that a court might consider the issue of communicative conduct. Picketing, in the sense of walking back and forth in front of a target, would probably be communicative conduct. Here, however, the issue is signs, which would seem more akin to traditional expression. Even if a court considered the issue to be one of communicative conduct, the applicable test is so similar to that for time, place, and manner regulations that courts seem to treat the two as interchangeable. The result would probably be the same.

SELF-ASSESSMENT

The first place to be led astray here is on the last issue addressed in the model answer. Although there is nothing wrong with discussing commutative conduct, and a brief discussion was included in the model answer, taking that as the main issue might lead you to waste too much time, and you will not be able to address some of the more important issues raised by the question. While keeping the discussion short, the inclusion of the issue at the end of the answer indicates a recognition of some potential relevance. If time were available, the test for communicative conduct regulation could be presented and applied.

The fact that the question asked about similar issues presented in two different places should have been taken as an indication that the places themselves are important. That would lead to the public forum analysis that was central to the question. Including two places might also be seen as a hint that the answers as to the two places may be different or at least that there are differences in the analysis.

In your public forum analysis, demonstrate your knowledge. Do not just say that the sidewalk is a public forum. Explain what constitutes a public forum, and then come to that conclusion. With regard to a designated public forum, talk about the difference between general- and limited-purpose–designated public fora.

Note the reference to Supreme Court cases in the model answer. Although there are differences between the hypothetical and the cases discussed, the cases have relevance and should be included in the discussion. If you know the case names, include them. But, even if you do not, a reference to the cases by description is worth something. That inclusion demonstrates your knowledge of the case law. The question also asks for your advice to the city, and it would be useful for your client to know that you have Supreme Court precedent on which you are basing your opinion.

VARIATIONS ON THE THEME

1. Suppose that the ordinance completely banned signs on the sidewalk in front of the renovated factory.
2. Suppose that the ordinance, in addition to banning signs in the interior pedestrian spaces, also banned the distribution of literature.

3. Suppose that members of the City Council, concerned about the rights of organized labor, exempted from the bans signs protesting the labor practices of companies with shops in the renovated factory.

Problem 5

HYPOTHETICAL

(45 MINUTES)

The State of Crockett is mostly rural and largely tree covered. Those facts account for a major portion of business income in the state. Tourism is an important part of the economy, with three distinct seasons. The winter attracts snowmobilers and cross-country skiers. The summer brings campers. Autumn draws two populations: those who want to see the fall colors, and deer hunters. In addition to businesses that would usually be considered part of the tourist business, hunting supply stores do significant business in the fall.

Oh My Deer is a group of animal activists who are opposed to hunting. This past fall the group engaged in activities intended to reduce such hunting. One group dressed in costumes designed to resemble deer and stood in front of stores selling hunting supplies. They were largely silent and did not block traffic on either the sidewalk or at the entrance to the store. Nonetheless, a number of shopkeepers indicate that they saw a reduction in business, including people who walked to the store entrance but decided not to enter.

The other group, the day before the opening of deer hunting season, went to areas that were easily accessed from the road and were popular hunting spots. They brought amplifiers and had a recording of a wolf call. They played the wolf call at high volume. The impact was to cause the deer to retreat into deeper woods that were not as easily accessible to hunters. There did appear to be a reduction in the number of deer killed that fall.

The legislature has, in the time since last hunting season, passed two laws. The first law bars appearing on city streets, other than on Halloween, in any animal costume. The second prohibits the use of any animal call or recording of an animal call, other than a duck call, at any place in the state. Oh My Deer comes to you for advice regarding the legal theory or theories on which they might challenge both laws, and the likelihood of success. What advice do you give?

SAMPLE ESSAY

The challenge will be under the First Amendment, as applied to the states through the Fourteenth Amendment's Due Process Clause. Although the freedoms of speech and of the press do not speak in terms of conduct, it is clear that communicative conduct enjoys some protection. The first issue here will be whether the two actions would be considered communicative. To be communicative, the person or persons engaged in the conduct must have intended to communicate a message, and there must be a reasonable likelihood that those seeing the conduct will understand the message. With regard to the wearing of deer costumes in front of the hunting supply stores, it is clear that there is intent to communicate a message to those who come to the store to buy supplies, and perhaps to those driving by on the street. It also seems likely that those who see the conduct will understand its antihunting message. The activity is likely to be considered communicative.

The playing of wolf calls is somewhat more problematic. It seems primarily intended to drive deer more deeply into the woods, but it could also be intended to communicate an antihunting message to any humans who happened to hear the recording. It might be argued that the intent is to communicate with the deer the suggestion that they leave the area. If so, the deer will likely understand the message, although it is unlikely that case law will be found addressing communicative conduct aimed at nonhumans. If it is argued that the wolf call is intended to communicate an antihunting message to humans, that message is likely to be understood by anyone who sees the activist and amplifier and does not believe it to be an actual wolf call.

Because the deer costumes would seem to be communicative conduct, the restriction will be tested under the *O'Brien* test. The most important aspect of that test is whether the restriction is aimed at the conduct or the content of the message. If it is aimed at content, the statute must meet strict scrutiny. If it is aimed at the conduct, the test is a sort of immediate scrutiny test: the restriction must further an important or substantial governmental interest, and the incidental impact on expression must be no more than is essential to further the government's non–content-based interest.

Here, it may be difficult for the government to establish an interest other than in the message. Picketing on sidewalks would normally be allowed, when it does not interfere with traffic flow along the sidewalk or into or out of the business. So, the government's concern would seem to be with the animal costume. It is hard to see what the concern over the animal costume would be other than in the message it conveys. It seems unlikely that a court would conclude that the deer costume made obstruction more likely, especially given the lack of obstruction the previous fall. A court is more likely to conclude that the state's interest is in limiting the antihunting message. If so, the state will have to meet strict scrutiny: it will have to demonstrate a compelling governmental interest to which the restriction is necessary. An economic impact on either the stores or the state tourism industry would not suffice, and the restriction should be struck down.

With regard to the playing of the wolf call, assuming that it is communicative, the state may point to an interest other than in the content of the message. The state's real interest is in loud noises and the limiting effect of those noises on deer hunting. If that interest is accepted as being the aim of the statute, the state's interest may well be important or substantial. Furthermore, it would not seem that the restriction was more extensive than necessary. It is limited to those noises that are likely to have the greatest impact on the deer.

If wolf calls are found to be noncommunicative, the statue would only have to meet rational basis. As plaintiff, Oh My Deer, will have to demonstrate that the restriction is not rationally related to any permissible governmental objective. It is unlikely that that burden can be met, because the restriction serves to protect the state's permissible interest in hunting tourism, and the statute would be held valid.

There is one other potential approach. It could be argued that playing the wolf call is not communicative conduct but is more akin to pure speech. Although those playing the wolf call are not themselves speaking, playing a wolf call, like showing a film, could be seen as expression protected by the First Amendment. If so, it is possible that the restriction could still be justified as a time, place, and manner restriction. The test for justifying time, place, and manner restrictions is similar to the *O'Brien* test. The restriction must not be content-based, must be narrowly tailored to a significant governmental interest, and must leave open ample alternative channels for communication. Here, the statute addresses a particular kind of noise, and although there might be concern over any loud noise and its impact on deer, this particular noise has particular impact. Because the focus on the content of the message is not a focus on human communication, it may not be considered content-based. The statute could then be seen as other than content-based, and both furthering, and in fact seeming narrowly tailored to, a substantial governmental interest. There are also ample alternate channels of communication for the message aimed at humans. Thus, under this test, too, the anti–wolf call statute may stand.

SELF-ASSESSMENT

Again, because it is a state statute, the Fourteenth Amendment must be mentioned in the discussion. It should have been clear that the question involved conduct, but it was also important to recognize the significance, and the difficulty, of the issue of whether the conduct was communicative. In many communicative-conduct situations, it will be obvious that the conduct was both intended to, and in fact did, convey a message. It is, however, always a good idea to consider the issue, even if only to dismiss it in a single sentence or a few short sentences. By considering the issue, you will recognize situations such as this in which the issue merits more extensive discussion.

As there were two scenarios in the facts, you should suspect, or at least consider, that there might be two different analyses applied. The two raised different issues here, so assuming that they were the same would have limited the discussion and led to a failure to consider certain aspects of the answer. It is also important to consider the possibility that any one set of facts might be approached using different theories. Here, the unclear answer with regard to communicative conduct regarding the wolf call led to different analyses, depending on which answer was correct. This is, then, also a situation in which answering the first question too definitely would have truncated the discussion. Because the answer with regard to communicative conduct was not clear, both analytic paths needed to be followed.

The last part of the model answer also serves as an example of what to do when you finish your initial analysis. If you had time, and after discussing communicative conduct, you should have considered whether there could be any additional theories not already covered. Use any remaining time to address those issues.

VARIATIONS ON THE THEME

1. Suppose that the statute prohibited all demonstrations in any downtown business district, adequately defining a business district.
2. Suppose that the statute prohibited all noises above a particular decibel level in or next to any forested area.
3. Suppose that the organization managed to obtain one thousand pounds of offal from the processing of deer carcasses, placed the offal on a tarp on the sidewalk of the state capital, and was prosecuted under a state statute prohibiting causing a threat to the public health.

Problem 6

HYPOTHETICAL

(30 MINUTES)

X-Boxed Wines produces a number of inexpensive, fruit-flavored boxed wines. The wines appeal to a younger group of consumers. Although it is illegal to sell alcoholic beverages to anyone under twenty-one, studies indicate that a significant number of those under twenty-one are attracted to, and are purchasing, the wines. The company's advertising employs cartoon characters modeled after some of the characters in popular video games, including games that the videogame industry rates as being appropriate for younger teenagers.

The State of Fillmore, believing that the advertisements have led to underage consumption of alcohol, has passed a statute prohibiting any use of cartoon figures in the advertisement of alcoholic beverages. The legislative history cites studies that teenagers are particularly attracted to cartoon figures in advertising, and studies that show that teenagers, when they manage to buy alcoholic beverages, tend to buy those beverages that are the most heavily advertised.

X-Boxed Wines wants to challenge the law as a violation of its free expression rights and has come to you for advice. What do you tell them regarding the likelihood of their success?

SAMPLE ESSAY

X-Boxed Wines' expression would seem to be an example of commercial speech. It indicates the offer of goods for sale, whether or not it also indicates the price. Commercial speech is not without First Amendment protection, as applied to the states through the Fourteenth Amendment's Due Process Clause, as long as it is not false or misleading and is for a legal product or service. Alcoholic beverages are legal product for adult consumers, and there is no indication that there are any false or misleading statements accompanying the use of the cartoon characters. Thus, the advertisements do enjoy First Amendment protection, but limits or infringements are tested in a less-stringent way than speech more central to the First Amendment interests.

To justify a limit on commercial speech the state must, under the *Central Hudson* test, demonstrate a substantial governmental interest. The regulation must also directly advance that interest and should not be more extensive than is necessary to serve that interest. Here, the state's interest in reducing or preventing underage consumption of alcoholic beverages is likely to be considered substantial. In a case involving advertising tobacco products, the Supreme Court so held with regard to the interest in preventing underage use of those products, and it would seem that the interest in limiting alcohol consumption would be equally substantial. The Court, in the tobacco case, was willing to conclude that advertising can drive consumption and, hence, limiting advertising is likely to reduce consumption. The same analysis would apply here, particularly in light of the evidence with regard to teenage attraction to cartoon figures and teenage consumption of the more heavily advertised varieties of alcoholic beverages.

The more difficult issue has to do with the closeness of fit between the limits and the substantial interest. Although the Court seems not to require the closeness demanded by strict scrutiny, it was this aspect of the test that led the Court to strike down a ban on the outdoor advertising of tobacco products within a particular radius of schools, playgrounds, and parks. The rule effectively banned outdoor advertising almost anywhere within the major cities of the state, showing a lack of close fit. In the interest of protecting children, it prevented adults from being exposed to information about a product that was lawful for them to buy.

If we apply the analysis to this statute, the impact on the ability to advertise to adults seems less constrained. It is only the form of the advertising that is limited, and the limitations seems to address a form of advertising that is particularly attractive to those for whom the product is not legal. It is true that in the tobacco case, it could be argued that it was a form of advertising (i.e., outdoor advertising) that was limited, but that limit prevented the reaching of adult consumers to a greater degree than the current statute. Where a statute limits only advertising that is particularly attractive to children (unlawful potential consumers), it would seem more likely to stand up to constitutional scrutiny than a ban on advertising more generally.

SELF-ASSESSMENT

First, remember to plead the Fourteenth Amendment, because the challenge is to a state statute. It is also, of course, important to note that this is commercial speech. A failure to do so would likely have led you into a strict scrutiny analysis because the restriction is content-based. Although the substantial interest in preventing underage use of alcohol would probably have served also as the compelling interest for strict scrutiny, the tie between the restriction and the interest must be stronger for strict scrutiny than it is for commercial speech and its intermediate scrutiny test. As you have recognized that commercial speech is involved, state the test to be applied. Where you remember the name of the test, use it.

The question is clearly drawn from the tobacco advertisement case, so that case provides a basis for comparison. When a question is clearly drawn from one of the cases you have read, be sure to discuss the case and exploit any analogy. (Where you do not remember the name of a case, a short statement describing the case, as was present in the model answer, still demonstrates your familiarity with the case law.) It would, however, have been a mistake to import the preemption analysis from the tobacco case. The facts given in the hypothetical provide no suggestion that there is a federal preemptive statute such as the one that limited the application of the tobacco advertising rules to cigarettes. It would also have been a mistake to conclude from the tobacco case that states cannot shield children from commercial speech aimed at products that are illegal for them to consume. You needed to discuss the shortcomings that led to the regulation being struck down in the tobacco case and analyze whether they applied here.

VARIATIONS ON THE THEME

1. Suppose that the statute was applied to a campaign by X-Boxed Wines using the same cartoon characters in a campaign directed to eighteen-to-twenty-year-olds, not intended to increase consumption but suggesting that this group campaign for a reduction in the drinking age to eighteen.
2. Suppose that, instead of the state statute, the federal government passed the ban on advertising any alcoholic beverages in a magazine the readership of which is at least 25 percent under the age of twenty-one. Should that ban survive a First Amendment challenge?

3. Suppose that the federal statute suggested applies only to magazines whose under–twenty-one readership is at least 80 percent. What then?

Problem 7

HYPOTHETICAL

(45 MINUTES)

You are an associate for the law firm that represents the Lakeside School District. You have just received an emergency telephone call from the principle of Lakeside High School. She has told you that, this morning, the school held an assembly for the student body at which nomination and campaign speeches for students running for offices in student government were given. In one of the speeches backing a particular student for student body president, the speaker emphasized the "Nordic good looks" of the candidate. The speaker also suggested that a number of the other candidates "just don't look American." The comments were met with a general murmuring, and several students seemed visibly upset.

The teacher who was assigned as the sponsor of student government had required that all speeches be submitted in advance. She had read the speech in question and had told the speaker that it would be in violation of school rules prohibiting racist or sexist speech that interferes with other students' abilities to obtain an education and participate fully in the activities of the school. She told the student to write a new speech and submit it to her. The student did so, and the new speech was approved, but at the assembly the student delivered the original speech.

The principal wants to impose some sort of punishment on the offending student, but she is concerned that she might run afoul of the student's First Amendment rights. She indicates that she does not believe the students actually have any free-speech rights in school, but she said she wants to check with you prior to imposing any punishment on the student. Are there any questions you might want to ask her, and what advice do you give?

SAMPLE ESSAY

First, it is not correct that students enjoy no First Amendment protection while in school. As the Supreme Court said in *Tinker*, students and teachers do not lose their First Amendment rights at the schoolhouse gate. But, those rights may not be the same as would exist outside the school setting. *Tinker* did involve core First Amendment speech, as it grew out of a protest against U.S. involvement in Vietnam. Although the speech at issue here may not be political in the same sense, the speeches were a part of student government, and *Tinker* might not be easily distinguished on that basis.

Probably the most important question to ask is whether there has been a history of racial disturbances at the high school. *Tinker* said that speech that interfered with the work of the school or the rights of others could be limited in the school setting. Although the school could not suppress speech out of speculation, if it could reasonably expect a real and substantial disruption of the educational process, speech could be limited. If we apply that rule to these facts, if there was concern that the speech would lead to a racial disturbance, it could be limited. And, the student, having been told that the speech was unacceptable, would have been in willful violation of the rule and could be punished. The best evidence that there was a real and substantial concern that the speech would cause a disturbance would be a history of such racial disturbances. If there is such a history, the principal is on solid ground in punishing the student. But, even if there is no such history, the principal may have the latitude to impose some sort of punishment.

The case that seems most on point here is *Bethel School District v. Fraser*, a case also involving a student assembly speech nominating someone for student government. There the speech, rather than containing material of racial concern, involved sexual metaphor. The circumstances, otherwise, seem the same, and the Supreme Court allowed the imposition of punishment in that case. The difference that does exist may be important, because the Court seems more willing to limit children's exposure to sexual speech than speech on other topics, but there are solid arguments that *Fraser* should apply.

The *Fraser* Court expressed concern that the speech there would be insulting to female students, and the speech here would be similarly insulting to students of non-European, or even non-Nordic, extraction. But, clearly not all insults lose First Amendment protection throughout school property. An important point, here, is that this speech did not occur just anywhere on school property. It was at a student assembly, and the speech might be seen as, in some sense, school sponsored. As with school newspapers, a school may have more latitude in regulating speech that could be seen as the school's, or at least as school sponsored.

There is one more recent case that may have relevance. In the "Bong Hits 4 Jesus" case, *Morse v. Frederick*, the Court held that a school principal had not violated the First Amendment rights of a student who was punished for displaying a banner with that message at a school-sponsored event. The Court said the school could punish speech that interfered with its educational mission, and included in that mission was conveying an anti-drug message. There was a necessary concurrence in that case that would place a limitation on the scope of the sort of "educational mission" that can be protected through the suppression of speech. A school could not declare its educational mission to include a political or moral position and suppress speech contrary to that position. That does not appear to be what the principal is attempting to do here. Although a rejection of racism clearly has political and moral dimensions, the case seems closer to *Fraser* then to the concurrence's concerns.

The principal can clearly take steps to disassociate the school from the speech. That could include an official rejection of the sentiments expressed and an apology to those who may have been offended. But, it would also seem that the principal can impose some disciplinary action on the offending student.

SELF-ASSESSMENT

Most questions on law exams will present situations that fall between the decided cases. It is important to try to identify all the cases that might be anywhere near on point and bring them into the answer. Here, *Fraser* is sufficiently close on its facts that one might ignore the other cases. But, bringing those cases into the discussion demonstrates a broad knowledge of the case law in the area. Of course, some judgment is required. Here, you would not want to waste time discussing all the important First Amendment cases, but starting with *Tinker* is a good idea. It is the foundational case in the area of in-school speech and a good beginning point. It also raised the issue of whether its test could be met, and the question for the principal that that raised. Not looking to the more general case and starting with

Fraser would have led away from another theory on how to resolve the issue. And, it would not have addressed the issue of what question to ask the principal.

It is also important to look at the principles that underlie cases. *Fraser* was about indecent speech in schools. If the point of the case was read too narrowly, the discussion of its extension to the hypothetical would have been missed.

The discussion of *Morse v. Frederick*, the bong hits case, also raises the issue of when to discuss a concurrence or a dissent. Dissents may not be worth much consideration unless a case can be made that the Court is moving in that direction. There is, nonetheless, nothing wrong with the discussion of a dissent, if there is time available and it is clearly indicated that it is a dissent. Even then, any relevance should be explained. It should also be recognized that it is to be undertaken only if there is time. If time is short, other discussions are likely to yield more points. Some of the same general points may be made for a concurrence, but there is an exception that is relevant here. Sometimes a concurrence is very important in explaining a decision. That was the case here, where a portion of the Court necessary to make up the majority wrote on the limits of the decision of the Court. Without the concurrence, the majority would only have been a plurality, so what the concurrence had to say was important and worth discussing in an answer.

VARIATIONS ON THE THEME

1. Suppose that the speech had emphasized the candidate's record of standing up to the school administration in support of student rights.
2. Suppose that, instead of commenting on the student's ethnic characteristics, the speech focused on the candidate's experience working for a political group, the major focus of which was opposition to affirmative action.
3. Suppose that the comments were not made in an assembly and that the student had, instead, stood up in the school cafeteria and made the same assertions.

D. OPTIONAL READINGS

The following sources present the topics covered in this chapter in more depth than the chapter introduction. The sources are in increasing levels of detail. The first provides an overview, the second provides more detail, and the third and fourth provide the greatest coverage of the material.

MICHAEL C. DORF & TREVOR W. MORRISON, CONSTITUTIONAL LAW (2010), 157–71.

ERWIN CHEMERINSKY, CONSTITUTIONAL LAW: PRINCIPLES AND POLICIES (4th ed. 2011), chapter 11, §§ 1–4, 6.

JOHN E. NOWAK & RONALD D. ROTUNDA, PRINCIPLES OF CONSTITUTIONAL LAW (4th ed. 2010), chapter 16.

JOHN E. NOWAK & RONALD D. ROTUNDA, CONSTITUTIONAL LAW (7th ed. 2000), chapter 16.

10 FREEDOM OF ASSOCIATION

A. INTRODUCTION

The freedom of association is not expressly mentioned in the Constitution, but it is one of the freedoms protected by the First Amendment. Associational freedom is necessary to the functioning of the freedom of expression, which is expressly protected by the First Amendment. Effective expression may well require an ability to associate with those of like belief. Indeed, a right to peaceable assembly is expressly mentioned, although the freedom of association goes well beyond a simple coming together. This variety of freedom of association for political purposes was the focus of *NAACP v. Alabama*, 357 U.S. 449 (1958), in which the Supreme Court held that association rights protected the membership list of the NAACP from compelled disclosure to the state.

Cases decided since *NAACP* have involved a right not to be associated with particular ideas or expression. There have been challenges, for example, to public employees being required to pay union dues when those dues are used to further the political goals of the unions. The dues requirements forced public employees to support ideas with which they might disagree. Although public employees may be required to support the nonpolitical purposes of their unions, they could not be forced to pay that percentage of dues that would go toward political ends. A similar result was reached with regard to dues to a state bar association.

Other cases have protected the rights of individuals not to be forced to state their agreement or association with the ideas put forth by the government. Thus, schoolchildren cannot be required to engage in a flag salute, and drivers may not be required to sport a state motto on a license plate.

There are also association cases that turn on a right to be associated, or not to be associated, with groups of people. For example, there are public employment cases in which the Court has held that membership in the political party in power cannot be a requirement for public employment, nor can people associated with the party formerly in power be fired when that party goes out of power, at least when the employees do not hold policy-making positions.

One of the more recent and interesting uses of the freedom of association has been in response to antidiscrimination laws. The right has been asserted when a court or antidiscrimination agency has ordered an organization to accept persons, against whom it had practiced discrimination, as members. These lower court and agency decisions have treated the organizations as though they were ordinary businesses or places of public accommodation. The organizations have gone to federal court, arguing that these applications of the statutes, though consistent with the terms of antidiscrimination law, were violations of the organizations' associational rights. That is, the organizations have argued that their freedom of association includes a right to discriminate. or more accurately a freedom not to associate on a particular basis.

B. READINGS

Before attempting the problem below, read the following material. If you have already read some of the material, review it. If you are working with a casebook, the book's edited copies should be adequate. If you are not working with a casebook, or if your book is missing one or more of the cases, the jump cites provided will guide you to the relevant material.

Wooley v. Maynard, 430 U.S. 705, 706–10, 713–17 (1977).
Rumsfeld v. Forum for Academic and Institutional Rights, 547 U.S. 47, 51–70 (2006).
Hurley v. Irish-American Gay, Lesbian and Bisexual Group of Boston, 515 U.S. 557, 559–80 (1995).
Abood v. Detroit Board of Education, 431 U.S. 209 (1977)
Keller v. State Bar, 496 U.S. 1, 4–17 (1990).
Johanns v. Livestock Marketing Ass'n, 544 U.S. 550, 553–67 (2005).
Rutan v. Republican Party of Illinois, 497 U.S. 62, 64–79 (1990).
Roberts v. United States Jaycees, 468 U.S. 609, 612–40 (1984).
Boy Scouts of America v. Dale, 530 U.S. 640, 643–61 (2000).
Christian Legal Society v. Martinez, 130 S.Ct. 2971, 2978–95 (2010).

C. PROBLEMS

Problem 1

HYPOTHETICAL
(30 MINUTES)

The Hart Club is an organization that, in its bylaws, limits its membership to males. The bylaws also limit the number of members to a maximum of one hundred, and the actual number of members has varied, over the past ten years, between eighty-three and ninety-seven. An invitation to join the organization requires a 90 percent positive vote of the present members. The organization owns a house in a forested area and holds retreats there one weekend each month. Members must attend at least nine of the twelve retreats each year.

The organization also engages in political activity. Its bylaws state that the organization is dedicated to preserving what is "the rightful dominance of males in family and community life." To that end, it has endorsed candidates taking positions against gender-based affirmative action and antidiscrimination laws.

The members of the organization typically are prominent members of the business community. Relationships among the members have led to business opportunities for the individuals and business deals between the companies for which they work. The organization itself also engages in a form of business. Because the retreat house is used only one weekend per month, it is operated for the remaining time as a bed-and-breakfast. The organization hires a property manager to run the bed-and-breakfast and provide services for the retreats. The income more than covers the cost of the house, and the surplus is used to fund the organization's political activities.

The state's antidiscrimination agency, noting the membership and bylaws, and having determined that the Club is a "place of public accommodation," has ordered the Club to cease in its discrimination against females. Rather than comply, the Club has filed suit in federal court alleging that the state order violates the constitutional rights of the organization and its members. You are a clerk for the federal judge assigned to hear the case and have been asked to write a memorandum on the issues presented. Discuss those issues.

SAMPLE ESSAY

The Hart Club's cause of action will arise under the First Amendment as applied to the states through the Fourteenth Amendment Due Process Clause. The First Amendment has been held to contain a freedom of association that includes, at least under certain circumstances, a right not to associate with others. If an order issued under a state statute violates that right, the order is constitutionally invalid.

Not all organizations enjoy this right: it is a right enjoyed only by two kinds of associations. The first is an intimate association. In a Supreme Court case, *Roberts v. United States Jaycees* (1984), the Jaycees were held not to be an intimate association because of the organization's size and the fact that it was generally open to all males within a certain age range. Being an intimate association requires that the association be small enough to allow a certain amount of intimacy among the members. It also requires a level of exclusivity befitting an association in which the members will have such close relationships. The Hart Club would seem both small enough and sufficiently exclusive to be considered an intimate association. The fact that the members spend a weekend together each month adds strength to that conclusion.

The other sort of organization to possess a sufficient freedom of association as to allow discrimination is an expressive association. This is exemplified by the Boy Scouts' case, *Boy Scouts of America v. Dale* (2000), in which the Supreme Court accepted the Boy Scouts' assertion that it had as a part of its mission the spreading of a message, at least among its members, of a philosophy at odds with the inclusion of an openly gay male in its leadership. Here, the Hart Club is organized, in part, to advocate male dominance. Although having female members might not be the direct conflict the Boy Scouts asserted, being forced to include females arguably weakens the Club's ability to assert its position.

Under either analysis, it would appear that the Hart Club would enjoy freedom of association that would be violated by the order of the state antidiscrimination agency. The only caveat here is with regard to the business aspects of the organization. Certainly, a large business could not simply add a statement of male dominance to its business mission and then be allowed to discriminate on the basis of gender. But, the Hart Club is not a large business. It is, nonetheless, a business in that it runs a bed-and-breakfast. Although it could not discriminate in the actual operation of the business by, for example, refusing to rent rooms based on race or gender, the question is whether it can discriminate in what is essentially ownership. That may not be clear. But, if the organization is nonprofit, it might be seen to be similar to the nonprofits that were parties to the other cases. The other business aspect involves the business contacts made through the organization. In that regard, the Hart Club would seem similar to any exclusive country club. The fact that members make business contacts would seem unlikely to cost the club its freedom of association.

Once it is determined that there has been an infringement of the club's freedom of association, it would seem that the state should be allowed the opportunity to try to pass the strict scrutiny test by demonstrating that the order issued was necessary to a compelling governmental interest. The state might argue that the elimination of discrimination is a compelling governmental interest to which this order was necessary. But, the Supreme Court cases also involve discrimination, and the cases turned on the nature of the association rather than the state's interest. This might be an indication that limiting private discrimination, when an organization has the freedom of association, is not an adequate interest.

SELF-ASSESSMENT

It is important to include the Fourteenth Amendment in the analysis here. The First Amendment applies to the federal government, and the Fourteenth Amendment is required to make it applicable to the states. It is also important to discuss alternative theories. Even having concluded that the Hart Club is an intimate association, and recognizing that that might be sufficient to resolve the case, there will likely be points available for discussion of the club's status as an expressive association. The facts regarding the size, selectivity and closeness of members should have made consideration of intimate association clearly necessary. But, there was a reason you were provided with facts regarding the club's political positions. The idea was to lead to the discussion of expressive association. Citations to cases, even by description if not by name, also demonstrate knowledge in the area.

In answering any question, it is important to at least think about all the facts that are given. Although, sometimes, facts may be thrown in as red herrings, do not simply dismiss them as such without considering whether they are relevant. Here, the business aspects of the organization provided an opportunity for at least a brief discussion, even without a final conclusion, as to whether sufficient business can take an organization that would otherwise have freedom of association outside of that protection.

VARIATIONS ON THE THEME

1. Suppose the Hart Club also ran its bed-and-breakfast, during non-retreat times, in a discriminatory manner. It would only rent rooms to "traditional families," families that it saw as demonstrating the male dominance that it advocated. Would it be protected in that discrimination?
2. Suppose that the Hart Club discriminated on the basis of race, not gender, but that its political positions were the same. What effect would that have on the analysis?
3. Suppose that the club had one thousand members and, instead of a retreat house, owned a hotel. The members were required to spend six weekends each year at the hotel, but it could be any weekends, so there were seldom any more than two hundred members staying at any one time.

Problem 2

HYPOTHETICAL

(45 MINUTES)

Jefferson State University imposes a mandatory fee on all enrolled students to support the programs of the Jefferson Students Association (JSA). The JSA uses the funds for a variety of purposes. Twenty percent of the funding is devoted to the costs of running the JSA, including advocating for the interests of students with university administration. This past year those interests have included such things as adequate student parking and the quality of care in the university student health center. Ten percent of the funding supports a university legal aid office, staffed by students and the clinical director from the university's law school, that provides legal advice to students. Fifty percent of the funding has been devoted to a speaker series sponsored by the JSA. The administration has required that the JSA, in the selection of speakers, include a variety of topics and present varying ideological viewpoints. The remaining 20 percent of the funding has, over the past several years, consistently been used for political advocacy. The JSA has lobbied the state legislature to increase funds for the University. It has also funded, and distributed on campus, election material favoring candidates who would provide that increased support.

Lisa Libertarian objects to the imposition of the fee. Ironically, she has come to see you, a law student working in the university legal aid office, for advice on whether she can obtain a court order that she not be required to pay the fee. If not, she at least wants to know if she can get some of the fee refunded to her. She asserts that she disagrees with the position of the JSA regarding legislative funding. She has also looked into the speaker schedule for the upcoming year, and she says she disagrees with the positions of half the speakers. You have explained to her that, because of the funding of the clinic, you may be seen as having a conflict, but she has waived any such conflict, as have the university and the JSA. What advice do you give her?

SAMPLE ESSAY

There are cases that at least partially support your position. Although it is unlikely that you would get an order barring the collection of the fee, you may be able to get a partial refund. Because there is state action in a state university imposing a fee, the imposition is subject to constitutional restraints. The constitutional provision at issue here is the freedom of association held to be a part of the First Amendment imposed against the state through the Fourteenth Amendment Due Process Clause. The variety of freedom of association to be argued is a right not to be associated with speech you find objectionable.

One of the cases most on point involves a public school system employee union in which the system required that its employees join the union and pay union dues. When the dues requirement was challenged, the Supreme Court refused to conclude that no dues could be mandated. The union performed services that were of benefit to all employees and were necessary to healthy labor–management relations. The union, though, also engaged in political activities. The school system could not require that school employees support those political activities. Were the employees so required, they would not only be associated with, but would be required to financially support, speech with which they disagreed.

A similar case involves mandatory bar association dues for practicing attorneys. There are bar association programs that practicing attorneys may be required to support, such as disciplinary committees and client reimbursement funds. However, if a bar association engages in political activities, the state cannot require attorneys to support those activities. The remedy, in both cases, was not an order that no dues or fees be collected but, rather, that the portion of the fees that were devoted to political purposes be refunded.

If we apply those principles to this case, there seem to be expenditures that students might be required to support. The 20 percent of the fee that is devoted to representing student interests to the administration resembles the portion of union dues that help maintain labor–management relations, so that support may be constitutionally imposed on the students. The 10 percent that supports the student legal aid clinic may be a little less clear. The funding is not for a program that is intrinsic to the nature of a student association, unlike the labor–management function of the union or the disciplinary function of a bar association. On the other hand, the clinic does not engage in political speech with which you have a right to disassociate. It provides individual advice to students. It seems likely that a court would allow the imposition of that portion of the fee that supports the clinic.

However, the portion of the fee that supports political activities looks problematic for the university and the JSA. As with bar association members or public-school employees, students should have a right not to be associated with, and in particular not to be required financially to support, political speech with which they might disagree. The remedy here, however, would not be an order that no fee be collected but only that you are entitled to a refund of the 20 percent of the JSA fee that supports those activities.

The 50 percent of the fee that support the speakers program is least spoken to by the decided cases. It might be seen as equivalent to support of continuing legal education by a bar association or educational programs provided by the teachers union, both of which would further legitimate goals of professionalism. Here, the speakers program may be seen as a legitimate part of the university's educational program. Although such educational decisions may often be made by faculty and administration, allowing student control over a portion of the university mission would seem proper. Furthermore, there is a difference in how the support is used. With the political speech of the union, the bar association, and the JSA, the member or student is being forced to support the speech of the organization, despite any disagreement with that speech. Here, it is not the speech of the organization that is being supported. It is, in a sense, speech to the organization or the members of that organization. This difference, along with the speaker program's contribution to the education of students, provides support for that portion of the fee.

In sum, it is unlikely that a court will order that the university not impose the free, but it is likely that that portion of the fee that supports the JSA's political activities would be ordered refunded.

SELF-ASSESSMENT

As with the previous problem, it is important to remember the necessity of including the Fourteenth Amendment's Due Process Clause to incorporate the First Amendment against the state. A brief statement that the university is a state actor is also worth making, although any extensive analysis would likely be a waste of time.

Where there are cases you have read that are relevant, it is good to spend some time discussing them. You could, instead, try to reproduce the reasoning that led to those results, but citing the cases and explaining how they are relevant demonstrates a command of the material. It also strengthens your arguments, because the cases highlight the precision of your analysis. It is certainly important, when relying on cases, to explain their relevance. It is equally important to recognize any differences between the decided cases and the hypothetical and to discuss how those differences affect the relevance of the cases and the result under the hypothetical.

It is, of course, unlikely that Lisa is interested in the Fourteenth Amendment incorporation of the First Amendment against the states. In the client discussion asked for in the hypothetical, you probably would not explain it and would simply discuss the First Amendment. Even so, in the context of an exam, demonstrate your knowledge and mention incorporation.

VARIATIONS ON THE THEME

1. Suppose that the administration had not imposed a requirement that the JSA be ideologically evenhanded in the selection of speakers, and the JSA has for the past several years and for the upcoming year selected only speakers representing a particular political ideology. What impact does that have on the analysis?
2. Suppose the political activities of the JSA were limited to promoting on-campus voter registration and a get-out-the-vote campaign. Are there any differences in your analysis?

D. OPTIONAL READINGS

The following sources present the topics covered in this chapter in more depth than the chapter introduction. The sources are in increasing levels of detail. The first provides an overview and some detail, whereas the second and third contain greater coverage of the material.

ERWIN CHEMERINSKY, CONSTITUTIONAL LAW: PRINCIPLES AND POLICIES (4th ed. 2011), chapter 11, § 5.

JOHN E. NOWAK & RONALD D. ROTUNDA, PRINCIPLES OF CONSTITUTIONAL LAW (4th ed. 2010), chapter 16, §§ 19–23.

JOHN E. NOWAK & RONALD D. ROTUNDA, CONSTITUTIONAL LAW (7th ed. 2000), chapter 16 § 41.

THE RELIGION CLAUSES

11

A. INTRODUCTION

There are two clauses in the First Amendment regarding religion. The first, the Establishment Clause, prohibits Congress from passing any law regarding an establishment of religion. The second, the Free Exercise Clause, bars laws, again those passed by Congress, infringing upon the free exercise of religion. Both are incorporated against the states through the Due Process Clause of the Fourteenth Amendment. It is also important to note that it is not only laws that are addressed. Practices in, for example, public schools must also comport with the requirements of the religion clauses.

Regarding the Establishment Clause, there are a number of tests that may apply to a particular factual setting. In fact, in some settings they may all need to be analyzed and applied. In the readings that are listed below you will find the *Lemon* test, the oldest of the tests that apply, as well as the endorsement test and the coercion test. When addressing an issue in which any one of the tests might apply, all three should be considered; some justices use one, others the second, and still others may use the third. You need to be familiar with all three. In addition to the three mentioned, there are situations in which the Court has applied a neutrality test. These are situations in which support does end up going to religious institutions, but the government is neutral and the determination as to how much support goes to each religion is the result of individual decisions made by, for example, parents using publicly funded school vouchers to send their children to a school of their choice, even when that choice is a religious school.

With regard to the Free Exercise Clause, there has been a general weakening of the protection the clause affords. As the law now stands, the general application of neutral criminal laws is not thought to raise any First Amendment problem at all, although as you will see, there may be heightened scrutiny when a law limits free exercise, while at the same time impacting some other constitutional right. The Free Exercise Clause is violated when the law prohibits the performance of an act specifically because of its religious nature. Such a law is not general and neutral in its application.

B. READINGS

Before attempting the problems in this section, read the following material. Actually, you may have already read most, if not all, of the cases. If you have a casebook, the edited copies found there will be adequate. If not, or if your casebook does not contain one or more of the cases, the jump cites are provided to guide you to the relevant material in the full reports.

Lynch v. Donnelly, 465 U.S. 668, 670–94 (1984).
Allegheny County v. American Civil Liberties Union, 492 U.S. 573, 578–679 (1989).
Lee v. Weisman, 505 U.S. 577, 580–99 (1992).

McCreary County v. American Civil Liberties Union, 545 U.S. 844, 850–85 (2005).
Van Orden v. Perry, 545 U.S. 677, 681–705 (2005).
Zelman v. Simmons-Harris, 536 U.S. 639, 643–63 (2002).
Locke v. Davey, 540 U.S. 712, 715–25 (2004).
Employment Division v. Smith, 494 U.S. 872, 874–90 (1990)
Church of Lukumi Babalu Aye, Inc. v. Hialeah, 508 U.S. 520, 523–47 (1993)

C. PROBLEMS

Problem 1

HYPOTHETICAL
(30 MINUTES)

The City of Vernal has, for the past dozen years, sponsored a spring sidewalk sale for merchants in the downtown area. For a number of years there was an increase in the number of customers shopping in the area around the town square, but over the past couple of years, sales have fallen off. The City Council, believing that the sidewalk sale had simply lost some of its novelty, decided to erect on the town square a display that it characterized as a "Springtime Celebration." The display has been put up each year for the past four years and has again increased the number of shoppers.

The display consisted of a number of things. There is a large robotic talking Easter Bunny and a number of colorful oversized plastic eggs. There is also a maypole festooned with brightly colored ribbons. Flowerbeds have been established in the square, and they have been planted with spring blooms. Additionally, several plant nurseries were recruited to sell flowering plants alongside the merchants already located in the area. The display has also included, in a central location, an 8-foot-tall Crucifix, a depiction of Christ on the cross. In one corner of the square, there is a natural rock formation. An artist volunteered to paint the illusion of a cave in the rock, and the large artificial rock was placed next to the seeming opening. Above that false opening was painted the sentence "He is risen."

The timing of the display has varied somewhat from year to year. It has, however, each year been scheduled so as to include both the first day of spring and Easter Sunday.

A national public interest group dedicated to the separation of church and state has engaged you to file suit to have the entire display removed. How do you analyze the situation?

SAMPLE ESSAY

The display raises an issue under the Establishment Clause, as applied to the states through the Due Process Clause of the Fourteenth Amendment. Given the cases in that area, there are three tests that might be applied. The first is the *Lemon* test that asks whether there is a secular purpose, whether the primary effect is the advancement or inhibition of religion, and whether there is an excessive entanglement between church and state. In looking for secular purpose, there is an issue over how narrow or broad that examination should be. If the question is the existence of the springtime display generally, there appears to be a secular purpose in attempting to bring more shoppers to the downtown area. If the issue is framed as the inclusion of the Crucifix and the depiction of an empty tomb, there may not be a secular purpose. These are explicitly religious images, and the purpose of including them might be held to be religious. Much the same can be said with regard to primary effect. The primary effect of the display as a whole may be to increase downtown shopping. The primary effect of the inclusion of the Crucifix and tomb are likely an advancement of religion. The third prong, excessive entanglement, seems to be less of concern, as there is no indication that either church or state are interfering with the operation of the other.

The second potential test is the endorsement test, which would ask if the display is an endorsement of religion. Does it indicate to believers that they are political insiders, and to nonbelievers that they are political outsiders? The inclusion of these strongly Christian symbols could well be seen as an endorsement. This is particularly true of the Crucifix, given its size and central location. Location has made a difference in Christmas displays, where a nativity scene simply set among many other displays was not seen as a violation of the Establishment Clause, whereas a nativity scene placed by itself in the central staircase of a courthouse was a violation. Although the seeming tomb may seem to be a closer question, given its lack of centrality, its explicitly religious message is likely to be taken as an endorsement.

The third potential test is the coercion test. Religious invocations have been held to fail this test when the price of avoiding the religious speech is being unable to attend something as important as a school graduation. The brevity of the display seems to make a difference in this test. Although it has been suggested that a Latin cross placed on the top of City Hall would constitute coercion, holiday displays seem noncoercive.

It should be noted that there is a great difference between the inclusion of a nativity scene in a winter holiday display and of the inclusions here. Christmas has become, to a large degree, a secular holiday; it is celebrated by people who are not Christian. There is, at least, a general celebration in the last week or two of the calendar year. Displays that recognize and further that celebratory feeling are not necessarily religious in nature. The inclusion of a nativity scene in the display has been seen as simply a reminder of the historical origins of the now-secular holiday. Under what is sometimes referred to as the "plastic reindeer test," a nativity scene surrounded by sufficient symbols of the secular holiday is not a violation of the Establishment Clause. The difference here is that Easter is not, by any measure, a secular holiday. Thus, surrounding symbols of the religious holiday by other indicia of spring may not be sufficient to avoid a violation of the Establishment Clause. The Crucifix is not a historical explanation of the origins of the societal inclination to celebrate spring. It remains a purely religious message.

SELF-ASSESSMENT

Although it would be clear that this is a case to be resolved under the religion clauses, it may not be clear, without some thought, which clause applies. Because this is not an instance of a government attempting to stop someone's religious practice, the Free Exercise Clause does not apply. Rather, it is a case involving government activity that has a religious tie, and the Establishment Clause is the appropriate analysis. Do not forget to include the Fourteenth Amendment as incorporating the First Amendment.

The major likelihood of error here would be in the assumption that the hypothetical is conceptually identical to the Supreme Court cases regarding nativity scenes. It did raise similar issues: the existence of a plastic, robotic Easter Bunny and colorful Easter eggs might be seen as sufficiently similar to the inclusion of a talking Santa Claus, reindeer, a wishing well and carolers to make the results the same. But, it is critical to recognize the importance of the fact that the Court recognized that Christmas has become celebrated as a secular holiday. If Christmas is celebrated by non-Christians, and the nativity scene is not the major focus and serves as a historical explanation, there is no violation of the Establishment Clause. Easter has not reached any secular status. It is celebrated only by Christians, so its inclusion is an explanation only of the religious holiday and not of any secular celebration.

It is also important in this area to apply all three of the tests that have been employed by the Court. The discussion of only the *Lemon* test would provide an incomplete answer. There are certainly points available for explaining and applying the endorsement and coercion tests. Do not leave those points on the table.

VARIATIONS ON THE THEME

1. Suppose the Crucifix was not part of the display, but the inclusion of the empty tomb and the "He is risen" legend remained in the corner of the square. What impact would that have on the analysis?
2. Suppose that the Crucifix was gone, the empty tomb remained, and a depiction of a Passover seder meal was included. The timing was also adjusted to ensure that the date of Passover was included. Any difference in results?
3. Suppose that the Crucifix was gone, there was no painting of an empty tomb, and the seder had not been added. What was left was the Easter Bunny, eggs, maypole and flowerbeds. What result then?

Problem 2

HYPOTHETICAL

(60 MINUTES)

The New Wave Movement, which characterizes itself as the religion of the new millennium, believes that God operates through cosmic forces and that there are places on earth that are critical points for this cosmic energy. The leader of the Movement has identified the peak of Mount Jackson, just outside the town of Marshall, as the strongest such site in the United States. The leader has determined that all children born to members of the Movement must be brought, within the first year of life, to the mountain peak and be dedicated to God. The identification by the religious centrality of Mount Jackson has drawn adherents to the New Wave Movement to come to live in Marshall, where they have developed a community on land owned by the Movement.

There has been a cultural clash between long-time residents of Marshall and the newcomers. The residents demanded of the city council that it do something to stop the growth of this new population. The council responded that it wanted to comply with the wishes of the long-time, and still majority, population, but that there was nothing it could do. The houses that had been built in the new community were in keeping with the zoning ordinance in effect at the time of construction. The New Wave Movement's church building had been constructed under the same requirements as all such facilities.

The presence of the Movement in Marshall has also drawn the curious. A significant number of people have come to the town to see the way of life of members of the Movement. The tourists have also taken to hiking the relatively easy foot trail to the peak of Mount Jackson. The result has been some minor degradation of the environment not involving irreparable damage or stress on any endangered species.

The town decided to build a mayor's retreat, named Camp Dave, just below the peak. It has established, "for security reasons," a no-trespass zone around the camp large enough to include the peak. In addition to security, the town indicated a need to protect the wild habitat. There are criminal penalties for anyone entering the zone other than city employees and invited guests.

The leader of the New Wave Movement has filed suit in federal court asking for an injunction against enforcement of the trespass law against adherents to the religion making their obligatory trek to the mountaintop to dedicate their children to God. You clerk for the judge hearing the case and have been asked for a pretrial memo setting out the constitutional issues the case may raise. What advice do you provide?

SAMPLE ESSAY

The major constitutional issue here arises under the Free Exercise Clause of the First Amendment, as applied to the states through the Due Process Clause of the Fourteenth Amendment. Members of the New Wave Movement are being prevented from engaging in an activity required by their religion. Although that is clearly a limitation on the exercise of religion, it is less clear that it is a violation of their constitutional rights. The case seems to fall in between the holdings of the two major, relatively recent, Supreme Court cases in the area, *Employment Division v. Smith* and *Church of Lukumi Babalu Aye, Inc. v. Hialeah*. Both those cases concern prohibitions on activities that were demanded by, or were an essential part of, a religion.

In *Smith*, individuals lost their jobs as drug counselors because of their use of peyote in ceremonies of the Native American Church. Although they had been in violation of the criminal law, the direct impact of their behavior was the loss of their positions and the denial of unemployment benefits, because the discharges had been for misbehavior. They claimed that the refusal to provide unemployment benefits violated their free exercise rights. The Court held that they were not protected by the Free Exercise Clause. Where a neutral criminal statute of general application prohibits an activity, the Court saw no constitutional issue. The fact that exercise was impacted made no difference.

In *Hialeah*, the city had prohibited animal sacrifice for religious purposes. The impact was on practitioners of Santeria, who could not engage in the sacrifice of chickens within the city limits. The Court saw this as other than a neutral statute of general application. It did not prohibit killing chickens for other purposes; it was only the religious killing of chickens that was banned. Thus, the Free Exercise Clause does provide some protection for religion, but only where a prohibition that limits exercise is specifically aimed at religion. Impact from a statute lacking that aim does not rise to the level of a constitutional violation.

Of course, where *Smith* applies, the statute or ordinance must still meet rational basis. And, where *Hialeah* applies, the governmental unit should be given the opportunity to attempt to meet strict scrutiny, which it is unlikely to be able to do if the statute is really aimed at religion.

The trespass ordinance at issue in this case seems to fall between the two Supreme Court cases. It is, on its face, neutral and generally applicable. So, under

Smith, it would seem to raise no issue under the Free Exercise Clause. But, unlike the statute in *Smith*, the ordinance here may be seen as aimed at the religious group. In *Smith*, the impact was the result of the inclusion of peyote in a list of generally prohibited drugs. There was no indication that the law was motivated by a desire to harm the religion, and impact was not sufficient. Here, given the history of interaction between the town and the religion, political pressure to limit the activities of the religion, and community dislike for adherents, the ordinance could well be seen as aimed at the religion. The incidental impact on the curious who also hiked to the mountaintop may not make this a law of general application, if the ordinance was motivated by religious animosity.

Looking at *Hialeah*, the ordinance there was, on its face, aimed at religion: it banned the religious sacrifice of animals. The ordinance in this case lacks that clarity of motivation on its face. Nonetheless, if it is aimed at religious practices because of some dislike for those religious practices, it should probably be seen as running afoul of the Free Exercise Clause. A willingness to have some minimal impact on others by using more general language should probably not affect the conclusion that the ordinance was aimed at religion.

This may then be seen as a case that will rest on factual issues. There must be an examination of the motivation of the town council. The town did declare that it was concerned about security and about degradation of the environment. If these are found to be the actual motivations, the ordinance should be seen as neutral and of general application. They would also satisfy rational basis in that they are permissible governmental purposes to which the trespass ordinance is rationally related. If, on the other hand, it is found that the council mentioned security and environment only to mask its true purpose, discrimination against religious practice, strict scrutiny will have to be applied. Although security may be a compelling governmental interest, it may be a question as to whether the no-trespass zone is necessary to that interest. The possibility of a tighter security perimeter, coupled with perhaps a low likelihood of threat, may make the larger area encompassing the peak too extensive. And, although preventing a really significant threat to environment might be a compelling governmental interest, the threat here seems to be minimal.

One other issue should be considered. The Court in *Smith* explained the heightened scrutiny that has been applied in some of its earlier free exercise cases. Part of that explanation was that some of the cases represented hybrid situations: they combine the Free Exercise Clause with other constitutional rights, primarily the rights of parents in the upbringing of their children. That was, for example, seen as justifying the Court's decision allowing Amish families not to send their children to school beyond the eighth grade.

It might be argued that this case, too, is a hybrid. Although it involves free exercise, the prohibition prevents parents from bringing their children to the mountain peak, which the religion demands for the children's dedication to God. Thus, there is an impact on decisions of parents with regard to their children. However, it seems unlikely that that would change the outcome here. The concern in the Amish case was with more education somehow interfering with an ability to live well within the Amish community. So the parental concern was not simply religious but was in providing a proper upbringing for their children. Here the parental interest seems a more purely religious interest, so any claim to being hybrid would seem to collapse into a free exercise claim.

SELF-ASSESSMENT

The facts given pretty clearly indicate the relevant cases. It should have been easy to identify the free exercise issue. Remember again that, because this is a state or local case, it is necessary also to include reference to the Fourteenth Amendment.

This is an example of a question in which you may have had more time than you would have thought necessary to answer the question. You might take that as an invitation to answer the question quickly and to leave more time for the other questions. However, it may be better to take the amount of time allowed as an indication of the depth expected of the answer. Here, the time allowed provided for more explanation of the relevant cases than might otherwise have been attempted.

It is not necessary to provide a clear and certain answer with regard to outcome. Having set out the legal issues, given that you are providing advice to a judge, you can discuss (as was done in the sample essay) the additional issues to be raised. The fact that you are asked for a pretrial memo might have been taken as a hint that you were expected to address the issues that needed to be determined at trial.

In discussing the relevant cases, it was important to recognize and present limitations on their application. There were issues, some factual, that raised questions with regard to the applicability of either of the two major cases. There was also an issue, hybrid nature, growing out of the Court's analysis in *Smith* that could easily have been missed. (By the way, the Amish case mentioned in the model answer was discussed in *Smith*. If you are interested in reading it, it is *Yoder v. Wisconsin*, 408 U.S. 205 (1972).)

VARIATIONS ON THE THEME

1. Suppose that the evidence of conflict between religious adherents and the town's population was the same as presented, but there was evidence of more serious environmental impact. Before enacting the non-trespass ordinance, the town had heard evidence that foot traffic on the mountain peak was leading to it being denuded of plant life and that as a result, there was a danger of landslide.
2. Suppose that the ordinance did not prohibit trespass but only prohibited the performance of any rites on the mountaintop.

Problem 3

HYPOTHETICAL

(45 MINUTES)

The schools in the city of Lakewood have been failing their students badly. The majority of students in the system have been unable to pass state minimal competency tests at all grade levels for the past five years. As a result, a number of alternatives have become available to parents dissatisfied with their children's education. Several private academies have opened, supervised by local colleges and universities or by boards of interested citizens and parents. In addition, there are a number of religious schools that have been in operation in the city for decades. All charge tuition: less than the per-pupil funding for public schools but more than many parents can afford.

The State of Lyceum, recognizing the problems in Lakewood, passed a law that any student in a failing district, and Lakewood has been held to be failing, may seek alternative education using state funding. The program provides a voucher to the parents of each school-age child in the failing district. Parents select the school they wish their child to attend, and if there is space in the school, hand over the voucher to the school administration. The school turns in the vouchers for funding from the state. Parents may continue to send their children to the public school system, in which case the school system receives the funding. Parents may instead choose one of the private academies, with the funding going there. The Lyceum Supreme Court has, however, ruled that any state funding going to religious schools is a violation of the constitution of Lyceum, and the vouchers may not be used for tuition at the religious schools.

One of the religious schools, and a number of parents who would like to use the vouchers to send their children to that school, have come to you seeking advice on their likely success in challenging the exclusion of the school from the program. What advice do you give?

MODEL ANSWER

The answer here is not clear. It is clear that voucher programs that provide children an education, especially where public education is lacking in quality, are constitutional. The Court has applied a neutrality test in this sort of situation. Although government is limited in the support it may directly provide to religious institutions, in this sort of school vouchers situation the support goes to parents. It is only through the decisions of parents, as to the schools their children will attend, that any money passes through to the religious schools. That is the sense in which the government is neutral. So, if the state of Lyceum had chosen to, and was allowed by its constitution to, include religious schools, there would be no violation of the Establishment Clause of the First Amendment, as applied to the states through the Fourteenth Amendment Due Process Clause.

The issue here is the constitutionality of the exclusion of religious schools. There is a case of at least some relevance. The state of Washington provided scholarships to academically promising students to attend college. But, as required by its state constitution, it prohibited the use of its funds to pursue degrees in devotional theology. The Supreme Court held that this did not violate the Free Exercise Clause. Explaining the interaction of the two clauses, the Court said that there are some actions that the Establishment Clause may allow but that the Free Exercise Clause does not demand.

Although the Washington case might seem to indicate that the state of Lyceum is not required to include religious schools in its voucher program, the issue may be more complicated. As with the Washington limitation, the Lyceum program does not interfere with anyone's ability to practice his or her religion. But, neither program would seem neutral with regard to religion. In fact, the Lyceum limit may have more impact than that in Washington. Under the Washington program, a student interested in becoming a minister might use a scholarship to attend one college, while also, at his or her own expense, taking devotional theology courses at another college. The unlikelihood of schoolchildren splitting their coursework between or among schools, and the seeming lack of provision for such a situation in the voucher program, may make this program more restrictive.

This program may also lack some of the justification of the Washington program. The Court noted general historical concerns over using tax dollars to support ministries. The Washington constitution demonstrated such a concern, and the limitation only with regard to supporting devotional ministry courses directly addressed that concern. Here, children receiving instruction in religious schools, even with neutral state support, would seem far less central to the historical concerns addressed by the Establishment Clause. It may be that the Washington case is not relevant to the results here, and there is some possibility that a court would find the exclusion of religious schools in the Lyceum program unconstitutional under the Free Exercise Clause.

There could also be some relevant Establishment Clause argument. Under the neutrality test, the program is not neutral, but if that test requires only that the government be neutral with regard to funds that end up in a religious institution, rather than neutral in who is eligible to be the final recipient, then the test could be met. Furthermore, under the *Lemon* test, the requirement that the primary effect of the program be neither the inhibition nor the advancement of religion might raise a problem. The primary effect of the program as a whole is to advance education, but the exclusion may be seen as an inhibition of religion. Although the endorsement test has generally been phrased as whether or not there is a message to adherents of a religion that they are political insiders, perhaps this reverse message, if seen as indicating to adherents that they are outsiders, could raise a problem.

Given the approach of the Court in the Washington case, free exercise may be the route to follow here. It is far from clear what the result would be from applying the Washington case's analysis to the Lyceum situation.

SELF-ASSESSMENT

This is a question that falls between two Supreme Court cases and between two provisions of the Constitution regarding religion. It is also a question for which the answer is not clear. Although it is usually the case that the analysis in your essay is more important than the answer, that will be even more so the case here. So the important part is simply to set out the arguments.

It might be tempting to answer this question based solely on the Cleveland schools' case and to conclude that not only may religious schools be included in a voucher program, but that they must be. That would clearly be an unwarranted extension of the conclusion in that case. It might also be tempting simply to apply the Washington case and conclude that the state may exclude religious schools. Although not the logical error of the first possibility, this too would be a mistake. The rationale behind the Court's decision in the Washington case must be examined to see if it applies here.

Where a question falls between identifiable cases from the Supreme Court, demonstrate your knowledge of those cases by indicating, briefly at least, the facts, the Court's holdings, and the reasoning behind the decisions. Once having done that here, it should have become clear to you the difficulties in applying either case. Even if you had not initially seen the complexity of this question, setting out the Court's reasoning would have led to that recognition.

Be sure, at some point in the essay, that you have identified the clauses involved and their application to the states through the Fourteenth Amendment. Although the question called for advice to the potential plaintiffs, and you would perhaps not discuss incorporation with an actual client, mentioning incorporation may be worth a point or points on an exam.

VARIATIONS ON THE THEME

1. Suppose that the Lyceum Supreme Court had instead ruled only that state support could not go toward actual religious instruction. The voucher program required that religious schools receiving vouchers from parents, and submitting them for payment, would self-report the percentage of time spent in actual religious studies, and the state would deduct that percentage of the payment that would otherwise be due.
2. Under the same ruling as in the first variation, suppose the state required that religious schools receiving vouchers must allow state inspectors to visit the schools to make their own determination as to the percentage of time devoted to religion, including time devoted to religion in courses not identified as religion courses, and to make a reduction based on that percentage.

D. OPTIONAL READINGS

The following sources present the topics covered in this chapter in more depth than the chapter introduction. The sources are in increasing levels of detail. The first provides an overview, the second provides more detail, and the third and fourth provide the greatest coverage of the material.

Michael C. Dorf & Trevor W. Morrison (2010), Constitutional Law, pages 171–85.

Erwin Chemerinsky, Constitutional Law: Principles and Policies (4th ed. 2011), chapter 12.

John E. Nowak & Ronald D. Rotunda, Principles of Constitutional Law (4th ed. 2010), chapter 17.

John E. Nowak & Ronald D. Rotunda, Constitutional Law (7th ed. 2000), chapter 17.

MIXED INDIVIDUAL RIGHTS PROBLEMS

12

There has, to this point, been a sort of artificiality in the way that the questions you have answered have been presented. The questions have been contained in chapters with identified subject matter. It was clear that a hypothetical in the chapter on equal protection raised an equal protection issue. Although you had to determine what prong of equal protection analysis applied, the constitutional provision at issue had already been identified. On a constitutional law exam you are unlikely to be given similar guidance. You will need to be able to identify, for example, whether the hypothetical raises an issue of equal protection or of substantive due process or, perhaps, both.

The hypotheticals in this chapter will require you to identify the broad subject matter of the questions. Indeed, they may present issues arising under more than one constitutional provision, and you will need to organize your answers to address all of the issues raised.

Problem 1

HYPOTHETICAL

(60 MINUTES)

The State of Bronchia has become concerned over the effects of tobacco smoke on fetuses and the resulting postnatal effects on children exposed to smoke in utero. Medical studies have established a correlation between fetal exposure to tobacco smoke and low birth weight, and low birth weight is correlated with infant health and a number of developmental problems in early childhood. Scientific studies have demonstrated that this problem exists not only whenever a woman who is pregnant smokes but also that there is no safe level of maternal smoking.

The state has passed a statute that prohibits smoking tobacco products by any woman who is pregnant and who knows, or recklessly disregards the likelihood, that she is pregnant. The statute imposes a criminal penalty. A woman, who has just learned that she is one-month pregnant, has sought an injunction in federal court against enforcement of the statute. What arguments might be offered on behalf of the plaintiff, and how successful are those arguments likely to be?

SAMPLE ESSAY

Because the act is addressed only to women, and there is an intentional difference in treatment, there would seem to be an equal protection issue. Gender discrimination has been held to be subject to intermediate scrutiny. The burden is on the state to demonstrate that the statute is substantially related to an important governmental objective.

It might, instead, be suggested that the classification and intentionally differential treatment is based on pregnancy, rather than gender, even if only women can become pregnant. If so, the level of scrutiny for such a classification must be examined. The first factor in that examination is whether those who are pregnant are a discrete and insular minority. Those who are pregnant are, at any particular time, a minority. The characteristic is also discrete: one either is or is not pregnant. There is, however, a lack of insularity; except in a maternity ward in the last stage of pregnancy, those who are pregnant live throughout society. If we turn to a history of discrimination, there has been discrimination, particularly in the employment setting, against those who are pregnant, although this may have lessened. As to a lack of political power, the analysis may rest on the analysis for women. Most women either have been, or may become pregnant, so whatever political power women have may also speak to representation of the interests of those who are pregnant. Finally, as to an immutable characteristic unrelated to merit or ability, the characteristic will, one way or another, eventually change, although it is largely unrelated to merit or ability.

It may well be that intermediate scrutiny should apply, which would lead to a nice symmetry between this classification and classifications based on the related characteristic of gender. If the class is seen as being suspect, or for that matter if the language in some of the gender cases of "exceedingly persuasive justification" is taken as indicating a more heightened scrutiny, strict scrutiny would apply. If, of course, the pregnancy classification is not seen as suspect or quasi-suspect, and it is based on pregnancy rather than gender, then only rational basis will be required.

First (applying intermediate scrutiny), the state must demonstrate that the classification is substantially related to an important governmental interest. The state's interest is in the health of newborn and the later development of children. Those concerns, and public-health concerns generally, would seem to address at least important governmental interests. The real issue here may be whether the classification drawn is substantially related to those interests. The statute does apply only to women, but women are differentially situated here. Furthermore, the reach of the statute includes only those women who are pregnant, and who know or recklessly disregard the probability that they are pregnant. Those who are pregnant have, through their activities, a particularly strong impact on the fetus and child. A classification drawn on that basis might be held to be substantially related to the state's permissible interest.

On the other hand, a statute could be effective without drawing a line based on pregnancy or gender. A statute that prohibited knowingly smoking within some number of feet from a fetus, written so as to include the woman carrying the fetus, might serve the same purpose. If that were adequate, then although the limits on smoking would be constitutionally acceptable from an equal protection perspective, the classification burdening only pregnant women would not be justified.

If strict scrutiny applies, the state will have to demonstrate that the classification is necessary to a compelling governmental interest. The health of children is likely to be held a compelling governmental interest, and the same analysis with regard to substantial relationship might also demonstrate necessity. Of course, if a court were to see the classification as not at all suspect and apply the rational basis standard, the plaintiff would have to demonstrate that the classification and statute are not rationally related to any permissible governmental objective. In light of the analysis of intermediate scrutiny, the plaintiff would not be able to carry this burden. It would seem fairly unlikely that the equal protection challenges would be successful.

There could also be a fundamental rights/substantive due process challenge to the statute. The plaintiff could argue that she has a privacy right to smoke during pregnancy. Establishing that right would require, first, an analysis of precedent. The abortion cases may well be relevant here. They establish that a pregnant woman has control over her own body and can, up to the point of viability, terminate her pregnancy. It might be argued that, because she can terminate her pregnancy, she can do the lesser harm to the fetus that would result from smoking.

This analysis requires a consideration of the right involved and the state's interest. In the abortion cases, the fundamental right involved the decision as to whether to procreate. That decision was recognized to belong to the woman, unless restrictions were necessary to a compelling governmental interest. The Court recognized two compelling interests: maternal health, which became compelling at the end of the first trimester, and in the potential life or personhood of the fetus, which became compelling at viability.

Here, the health interest is not in maternal health but in fetal health for those fetuses that eventually become persons and the health and development of those persons. This health, as again with public health generally, may be a compelling governmental interest. Furthermore, it may become compelling, not at the point at which abortion becomes less safe, but from conception. If so, the statute addressing only those who know that they are pregnant or recklessly disregard that fact would appear to be narrowly tailored, or necessary, to the compelling interest.

The interest in potential life or personhood of the fetus, that became compelling only at the point of viability, is somewhat different from the state interest in the health and development of those fetuses that eventually become persons. Where the interest is in life itself, the Court held that the interest only becomes compelling at the point at which the fetus is viable. The holding seems to be that, up until that point, the issue is whether the fetus will become a person, and the decision is the woman's. Here, the issue is not whether the fetus will or will not become a person and whose decision that is. Rather, it is interest in those fetuses that do come to term and the health of the resulting child. Assuming that that interest is compelling, it becomes compelling at the point at which it is necessary to address the interest, and that may be far earlier in pregnancy.

Alternatively, it might be argued that there is a fundamental right to smoke. This approach would seem unlikely to be successful. There is no precedent in that direction. Although people have historically been allowed to smoke, it might be seen simply as a failure to outlaw the practice, rather than a tradition of protecting the practice. And "implicit in the concept of ordered liberty" approach would also seem unlikely to be successful. It would seem that a general ban on smoking would match bans on other drugs and alcohol.

SELF-ANALYSIS

The first thing to recognize here was that there is a classification drawn. People were put into two classes, those who are pregnant and those who are not, and are treated differently. That should always lead to, or at least the consideration of, an analysis under the Equal Protection Clause. The fact that the classification is based on pregnancy might have led directly into the analysis of how to determine whether a classification is suspect, quasi-suspect, or not at all suspect. However, the argument that the classification is based on gender was at least worth a mention and gave you the opportunity to demonstrate that you knew the standard that applies to gender discrimination.

The examination of the classification as based on pregnancy went through the usual analysis for determining how suspect the classification is. You might have simply argued that because only women can be pregnant, the treatment of the two classifications should be the same. Even if that is the final conclusion, going through the analysis allowed you to demonstrate that you know how that analysis works.

It is always best not to come to a firm conclusion when the Court has not offered a clear conclusion. By not concluding decisively just how suspect the classification might be, you are able to state and apply all three tests used in equal protection analysis.

The fact that the issue surrounds pregnancy should also have led you to consider the possibility of a fundamental rights analysis. Many of the cases in that area focus on procreation, and that is at least implicated here. It might have been tempting to conclude that, because the woman has a right to abort, anything else is allowed. But a better analysis would look at whether the reasoning of the abortion cases carries over to this case. Whatever conclusion you came to on that issue, the analysis would have demonstrated your command of the material.

The consideration of whether smoking is a fundamental right was saved until last, because it seems less important than the other issues. It is the sort of thing that, if you have time, might be addressed and might earn a few points. It should not take you away from the issues that are more central.

It is also important not to fight the hypothetical. Even if you do not believe that smoking has an effect on health generally or on fetal health, arguing that point is a waste of time. The facts say there is a health effect; accept that and go on.

Problem 2

HYPOTHETICAL

(60 MINUTES)

The University of Pacifica at Barkeley is a state university considered highly competitive in terms of admissions. For a number of years, it has required applicants to have taken four years of high school English, including literature; three years of a foreign language; four years of mathematics; courses in the histories of the United States and the world; a government course; and three years of science, two of which must be biology and chemistry. Three years ago, the university issued a prospective interpretation of its requirements. The more-specific requirements would apply to students then entering their high school freshman year.

Future applicants must have their guidance counselors provide a curriculum guide to the university, so that the content of courses can be examined. The interpretations made clear what sort of courses satisfy the admission requirements. The U.S. and world history courses must cover the topics generally. In particular, several courses taught by several Christian schools in the state, The Role of Religion in the History of the United States and The Role of Religion in the History of the World, have been ruled too specific to meet the social studies requirements. Another commonly taught course in the Christian schools, The Role of Religion in Government, has also been held not to be broad enough in its coverage of government. Although the university has accepted courses in which the Bible is studied as literature, and courses in which a variety of religious texts are examined, the Bible Studies courses at the same Christian schools have been held to be religion courses, rather than English or literature courses. Finally, with regard to the science aspect of the admission standards, the university does not consider any course that does not include the study of evolution to meet its biology requirement, because it considers evolution to be the cornerstone of modern biological science.

The university has also announced that all incoming students will be required to sign a statement asserting their agreement with the theory of evolution. Anyone refusing to sign will be denied the right to matriculate. Furthermore, any student later taking a public position against the theory of evolution will face disciplinary action, possibly including dismissal from the university. The university explains that its reputation as a prestigious scientific institute, acquired through great effort over a long period of time, has been damaged, and the university held up to ridicule, due to student advocacy of antievolutionary positions.

Several students, who are now seniors at Christian schools, have come to realize that they will be denied admission, despite high GPAs and SATs, because the courses they have taken do not meet the course requirements. (There is no notice issue, as the requirements have been in place since they entered high school.) They have filed suit in federal district court seeking an order that the university be required to accept the disputed courses and proceed to evaluate their applications along with those of students from other high schools.

There is also a group of fellow students who have taken both the religious-based courses and other courses that do meet the requirements and are likely to be admitted. They seek an order that they not be required to sign the evolution statement, and that the rule against advocating antievolution positions be declared unconstitutional. You are clerking for the judge scheduled to hear the case, and you have been asked to provide a memorandum regarding the arguments that could be offered and your analysis of the likelihood of their success. How do you respond?

SAMPLE ESSAY

The first issue to be examined arises under the Free Exercise Clause of the First Amendment, as incorporated against the states through the Due Process Clause of the Fourteenth Amendment. The students will claim that the refusal to count the courses they have taken toward the admission requirements prevents them from engaging in activities required by their religion. There are two problems with this approach. The first has to do with the protection the Free Exercise Clause does and does not provide. The second has to do with whether there has, in fact, been any interference with their religious freedom.

In *Smith*, the peyote case, the Court held that a neutral, generally applicable criminal law does not even raise a First Amendment issue. As reinforced by the *Hialeah* case, it is only when a law is aimed at religion that there may be a violation of the First Amendment. Although those cases were criminal ones, it would seem that a criminal statute would have a greater impact on religious practice than this sort of admission requirement, and the result should carry over here.

There may be an argument that these admission requirements are, in fact, aimed at religion, so that *Hialeah* is the appropriate case. In response, the university's position would be that the admissions requirements are aimed at assuring that incoming students have an adequate educational background. Any impact on religion would be incidental.

There may also be an argument that this set of admission requirements should be considered to be among the hybrid situations that were distinguished in *Smith.* Education requirements, as applied against the Amish, were seen as violating a combination of free exercise rights and the rights of parents to determine the education their children will receive. There is, however, a difference here in that students are not being required to participate in any educational program. The university is simply refusing to accept some of the courses they have taken as meeting admission requirements.

There will also be a question as to whether these requirements even have an impact on the free exercise of religion. The students are not prohibited from taking these courses with religious content. The university is simply requiring a combination of courses toward which these at least quasi-religious courses do not count. But, there is nothing prohibiting students from taking these courses in combination with courses that do satisfy the admission requirements.

Even if this were a free exercise concern, the university would have First Amendment principles backing its position. In the affirmative action cases, the Court has recognized that the universities have such a right to take steps to enrich the academic debate. If that interest justifies taking steps to assure a diversity of views in the student body, it might be seen also to justify assuring that all the students admitted have the academic background required for effective participation. This would justify the requirements of certain courses, although it would seem not to justify a position that students who had taken those required courses as well as the religious courses not be admitted.

There might be an argument offered that there is an Establishment Clause issue in that there is an establishment of nonreligion or religions that accept evolution. Although perhaps a weaker argument, it may need to be analyzed. Under the *Lemon* test, the purpose seems to be secular in requiring an adequate academic background. The primary effect also appears to be neither the advancement nor the inhibition of religion. It requires adequate background knowledge and does not prohibit taking religious-based courses. There might be some entanglement with regard to the curriculum guide, but the university is not setting the curriculum, but only examining it to see if it meets the requirements of the university. There also does not appear to be an endorsement of irreligion, in that it is not a general message to those who have religious beliefs that they are political outsiders. Nor does there seem to be coercion in the direction of irreligion, in assuring that the required courses have been taken. All in all, free exercise seems to be the more appropriate issue.

Although it seems that the students are likely not to be successful on this first approach, those students who are likely to be admitted and thus seeking the order that they not be required to sign the statement or refrain from expressing their ideas, assuming they have standing, are more likely to prevail. The standing issue may actually be of concern here, because they have not been admitted at this time. There may be a ripeness concern that would require that they wait until they have been admitted.

Requiring students to sign a statement that they agree with the principles of evolution would seemingly run afoul of the association right not to be associated with ideas. This would seem equivalent to requiring schoolchildren to salute the flag and, thereby, express their agreement with the sentiments contained in the flag salute. It would also seem similar to requiring that drivers carry a state motto with which they disagree on their license plates. In both cases the Court recognized the right to refuse to assert a position. These cases would seem likely to lead to the same result here.

It is true that the state would have to be given an opportunity to meet strict scrutiny. The university will be given the chance to demonstrate that there is a compelling governmental interest to which the requirement is necessary. Requiring statements of patriotism would not seem to be adequate. An interest in reflecting state pride, even coupled with the interest in identifiable license plates, was not adequate in a previous case. It seems unlikely that concerns about the academic reputation of the university would, then, suffice. Even if there is a compelling interest in the academic reputation of the university, it would not seem to be necessary to require signing the statement.

The requirement that students not, after their admission, take public positions against the theory of evolution also seems likely to be unconstitutional. The rule is a ban on speech, and the speech does not fit into one of the unprotected categories, such as libel, obscenity, or fighting words. It is, then, protected speech, and it may be limited only if it presents a clear and present danger of unlawful activity or, in some other way, strict scrutiny can be met. There is clearly no advocacy of unlawful activity, and the same analysis that met the statement requirement would indicate that this limit on speech could not meet strict scrutiny.

SELF-ANALYSIS

First, the essay mentioned standing only very briefly. Certainly, if your Constitutional Law course was not limited to individual rights and included standing issues, you should devote more to this discussion, focusing on the standing of students who have been neither admitted nor denied admission. If standing issues were not included in your course, it took little time to note the standing issue, and it might be worth some credit.

As we turn to the first challenge, it should have been clear that the challenge would arise under the religion clauses of the First Amendment. It is always a good idea also to recognize the role of the Fourteenth Amendment, when the contested action is one undertaken by a state or local government, including an entity such as a state university. Some judgment is required as to which clause to apply. If there is time, it is not a bad idea to discuss both, but put more of your effort into the clause you think more relevant.

In discussing free exercise, there were relevant cases, and discussing those cases shows your command of the material. The cases will also indicate the sort of analysis to be undertaken and the tests that may be applied. The amount of time available for a question is a good indication of the depth expected in the discussion. There was significant time allowed for this question, so it was reasonable to go into as much detail as was contained in the model essay.

The reference in the model essay to the Supreme Court's rationale for its affirmative action decisions may have seemed a stretch, but it did indicate a university interest in the quality of the academic debate. That was also implicated here, so the mention was not irrelevant. Where something is not irrelevant, there is no harm in mentioning it, and it may earn some points.

The Establishment Clause may not have quite the same relevance, but it still leads to a viable argument. That being the case, the only harm that a discussion of the clause can do is to take time that you might use elsewhere. The short discussion in the model answer did not take much time, while demonstrating an understanding of the relevant tests.

With regard to the students likely to be admitted concerning signing statements and not, in the future, speaking against evolution, there were two issues to consider. The hypothetical itself should have led you to realize that it was likely that there would be two theories to address. The facts required signing a statement and not speaking in the future. The existence of two requirements should at least have led you to consider the possibility that they were two different treatments of the issue.

With regard to signing the statement, you should have remembered a case that protected individuals who did not want to be associated with particular speech. Briefly discussing that case (*Wooley v. Maynard*) demonstrates an understanding of the case law and provides arguments directed at the result in the hypothetical under consideration. If you remembered the name of the case, it would be good to include it in your answer. If not, treating it as done in the model answer still shows knowledge.

With regard to the prohibition on future statements against evolution, the free speech issue should have been clear. You should state why the speech is protected (by showing that it is not an unprotected category), and what would be required to justify limits on the speech. Having done so, make sure to take the time to apply the test.

There might have been an inclination here to discuss prior restraints. If you had time remaining, it would certainly be a way to use that time. But, the discussion should explain why this is not really a prior restraint. It is not a requirement that statements be submitted before they are made. It is simply a statement by the university that there will be penalties applied to certain speech. Although that is clearly a likely violation of free expression protections, it is punishment after speech or publication, rather than the prior clearance or the injunction that would constitute a prior restraint.

Problem 3

HYPOTHETICAL

(60 MINUTES)

It is the year 2050, and medical research on reproduction through cloning has progressed in Europe to the point of becoming a regular medical procedure. Human beings have been created from cloned tissue, have been born, and have grown to middle adulthood, with no indication of any medical difficulties or abnormalities. The same technology exists in the United States, and U.S. physicians have learned the techniques used in Europe. No reproductive cloning of humans has occurred here, because such cloning has been banned by the federal Food and Drug Administration (FDA) as medically unsafe. Based on the European success and the number of trained U.S. physicians, the FDA has recently dropped its ban on reproductive cloning.

When the FDA announced its proposed rule change, there was a strongly negative reaction from a number of religious groups. The FDA made the rule change, but just before its effective date, the State of Adams placed its own criminal ban on the procedure, with the law's sponsor saying that, although the procedure may be safe, physicians should not be allowed to play God.

Barbara Baker is a twenty-five–year-old woman who lives in Adams. Her husband and only child were involved in a serious automobile accident. Her husband was killed in the accident and, in the resulting fire, his body was completely incinerated. Their daughter was rescued from the auto before it exploded but suffered grave, and ultimately fatal, injuries. The daughter was conscious and recognized her situation, and that her mother had lost her husband and might lose her only child. The daughter said that she wished they were in Europe, so that they could use one of her cells for her mother to have another child.

Before the daughter's death, several cells were removed and preserved in a manner that would allow their use for cloning. Barbara Baker wishes to proceed with cloning in which she would be impregnated with the clone (her egg with the nucleus replaced by a nucleus from one of her daughter's cells). She wants to have another child. Although she could be artificially inseminated, she wants the child to be both hers and her deceased husband's, and this is the only way to accomplish that goal. Barbara has a physician and hospital ready to perform the procedure, but both are deterred by the state statute. Barbara has come to you for legal advice. She would like an order from a federal court that she has a U.S. constitutional right to proceed, and that the anti-cloning statute is unconstitutional. What advice do you give her?

SAMPLE ESSAY

There are two approaches to arguing the unconstitutionality of the anti-cloning statute, either one of which has some chance of success. One approach would be to argue that there is a non-textual right to reproduce through cloning. The other is to argue that the passage of the statute is a violation of the Establishment Clause of the First Amendment, which applies to the states via the Fourteenth Amendment.

The Supreme Court has provided a model for the analysis that goes into the consideration of the recognition of a non-textual right. The first step in that analysis is an examination of precedent to see if those precedents support the right claimed. The cases recognizing non-textual rights have tended to focus on sex, procreation, and family relationships. The issue here is one of procreation. Most of the cases regarding procreation (those regarding abortion and the use of contraceptives) have seemed to involve a right to avoid procreation. But, there is an early case involving forced sterilization that acknowledged a fundamental right to procreate, although that acknowledgment did not consider technological means. So, there may well be precedent supporting the right claimed.

If a court does not accept that the precedent demands an order barring enforcement of the law, the next step in the analysis is to look at history and tradition. In this step there is a question of how specific the tradition must be, with the Supreme Court looking for rather specific tradition. If the court looks for a tradition of protecting procreation, the cases themselves indicate that it exists. If the court will accept only a history or tradition of protecting the right to reproduce through cloning, it is not likely to find it. Although that history or tradition is lacking because of a now-changed state of medical science, changes in the availability of DNA evidence did not lead the Supreme Court to conclude that a more limited history or tradition should be viewed more expansively.

There may be a middle ground here that would persuade a court, even a court looking for specific history or tradition, to accept that such a history or tradition exists here. The argument would be that we have a history and tradition of allowing reproduction through the use of all available, safe medical technology. When artificial insemination became available, society came to accept it. When in vitro fertilization became available, society came to accept it. There is now a new technology that is also medically safe, and our acceptance of all available reproductive technology would, traditionally, include it.

If the court will find neither precedent nor history and tradition to have established the right, we are left to argue that the right to reproduce through cloning is "inherent in the concept of ordered liberty." In other language, the argument would be that this right is one recognized in all countries deserving to be called free. This is a rather indefinite test, and it is one not liked by judicial conservatives. Nonetheless, there is some chance that a court might accept it. In this regard, it would be useful to note the current prevalence of reproductive cloning in Europe. There are cases involving same-sex activity and the juvenile death penalty in which the Supreme Court, to the consternation of the conservative end of the Court, has looked to the law in Europe and emerging values. The fact that reproductive cloning is allowed in European countries, countries deserving to be called free, and countries that enjoy ordered liberty, might give the court guidance as it did in the Supreme Court in *Lawrence*.

If the court finds that there is a fundamental right, the state would still be given the opportunity to meet strict scrutiny. It would have to demonstrate that the ban is necessary to meet a compelling governmental interest. The only compelling interest here would, it would seem, be one involving health and safety. Public health is generally seen as being a compelling interest, but the ban would not seem necessary to that interest. The FDA has determined that the procedure is no longer medically risky, so if there is a fundamental right, the ban should not meet the necessity requirement. It is true that the Supreme Court, in the "partial-birth" abortion case, did allow the medical fact-finding of Congress to override what seemed to be the view of the medical community, but that was Congress, rather than a state legislature. Furthermore, the statement by the bill's sponsor that the bill should be passed despite the safety of the procedure would indicate that it was not based on medical fact-finding.

If there is no fundamental right, then the law must meet only the rational basis level of scrutiny. Getting the law struck down will require showing that there is no permissible governmental interest to which the law is rationally related. That is an extremely difficult test to meet, and meeting it seems unlikely. The only potential approach would be to argue that the dissent by Justice Scalia in *Lawrence*, the same-sex sodomy case, properly characterizes the majority opinion as holding that morality is insufficient to provide a rational basis.

If the court will not accept that the statute is a violation of a fundamental right, or that it fails to meet a rational basis, it might be argued that the adoption of the statute was a violation of the Establishment Clause. In addition to the statement by the bill's sponsor, the fact that the state law was pushed by religious groups might lead to such a conclusion.

Applying the *Lemon* test, the first question is whether there is a secular purpose to this statute. The statute may well fail this prong of the test. Although many statutes touching on medical issues would seem to have a secular purpose in assuring the safety of patients, the FDA conclusion on safety coupled with the bill sponsor's statement and its seeming initiation by religious groups might be seen as denying that there is a secular purpose. This would put the case in line with Supreme Court decisions holding unconstitutional state statutes barring the teaching of evolution or requiring that, when evolution is taught, an alternative view that at least mirrors the biblical view of creation also be taught. If there was no secular purpose there, there would appear to be none here. There is also a Supreme Court case in which a statute calling for a moment of silence and suggesting voluntary prayer was justified by its legislative sponsor stating that it was his intent to put voluntary prayer back in school. The statement played a role in the Court striking down the moment of silence, and the sponsor's statement could have the same effect here.

If the court were to find a secular purpose, the next issue is whether the primary effect of the statute is to advance or inhibit religion. There is no inhibition of religion, but a ban on the reproductive practices at issue may advance religious views, if not religion itself. Finally, the test asks whether there is an excessive entanglement of government and religion. Here, other than the passage of the statute, neither the government nor religion seems to be engaged in the workings of the other.

An alternative to the *Lemon* test is the endorsement test. That test asks whether the statute could be seen as an endorsement of religion; that is, does the statute send a message to religious adherents that they are political insiders and to nonbelievers, or at least nonbelievers with regard to the particular religion, that they are political outsiders? The adoption of the statute that requires the adherence of everyone to the religious beliefs of a particular group, especially when there does not appear to be a secular purpose, might well be seen as sending such a message.

Finally, there is the coercion test. Although the statute would coerce individuals not to engage in practices that are disapproved of by the religious groups that motivated passage of the statute, it might not be seen as a violation of the test. The test seems to be applied to cases where an audience is required to sit through a religious message in order not to be excluded from an important activity, or cases in which there is a permanent, as opposed to seasonal, governmental display of religion. That may well not be the case here.

SELF-ANALYSIS

The most obvious issue in this question was the existence or not of the non-textual fundamental right. It was clear that the client wanted a court to recognize that she had a right to reproduce through cloning. Perhaps the most likely strategic mistake to have made would have been simply to state that the Supreme Court has not recognized such a right. Although that is true, neither has the Supreme Court declared such a right not to exist. As the question is open, it clearly calls for an explanation as to how rights are recognized. To that end, the model essay followed the route that the Court has taken in a number of cases.

In looking at precedent, be sure to mention any relevant cases. Anything you can do to demonstrate your knowledge of the case law is likely to be recognized. In looking at history and tradition, it was important to recognize the distinction between general and specific. The model answer then showed some ability to think creatively in its attempts to frame a history or tradition that would support the claimed right in a specific manner. Although recent cases do not put much focus on the "inherent in the concept of ordered liberty" test, thinking about that might have led you to consider what those countries with ordered liberty have done and to bring into the argument a mention of the European experience. Mentioning that the Court has looked at practices in Europe justifies that inclusion in the analysis.

There could have been an issue here with regard to any rights the daughter might have had with regard to her genetic material not being used in the procedure. Although there would be nothing wrong with stating that position, any great depth in the discussion would probably have been a waste of time. When a fact is given, at least consider its relevance. Here, the facts indicated that the daughter told her mother that she wished they were in Europe so that her genetic material could be used to produce another child. The inclusion of that fact would seem intended to remove the issue of the daughter's consent from consideration. Anything more than simply stating the concern over the daughter's consent but then noting that consent seems to be there would probably go beyond what was expected and would not be given points.

There were also facts given that would indicate that this was not only a fundamental rights question. The discussion of the activism of religious groups in the adoption of the statute and the statement by the bill's sponsor should clearly be seen as having relevance beyond the issue of fundamental rights. The involvement of the religious group, and the religious statement by the sponsor, should lead you to consider whether there is an issue arising out of the religion clauses.

The decision of which of the Religion Clauses to apply may not have been as clear. Here, the similarity of the facts to the evolution and moment-of-silence cases should have led you in the direction taken. Briefly stating the nature of those cases again demonstrates your knowledge of the case law. After you recognized some potential applicability of the Establishment Clause, it was important to recognize that there are three tests under that clause. All three should have been stated and applied. Even when one of the tests appears to be less relevant, as with the coercion test, stating it and saying why it has less relevance demonstrates your command of the material.

It should also have been clear that the Free Exercise Clause was not really relevant here. No one has had his or her religious beliefs or practices attacked or limited. Had the client somehow asserted that her religion demanded reproduction through cloning, then free exercise would have been relevant, although it would have been dismissed quickly, because the statute involved was neutral (at least with regard to an attack on religion) and of general application.

Problem 4

HYPOTHETICAL

(30 MINUTES)

The State of Alopecia has had trouble providing adequate prison space for its adult convicts and adequate institutional space for juvenile offenders. To address the problem it has turned several juvenile facilities into adult prisons and has turned to the private sector to provide facilities for juvenile offenders.

Corrections Corp. has contracted with the state to operate such a juvenile facility. The residents are all youths who have committed crimes and have been sentenced to juvenile detention. The corporation receives compensation from the state for each juvenile detained. The state regulates and regularly inspects the operation of the facility. In addition to state regulations regarding the operation of the facility, the corporation may also adopt rules for residents, which are subject to disapproval by the state.

Corrections Corp. has adopted rules for the appearance of its residents, and those rules have not been disapproved. One of the rules involves hair length.

Oddly, the rule specifies a minimum length. The director of the facility had become concerned with the number of youths who had shaved their heads, using electric razors provided for facial hair. The concern was that this fashion might be the beginning of a "skinhead" group. Such a group would run counter to the values the facility was trying to teach and could lead to fights within the population of residents. The rule specifies that hair must be at least 1/2-inch long on the entire scalp, although an exception is provided for anyone medically unable to grow hair.

A group of residents has challenged the rule. They claim that their hair length is not intended as a political or associational statement, but they still assert a constitutional right to have short hair. Discuss the likelihood of their success.

SAMPLE ESSAY

The first issue here is whether the Constitution applies at all. The Constitution provides limits with regard to what government can do to, or demand of, an individual; it does not speak to interactions between private entities or individuals. Thus, there must be a consideration of whether or not Corrections Corp. is a state actor and is then subject to constitutional limitations.

Corrections Corp. does, at least with regard to this facility, receive all its funding from the state government. But, there are many companies, such as producers of warships or tanks, that may contract only with the government and that receive all their funding from those contracts, but that would not seem to make them state actors. Indeed, a special needs school was held not to be a state actor even though almost all its funding came from governmental entities. It is also true that Corrections Corp. is subject to regulation by the state, but so might be a variety of businesses that would not seem to be so closely tied to government as to be state actors. Corrections Corp. also has to submit the rules it adopts for this particular detention facility to the state, but utilities usually have to submit rules to state regulators, and it would not seem to make them state actors.

The best argument that Corrections Corp. is a state actor comes from the business in which it is engaged. It is not just that it is a business in which the government is also engaged. Both the government and private entities operate schools and hospitals, but that does not mean that schools and hospitals operated by private entities are state actors. The difference here is that Corrections Corp. is performing an exclusively governmental function. Only the government can commit an individual to a detention facility. In most cases the government commits the person to its own facility. But, when it exercises its exclusive power in committing someone to a facility run by a corporation, that corporation is engaged in such core and exclusive governmental activities that it is likely to be considered a state actor.

If Corrections Corp. is a state actor, then the detainees can argue that there is a violation of their constitutional rights in requiring that their hair be at least 1/2 inch long. Their argument would be that there is a non-textual, but fundamental, right with regard to personal appearance. In analyzing that claim, the first consideration is precedent. The fundamental rights cases tend to speak to issues of sex, procreation, and family relationships. They do not seem to speak to the claimed right at issue here.

As precedent is lacking, the next consideration would be whether there is a history or tradition of protecting the claimed right. There is an issue here with regard to general versus specific in identifying the history or tradition. Although we may have a general tradition of allowing people to make decisions with regard to personal appearance, the examination of specific history or tradition would seem to lead to the opposite conclusion. The examination of specific history or tradition would ask whether we have a history or tradition of allowing inmates, or juvenile inmates, to make their own decisions with regard to appearance. History and tradition would seem to speak in the opposite direction. Finally, with regard to "inherent in the concept of ordered liberty," there may be something inherent in allowing the ordinary person to make these decisions. Here, however, the situation is one in which there is a general lack of liberty, ordered or not.

If there is no fundamental right, then only rational basis scrutiny applies. The inmates would have to show that there was no permissible governmental purpose to which the rule was rationally related. The stated concerns would clearly satisfy that test. If there is a right, then the burden would be on the state or the institution to show that the rule is necessary to a compelling governmental interest. Although a difficult test to meet, it might well be met here. Concerns about security and safety within the prison system would seem compelling, and the only issue would be whether this rule was necessary to that interest.

Given what seems to be a general concession that detention facilities can, for example, limit long hair for security reasons, the result would seem to carry over toward requiring minimal hair length. The only potential difference would be that limits on long hair may be motivated by concerns over objects being hidden in that hair, whereas that concern is lacking here. Nonetheless, the concerns are not simply over fashion but over safety and security. It is unlikely that a court will declare the regulation invalid.

SELF-ANALYSIS

This question requires some thinking about strategy. In many situations, it might be wasted effort to talk about state action, but here there is a real question. You could have gone right to the analysis based on exclusive governmental function, but the model essay, in mentioning and dismissing other potential bases, might well have earned more points. If you were a judge writing an opinion, you might even have skipped the analysis of state action. You could have resolved the case simply by concluding that, even if Corrections Corp. is a state actor, there would be no violation of any individual right. In that regard, the discussion of state action was not necessary. But this is an exam, not a judicial opinion. There were points to be earned for state action, so the discussion was important.

Having resolved the state action issue, you had to turn to the consideration of the claimed constitutional right. Of course, even if you had concluded that Corrections Corp. was not a state actor, you should still have proceeded to the discussion of the potential right, leading into it with "But if Corrections Corp. were to be held a state actor ...."

In terms of the existence of the right, follow the precedent, history and tradition, and ordered liberty analysis. Do not forget the distinction between general and specific history and tradition. As is usual, it is best not to come to too firm a conclusion. You want to be able to discuss the test that applies if there is such a right, and the test that applies if there is no such right.

You may know case law that touches on the issue here. If you read the Supreme Court case involving hair length and police officers in your course, discuss that case and its application to the hypothetical. Never pass up an opportunity to show your knowledge of case law having any relevance to a question.

The time allocated to a question can also be a hint that can help you decide what to discuss and in how much depth. The discussion of the right itself would seem unlikely to take the full thirty minutes. That should be taken as a hint that there should be some discussion of state action. On the other hand, the discussion of state action seems unlikely to have taken thirty minutes. That should lead you to recognize that you should spend some time discussing the claimed right and not simply dismiss it out of hand.

Problem 5

HYPOTHETICAL

(60 MINUTES)

Dire Straights High School has an annual senior prom at the end of the school year. The school has a dress code for the prom that requires the boys to wear tuxedos and the girls to wear gowns. Students may buy single or couple tickets, with couple tickets costing less than twice the price of a single ticket. After a year in which all those who would have bought single tickets paired up to save money by buying couple tickets, the school administration decided that a couple would be defined as a male and a female. The school also said it had a preference for the behavior it found among those actually on dates.

The school also delays production of each year's yearbook, so that pictures from the prom can be included. Yearbook staff, who are enrolled in a journalism class devoted to production of the yearbook, take pictures of individuals and couples at the prom for inclusion in the yearbook, along with pictures and stories regarding other activities from the year.

Sally Sappho is a lesbian member of the senior class. She has informed the school administration that she intends to attend the prom with her girlfriend. She has also said that she intends to wear a tuxedo, rather than a gown. The administration responded by refusing to sell her a couple's ticket, although it said it would sell her two single tickets. They have also informed her that she will not be admitted if she does not wear a gown.

The yearbook staff, in support of Sally, decided to set up its station for photographing couples outside the door to the venue for the prom. That way, even if Sally and her girlfriend are denied admission, they can still have their pictures taken for inclusion in the yearbook. The school administration responded to that plan by telling the staff that, although they can take any pictures they wish, any nonconforming pictures will be deleted before the yearbook is published.

Sally and a delegation from the yearbook staff have arrived in your office seeking advice. Sally wants to challenge the refusal to sell her a couple's ticket. She also wants to challenge the dress code. The yearbook staff wants to challenge the decision to pull any nonconforming pictures from the yearbook. What advice do you give them regarding the arguments available and the likelihood of success?

SAMPLE ESSAY

Sally's challenge with regard to the refusal to sell her and her girlfriend a couple's ticket would seem to raise an Equal Protection Clause problem. The classification involved might be seen as being based on gender. If so, intermediate scrutiny will apply. The school would have to demonstrate that its policy is substantially related to an important governmental objective. Although there is language suggesting that "an exceedingly persuasive justification" is required in cases of gender discrimination, the Court has left the test at intermediate scrutiny. If the school is interested solely in maximizing its revenue, that might not be seen as an important objective. If, instead, there have been concerns over behavior here by couples who showed up, in situations that were not really dates, there might be more likelihood of success. Here, however, Sally and her girlfriend would in fact be there as each other's dates.

It might instead be argued that the classification involved distinguishes between same-sex couples and opposite-sex couples. That would raise the issue of the level of scrutiny to be applied when there is intentional discrimination on the basis of sexual orientation, if indeed this was intentional discrimination on that basis. To determine the level of scrutiny, there are a number of factors to examine. The first is whether those with same-sex orientation are a discrete and insular minority. The group would appear to be a minority, but there is largely a lack of insularity. With regard to the yes-or-no issue of discreteness, there are those who are bisexual, but they might be seen as having both a same-sex and an opposite-sex orientation. Thus, the question of whether someone has a same sex-orientation might be one of yes or no.

A second factor is a history of discrimination. Although perhaps lessening, that history exists with regard to those with same-sex orientation. Third, is there a lack of political power? Whether there is underrepresentation may be unclear, as sexual orientation is not an obvious characteristic, but the existence of discriminatory laws might be taken to indicate a lack of political power. Finally, there is the issue of whether sexual orientation is an immutable characteristic unrelated to merit or ability. Although some may dispute the conclusion, sexual orientation would not seem to be a choice or to be subject to change. The characteristic certainly seems unrelated to merit or ability.

If this analysis adds up to classifications based on sexual orientation being suspect, strict scrutiny will apply. The school will have to show that its policy is necessary to a compelling governmental interest, and there was no suggestion of such a compelling interest. If the classification is quasi-suspect, intermediate scrutiny will apply. The school will have to show that its policy is substantially related to an important governmental interest. That result is likely to be the same as those discussed in the consideration of a gender basis for the challenge. If the classification is not at all suspect, the proper test is rational basis. The burden will be on Sally to show that there is no permissible governmental interest to which the policy is rationally related.

The plaintiff's burden in showing that there is no rational basis is extremely difficult. It was met in a Supreme Court case regarding sexual orientation, but that result may not apply here. The Supreme Court case involved a state constitutional referendum that would not allow any antidiscrimination statutes that protected individuals on the basis of sexual orientation. The Court saw the animus in adopting the provision as based on a dislike for those of same-sex orientation, and said that dislike for a group cannot be a permissible governmental interest. If the school's interest here is on minimizing the number of couple's tickets sold, and thereby maximizing its revenues, that might be seen as not based on a dislike for any group.

The requirements that Sally wear a gown, rather than a tuxedo, is best challenged as gender discrimination in violation of the Equal Protection Clause. As the girls are required to wear gowns and the boys are required to wear tuxedos, this policy might be seen as intentional discrimination on the basis of gender. Gender discrimination is tested under intermediate scrutiny. The school system will have to show that the policy is substantially related to an important objective. The school system might argue that its objective has to do with decorum. Part of the prom experience is having the students arrived formally dressed. That could be seen as important objective, and the issue would then be one of whether the policy was substantially related to that objective. Formal wear might be required without this gender-specific policy, but the school's response would probably be that girls showing up in tuxedos and boys showing up in gowns would detract from the decorum it seeks. It may not be clear how a court would rule on this justification.

The yearbook staff may not have much chance of success. It is true that *Tinker* said that students do not lose their First Amendment rights at the schoolhouse gate, and said that speech may be limited only when it threatens substantial disruption or interferes with the rights of others. If that were the only case, the yearbook staff would seem to have a good chance of success, as publishing the pictures would not seem to raise those concerns. There is, however, a school speech case that is more on point. That case involved a high school newspaper published by the school's journalism classes and the principal's decision to pull two pages from the paper, before distribution, because of concerns over stories on those pages.

When the newspaper staff brought suit alleging violation of their First Amendment rights, they were not successful. The Supreme Court held that the newspaper was not a public forum but was, instead, a publication of the school. As it was the school's newspaper, produced in class, the school, as its publisher, had a right to determine that the material was not suitable. If the situation is not to be controlled by this case, it can only be if the yearbook is not seen as a publication of the school. If it were an independently produced publication, there would likely be a violation of First Amendment rights. Where, as seems likely here because it is produced in class, the yearbook is more accurately seen as a publication of the school, the school administration would have the right to limit the pictures, at least with regard to any challenge by the yearbook staff. If the decision to withhold the pictures were challenged by Sally, the analysis would seem to follow that for her complaint.

SELF-ANALYSIS

It should have been clear that there were at least two issues here. The existence of two different plaintiffs, an individual and a group, provides a good indication of that. With regard to Sally, it should be obvious that she is being subjected to differential treatment, even if it is not as immediately obvious upon what basis the school is discriminating. From the facts, we know that she is female and that she has a same-sex orientation. That should be seen as an indication that there may be two different approaches. Look to both of them. There are also two different rules being applied to Sally: the requirement that she buy single tickets and the requirement that she wear a gown. That, too, was an indication that there would different directions in which to proceed.

In analyzing gender as a basis for discrimination, there is no need to go through the analysis for determining how suspect the classification may be. The Supreme Court has already determined that intermediate scrutiny applies. Simply state the test and apply it. The additional reference to "an exceedingly persuasive justification" is simply to demonstrate knowledge of the Court's opinions.

In looking at how suspect discrimination based on sexual orientation is, do not make the mistake of simply stating that the Supreme Court has not determined that the classification is either suspect or quasi-suspect and has not demanded heightened scrutiny. The Court's case in this area simply did not require heightened scrutiny to find a violation of the Equal Protection Clause. That is not the same as saying that heightened scrutiny would never be applied.

As is usually the case in an exam situation, you will do better if you do not come to firm conclusions at intermediate points in an essay. If you had concluded that discrimination based on sexual orientation must meet strict scrutiny, you would not go on to consider the intermediate scrutiny and rational basis tests. The same would be true if you firmly concluded that any other level of scrutiny was correct. You can state what you think the level of scrutiny should be, but then go on to consider what would happen based on other conclusions.

Once you state the tests, apply them. Your conclusions are likely to be less important than your analysis. If you have raised all of the relevant factors, that should get you the points available. Stating the result of the state constitutional referendum case demonstrated knowledge of the case law. Recognizing, however, that there is a difference between that situation and this showed an ability to think about the application of the Court's opinion.

When we turn to the issue raised by the yearbook staff, we see there was a case that was relatively close on its facts. The school newspaper case was sufficiently like the yearbook situation here that it is likely to govern the result. Although you might have discussed only that case, the mention of *Tinker* is sufficiently vital, because it is such an important case in the area of school speech, to have been worth some credit. Once again, never pass up an opportunity to demonstrate your knowledge of relevant case law.

TABLE OF CASES

CPSIA information can be obtained at www.ICGtesting.com
Printed in the USA
BVOW04s0255140416

444144BV00009B/19/P